Farewell to Feethams

a collection of Darlington FC memories

by Ray Simpson and Andrew Wilkinson

First published in August 2002 by The Northern Echo, Priestgate, Darlington, Co Durham DL1 1NF. The Northern Echo is part of Newsquest (North East) Ltd which is a Gannett company

The authors assert the moral right to be identified as the authors of this work

British Library Cataloguing in Publication Data
A catalogue record for this book is available from the British Library

ISBN 0-9540518-4-X

Printed by Gate Press, Darlington

Contents

Front Cover Pictures:

Main Picture: Colin Sinclair scores against Huddersfield in 1976.

Top 1: Frank Gray's penalty enters the net to help clinch the 4th Division title in 1991

Top 2: Mark Prudhoe

Top 3: The 1990-91 Fourth Division championship team

Top 4: Andy Toman

Top 5: David Cork scores against Rochdale.

Bottom 1: The Feethams groundsman inspects an icy pitch

Bottom 2: David Cork raises the Vauxhall Conference Trophy

Bottom 3: Feethams before the ground was built

Bottom 4: Feethams as it is now

Bottom 5: Fans celebrate winning the Conference

Picture credits: *Northern Echo picture archive, Marty Horn (private collection), Joyce Owers and Malcolm Noble.*

2

Acknowledgements

We are indebted to many people for their help and encouragement. Frank Tweddle's statistics book, the Definitive Darlington FC, was a mine of information while we were researching facts and events. Without it, we would have been lost, and our copies are now dog-eared as we have referred to them so often.

Frank also allowed us to use photographs from his Centenary book, a marvellous gesture, and one we greatly appreciate.

Football historian Leigh Edwards kindly supplied us with addresses and phone numbers of many of the players interviewed.

The staff at Darlington Library, especially the lady who fixed the microfilm reader after one of the authors broke it, gave valued help. Their meticulously kept files made our research smooth, easy and enjoyable.

We are grateful to Peter Barron, editor of the Northern Echo, and Nick Loughlin, sports editor, and, from the commercial department, Trish Taylor. We are indebted to the Echo's Richard Simpson, Dave Pottage and Peter Ashmore for design skills, patience, enthusiasm and encouragement.

Paul Addison, Len Brewer and Ian Kenyon of BBC Radio Cleveland gave valuable support, as did former Middlesbrough Evening Gazette editor Paul Robertson.

Thanks to the fans, players and officials for giving their time - and in some cases photographs - and for speaking so openly and enthusiastically. The time spent talking to them was the most rewarding part of the project.

And special thanks to our dedicated back up team of Audrey, Hayley and Andrew Simpson; Pat, Adam and Laura Wilkinson.

Introduction

THE sun shines resplendent on Darlington's new stadium in Neasham Road. The new ground is not complete, and quite when it will be is yet to be confirmed. And so the journey of Darlington FC continues on its uncertain route.

But then nothing at Feethams in well over 100 years has ever been certain. Perhaps that's the appeal - the magnet that draws fans back time and again.

The conflicting emotions of hope, disappointment, despair, and delight revolve with inexorable momentum.

This book is not a history of that cycle, but a dip into it, to extract and record for posterity (we hope) some of the thoughts and feelings of those carried along on this strange voyage. Perhaps the players are the lucky ones - they have been able to get off. Many of the fans - certainly the ones in this book - are trapped. Once on the ride, there is no disembarking. There wasn't even a government health warning when we clambered aboard.

But it has been heartwarming to discover that, for the most-part, the memories are not bitter, but amusing and optimistic.

It is both surprising and encouraging to discover how for many players, their time at Darlington was the best of their careers. And even those for whom that was not the case, left with some special memories.

The players featured are not necessarily the best to pull on the Quakers shirt. They were selected partly at random, some because of their major contribution, and others because of the different eras in which they played.

We felt it appropriate to include the thoughts of some who were here only fleetingly and played just a handful of games, and others for whom the club was their home for several years. Those omitted are not left out because their contribution to the club has been any less important.

The fans are a mixed bunch too! Some were interviewed, others compiled their own stories. All had a desire to be included, that stands as a tribute to their passion for their team. And even if some of the football has been forgettable, the friendships forged have made it all worthwhile.

Ray Simpson and Andrew Wilkinson, August 2002.

3

4

Chapter 1

Darlington FC - the story so far

LUNCHTIME at a cafe in Appleby on a June day in 1999 may seem far removed from Feethams. Indeed a conversation which was overheard that day would probably not have taken place on any previous summer's day in Appleby in the Quakers' 117 year history.

A Darlington fan was in the cafe. Three local men sat down on a nearby table, and continued their conversation.

They were discussing where to place their loyalties the following season. It became clear that two were converts from Carlisle to Darlington.

The third insisted he would stick with Carlisle.

His friends said that the extra distance to Darlington would be worth travelling because not only had George Reynolds slashed admission prices, but the Quakers would have a better season - and it seemed better future - than Carlisle.

It was clear then that the influence of Quakers' new owner, barely a month in the role, was considerable. He had predicted that he would draw fans from all over County Durham. Now it seemed, they were being lured from across the Pennines.

Our supporter left before hearing whether the third man had pledged to join his companions in heading east.

But the vision of Reynolds aimed to make Darlington a magnet it never dreamed of being way back in 1883, when the club was formed.

Feethams (said to be named after a firm of local solicitors) had been used for football since being rented from John Beaumont Pease in 1866, though Darlington Football Club was not officially formed for another 17 years.

It was founded at a meeting in Darlington Grammar School on July 20 1883, and although the first match was played at North Lodge, almost immediately the club moved to Feethams. Few Football League clubs have had the same home for as long as the Quakers.

Darlington became the major club in the Southern Section of the Durham Football Association. In 1885 they won the Durham Senior Cup, beating Sunderland in the final.

The following season Darlington made their first FA Cup (then known as the English Cup) appearance. They were walloped 8-0 by Grimsby, and have never suffered a bigger FA Cup defeat - though six years later they hammered Scarborough 13-1, a victory that remains their biggest.

A 5-0 home defeat by arch rivals Darlington St Augustines didn't go down well with the Feethams faithful.

In 1889 Darlington became one of the original 10 members of the Northern League.

Two Newcastle teams (East End and West End) and two Middlesbrough teams (the current club and Ironopolis) were members. Darlington first won the league in 1896.

Good players were signed, among them Charlie Roberts, a centre half. After being transferred to Grimsby, he later joined Manchester United for a then huge £400. In 1904/5 he played three times for England.

Darlington became professional in 1908, and joined the North Eastern League. In 1911 Quakers reached the last 16 of the FA Cup, beating Hartlepool, Wingate, Bishop Auckland, Shildon, and Derbyshire team Blackwell Colliery in the qualifying rounds.

Darlington then created one of their biggest upsets when a goal from Fraser gave them a 1-0 win at First Division Sheffield United - one of the few times in the history of the competition that a non-league side has won away at top flight opposition.

Around 5,000 fans and a band were waiting to welcome the team home. For the visit of Bradford Park Avenue of the Second Division, 12,030 fans packed Feethams to see Darlington win 2-1 with goals from Cornock (his eighth of that season's competition) and Dodds. They lost 3-0 at home to Swindon in the next round.

In 1912/13 Quakers won 31 of their 38 games to win the North Eastern League, conceding just 23 goals, a League record. In 1914 Darlington were winning a cup replay 2-1 against Port Vale at Feethams, when the game was abandoned owing to darkness.

5

During the First World War the club survived financial trouble, being rescued by Darlington Forge Albion, whose chairman, J B Haw took over the name, ground and affairs of Darlington FC. The new board completed the stand at Feethams. The club became a limited company.

By then Darlington had another big Sheffield scalp, having won 2-0 at Wednesday. George Stevens and George Malcolm scored in front of 52,000 fans. Over 42,000 saw Quakers lose at Birmingham in the next round. Quakers did, however, win the Durham Senior Cup that season, beating Durham City at Roker Park, Aaron Travis scoring the only goal.

The following season Darlington won their last six games to clinch the North Eastern League. That success earned them their Football League place - in the newly formed Division Three North.

On August 27, 1921, a crowd of 8532 packed Feethams for the first Football League game, goals from Hooper and Dixon giving the following side a 2-0 win over Halifax; Tommy Greaves, Hugh Dickson, Tommy Barbour, Percy Sutcliffe, George Malcolm, Alf Dolphin, Bill Hooper, William Edmunds, Arthur Wolstenholme and Thomas Winship.

Home and away games were played consecutively, and Darlington went to

Darlington v Chesterfield in 1923 was played on the Cricket field owing to the football ground being frozen

Halifax and lost 5-1. But they came to terms with the new league and finished runners up to Stockport County - not enough for promotion because only the champions were promoted in those days.

A year later they paid Dundee £80 for David Brown, who scored 74 goals in just 97 league appearances for Quakers. He scored 27 times as Darlington were unbeaten at home in the following season. They even played one game on the cricket field - a 2-1 win over Chesterfield - as the football ground was frozen (relations with the cricket club were obviously less frosty then!). The football club issued 5,000 £1 shares to keep themselves afloat, and the next season Brown notched 39 goals, to create a new Third Division record. Darlington won the title to win promotion to the second division.

Incidentally, if you think Darlington should have done better over the years, take a look at the teams who finished behind them in the Third Division North - Nelson were runners up, followed by New Brighton, Southport and Bradford Park Avenue, all gone from the League.

August 29, 1925 was the date of the first Division Two game at Feethams and 12,868 supporters saw a goalless draw against Nottingham Forest.

Quakers finished 15th, not realising that it would be their highest-ever placing. The average league crowd at Feethams was 9047.

The following season they were relegated, and have never returned to the top two divisions.

In a nail biting finish they had to beat fourth placed Chelsea at home, and hope other results went their way. But Chelsea equalised 40 seconds from time in a 2-2 draw.

The following season there was little to cheer other than a record 9-2 win over Lincoln City at Feethams - Tom Ruddy missing a penalty to deny Quakers double figures. At the end of the season Jack English, manager since Darlington joined the league, left for Nelson.

In 1933 Darlington finished bottom for the first time, and had to apply for re-election, a feat achieved with 47 votes, Scarborough being the nearest challengers with just four.

A year later Darlington won the Third Division North Cup - a tale told elsewhere in this book.

The 1939/40 season was cut short by Hitler (not some over zealous referee, but

The West Stand was destroyed by fire in 1960

the real Adolf Hitler). Darlington had been unbeaten in their opening three games, when Football League activity was suspended on September 3.

Regional leagues were formed, and star names played for Darlington, many from Catterick Camp. They were paid 30 shillings a game, and among them were Jack Robinson, Sheffield Wednesday's international forward. During the war years Darlington were in the same league as Newcastle United, Leeds and Huddersfield, so played these clubs for the first time.

Among memorable victories for Quakers were a 6-2 triumph against Boro at Ayresome Park, and a 5-4 win at St James's Park.

Darlington then hammered the Magpies 8-2 in the League Cup, with a team full of guest players. It was: Tapken (Manchester United), Tooze (Coventry), Dowen (Hull City), Wharton (Portsmouth), Thyne, Birse (Hibernians), Rudkin (Grimsby), Billingham (Burnley), Brown (Brentford), Stubbs, Mullen (Wolves).

In October 1944 Bob Thyne became the first Darlington player to be picked for an international. He played for Scotland against England, replacing Bill Shankly.

During war time football, the match programme advised fans (who had to carry their respirators) that in the event of an air raid they should go home if they lived near the ground. Otherwise they were to spread around the ground and not crowd together.

In the final season of war time football, the leagues were split again, and Darlington won their league of 10 teams. Harry Clarke scored 40 goals that season, and was later sold to Leeds for £5,000.

A few years later manager Bob Gurney snapped up Brian Henderson, Ken Furphy and Ron Greener, who went on to make massive contributions. Charlie Wayman came from Middlesbrough. He was a prolific scorer who held the league's post war goalscoring record of 342 before he joined Darlington, where he added 14 in 23 games before retiring.

Darlington made history when their FA Cup game at Carlisle in November 1955 became the first between two league sides to be played under floodlights.

The 1957/8 season was the final one before the new national third and fourth divisions were introduced. But Quakers finished 20th and found themselves in Division Four. Coventry were the first visitors in the new league.

The following season Brian 'Cheyenne' Redfearn became one of the few players to score four times in a game for Darlington. His feat came in the 5-2 win over Notts County at Feethams in December 1959. Since then Colin Sinclair, Alan Walsh and David Cork have all netted four in a game.

Floodlights were installed, the West Stand was destroyed by fire, and a new stand was built and became known as the Tin Shed.

A couple of seasons later Jim Lawton set a club record by scoring in nine consecutive league games. The games were spread over many months as the big freeze prevented Darlington from playing at Feethams between December 22 and March 11.

Quakers suffered their heaviest ever defeat in 1964, losing 10-0 at Doncaster. But in 1965/6 Darlington won promotion for the first time in 41 years, being pipped for the title on goal average by Doncaster Rovers.

Strangely the first Third Division manager to visit Feethams was Ken Furphy, whose Watford side were beaten 1-0, John Peverell scoring. But Darlington were relegated after a string of injuries. Bobby Cummings broke his leg, Les O'Neill broke an ankle, and winger George McGeachie's career ended with a knee injury.

In 1969, under Ray Yeoman, Darlington missed out on promotion by a single place, after being unbeaten for the first 14 games. They were the last unbeaten team in the entire league, and didn't lose an away game until February 24. They led the table until March before losing five in a row.

7

Farewell to Feethams | a collection of Darlington FC memories

They could have clinched promotion on the final day of the season by beating Bradford at Feethams. But City won 3-1. In the following two seasons the club had to seek re-election.

In 1975 Elton John was a visitor to Feethams, his Watford side losing 1-0 to an Eric Young goal, but still the side struggled, and on January 24, 1982, the board revealed that unless £50,000 could be raised within six weeks the club would fold.

The Evening Despatch newspaper launched a centenary appeal. Sunderland came to play at Feethams, as did a Southampton side skippered by England captain Kevin Keegan.

The money raised from the game and from the town rallying round saved the club. The irony is that soon afterwards the Despatch folded!

Darlington won promotion to the Third Division in 1985 under Cyril Knowles. At the higher level a run of eight successive defeats was followed by a sequence of 13 games without defeat. Such was the turnaround, that a 7-0 defeat at York in October was followed by a 6-0 win over Swansea in November.

But the following season Darlington were relegated. And disaster was just around the corner. In 1989 Darlington lost their League status, only to return immediately from the GM Vauxhall Conference.

They went on to win the Fourth Division title. Ironically their first home defeat in the Fourth Division Championship season, came from a Peterborough side managed by Dave Booth, who had not won a home game when Darlington manager for most of the relegation season. As he disappeared up the Feethams tunnel at the final whistle, one wag shouted: "Booth, this is the first time you've ever won here!"

Relegation back to the basement swiftly followed, despite a record outlay of £95,000 on striker Nick Cusack.

Soon another financial crisis loomed, which almost led to the club relocating to Gateshead as part of a tie up with Newcastle. Quakers' chairman John Brockbank had kept the club afloat virtually single handed, and there was difference of opinion in the boardroom as to whether the club should secure its future by a move north, or battle on independently. The latter course was chosen, and the club went into the hands of St Philips Trust, a Gibraltar based organisation.

In 1996 Darlington reached the play-off final, losing 1-0 to Plymouth at Wembley.

But after a 1-0 home defeat against Barnet the following season, the fans turned on general manager Steve Morgon, chanting for him to leave the club.

The reason was mistrust of many fans. Despite reaching Wembley and boosting the finances with the sale of Mike Pollitt, Matty Appleby and Gary Himsworth, many supporters were no longer happy with the running of the club.

They were bemused by the decision to alter the sponsorship name on the shirts to 'Soccerdome', the new shirts being worn for the first time at Wembley. The club planned to buy the Cummins Engines site in Yarm Road and turn it into Soccerdome, a sports set up comprising 20 indoor and 12 outdoor six a side pitches, plus floodlit full size pitches.

But the plan never materialised beyond the concept stage, and soon after the protest, Morgon did depart.

But while owned by St Philips Trust the club had enjoyed success. What the fans wanted was a more 'up front' owner, not a trust that they couldn't relate to.

Mike Peden was next at the helm, and under him, in 1998 the new 3,500 all seater new East Stand was built, complete with bars, restaurant and executive boxes. But again the club was in deep financial trouble.

In stepped local millionaire businessman George Reynolds with plans to build a new stadium and take the club up through the divisions.

He was exactly what supporters wanted. A man who appeared prepared to lead, and fund his ambition.

The stadium was soon to appear on the Neasham Road skyline, but getting out of the Third Division proved trickier than anticipated.

After seemingly having promotion all but wrapped up in the 1999/2000 season, a slump of seven games without a win plunged the club back into the play-off zone - and another Wembley defeat.

Striker Marco Gabbiadini, regarded by many as the best striker the club ever had, left for Northampton.

The following season the team struggled, though it did win at First Division Nottingham Forest in the Worthington Cup.

Early in season 2001-02 Tommy Taylor, an experienced manager arrived, determined to leave Feethams for Neasham Road with a winning team.

Ian Banks 1994-95

League appearances	39	Goals	1
Other Games	7		

IAN had an unusual debut for Darlington - it started late and finished early. The experienced midfielder was signed by Alan Murray in the summer, and eagerly awaited his debut against Preston at Feethams in what was to become his final season of league football.

But the opposition didn't show up until 2.55. The coach got stuck in traffic, and tried to take a short cut through the dales - allegedly the idea of manager John Beck, but it turned out a bad one.

Ian recalled: "My nerves were nothing compared to how referee Uriah Rennie felt. It was his first league game and I remember him pacing up and down. When we started - I think it was around 3.30 - he was uptight. He booked me after five minutes. It was a fair tackle on Paul Raynor but he fell into the advertising boards.

"My debut came to a sudden end, for Uriah sent me off early in the second half. A Preston player went down, so I knocked the ball just a few yards to where I felt the foul took place.

"The ref decided I had kicked the ball away and gave me a second yellow card. The lad needed treatment so they couldn't have taken a quick free kick anyway.

"Later several players kicked the ball further than I had done after the whistle, yet escaped.

Ian Banks

"But I had my say afterwards on Alan Brazil's sports show. The subject was referees so I had my 10 minutes worth about Mr Rennie!

"Later on as a Premiership referee, he controversially sent off Alan Shearer in the first game of the season, so I'm in good company."

However Ian had a good season. He had played for several higher division sides, and had been a team-mate of Gary Lineker at Leicester, the two of them playing snooker together in Willie Thorne's club.

Converted from midfield to a sweeper, Ian was a key figure, organising the Darlington youngsters around him.

One of his best games was against another former club, Barnsley, as Darlington drew 0-0 at Oakwell against a side two divisions above them, only to bow out of the Coca Cola Cup on away goals.

"Along with Bernie Slaven I was the old head trying to keep the youngsters right. Alan Murray had tried to sign me for Hartlepool when he was there, so once he was at Darlington and I was freed he jumped in.

"A former Barnsley team-mate Paul Cross was at Feethams. He rang me and helped make my mind up. Darlington played good football. We had the pace of Robbie Painter up front, and Matty Appleby and Sean Gregan were two youngsters who clearly had a bright future.

"We used to batter teams but lose 1-0. We didn't quite have the know-how, especially after Paul picked up a knee injury that ended his career.

"The following season, after I had left, the team reached the play-off final, so that shows the potential. I was there a year too early.

"There was a lot of politics going on and Murray left. When Eddie Kyle was given a short spell as caretaker manager I helped him with the coaching.

"He said if he got the job I would have been player coach, but the next thing I heard was in the form of a letter which said that due to the budget they couldn't keep me. I was 34 and would have had another season."

While at Darlington, Ian scored his 100th goal - a sweet left foot shot in a 4-1

9

win over Northampton. He had been moved back into midfield for that game, and showed he had not lost his touch.

He is now assistant manager at Bradford.

An interesting footnote is that in Uriah Rennie's first ever Premiership game, the floodlights failed, so his debuts at both levels were held up!

Fred Barber 1982-86

League appearances 135	Other Games 28

LOCALLY born Fred always wanted to play for Quakers, although he nearly went to Rochdale.

"I was offered a two year apprenticeship by Darlington, but then the Rochdale manager, Peter Madden, offered me a two year apprenticeship followed by one year as a professional," said Fred.

"I accepted Darlington's offer, because I lived nearby and wanted to play for my home town club. I was a regular in the reserves, and it toughened me up, because they played in the Northern League at that time."

Fred Barber with fan Paul Hodgson

One day, in his second season in the reserves, Fred went on an outward bounds course to Hexham with the rest of the apprentices.

"On the Thursday night, Brian Honour and I were told that we had to report for first team training the following day. I was told that Pat Cuff, the first team keeper, had suffered an ankle injury, so I would be playing.

"I banned all my family from going to the game, against Stockport at Feethams.

"Five minutes into the game, Tommy Sword, their big centre half, headed towards the bottom corner, and even though I got my hand to the ball, I couldn't stop it going in.

"As I turned round, there were four of my cousins all standing behind the goal, saying 'never mind'. I was very embarrassed.

"Fortunately, it got better for me as the game went on, and I made a goal for Alan Walsh, with a long punt up the field. We won 3-1.

"I was voted man of the match, and when I went to the boardroom for my award, I was asked about a council van parked at the back of the car park – and there were my cousins waiting to give me a lift!"

Fred had a glorious start to his Feethams career. "I won four man of the match awards in a row. We drew 0-0 at Hull when they had Billy Whitehurst and Emlyn Hughes in their team, beat Hartlepool, but lost at Wimbledon.

"At the end of the month, I got a trophy for best goalkeeper in the division from Match magazine."

As all keepers know, there are downs as well as ups. The following season, after Cuff had been released and Fred was first choice keeper, Quakers were hammered 7-0 at York City.

"I let a really soft goal in, and afterwards Billy Elliott told me that if I'd done that on my debut, then I wouldn't have played any more for the first team.

"I was booked for timewasting by George Courtney after ten minutes, when we were losing two or three nil, and when George sent his report in, he got my name wrong. He'd put my brother's name, Paul, down!

"Afterwards, we are all invited to see the Lord Mayor of York, who just happened to be a Darlington fan. We couldn't turn the invitation down, so of course I got all the jokes – like what do you want to drink, Fred? Seven up?"

Cyril Knowles took over from Elliott for the start of the 1983-84 season, and drove his players hard. "We played at Torquay in a midweek game, and in those days, we went there and back in the same day.

"I saw my milkman when I went out in the morning, and I saw him again when I arrived home the following morning.

"Cyril didn't think we had played well, so he had us all in for training the day after the match.

"Cyril was a hard man, and ruled by fear. He used to like playing "murderball" in the Sports Centre as part of the warm up, and tackles used to fly everywhere."

Fred was the hero of possibly one of Quakers' biggest giantkillings, the FA Cup win over Middlesbrough in January 1985.

The first game was at Ayresome Park, and Fred says: "Irving Nattress put a header towards the top corner, and I took off and managed to push the ball over. I didn't realise how good a save it was until I saw the picture in the Echo the following Monday."

Quakers drew 0-0, and the replay was three days later, with 14,237 packed into Feethams.

"There was a lot of trouble that night. We went into a 2-0 lead, and then Boro fans invaded the pitch from behind my goal at the Polam Lane end. It took about fifteen minutes to clear them, and when we went back on the field, there were flick knives and all sorts scattered around my goalmouth.

"It unsettled us, and they took advantage and pulled a goal back. But we held on."

That set up Quakers for a fourth round tie with Telford who were then in the Alliance Premier League. And, indirectly, a move to Everton a year later for Fred.

"We drew 1-1 with Telford at our place, and lost 3-0 in the replay. About a year later, Wales were playing Northern Ireland on the television, and Wales keeper Neville Southall, who played for Everton at the time, injured his ankle ligaments.

"At 10.30 the same night, Cyril phoned me up, and told me that Everton wanted to speak to me. I thought it was a wind-up, but he told me to hurry up, as their manager Howard Kendall wanted to see me.

"I didn't have a car at the time, so John Craggs drove me down to Everton and I quickly agreed terms with Kendall.

"I couldn't believe that he had signed me, and he said that he had watched me play for Darlington that night at Telford, and he could remember me for the spring in my legs, which he thought made up for my lack of height."

Fred is now a goalkeeping coach at several clubs in the north west of England.

Dave Barton 1983-84

| League appearances | 49 | Other Games | 11 | Goals | 4 |

DARLINGTON manager Billy Elliott signed Dave Barton, originally on loan in February 1983, along with his Newcastle team mate Kevin Todd.

Dave stayed for just over a year, before an injury ended his professional career.

But he nearly didn't stay at Feethams after his loan.

"We used to go into training and play table tennis or snooker," says Dave. "I couldn't understand that, so Kevin and I used to do our training in Newcastle, and join up with Darlington for matches."

At the end of the 1982-83 season, Dave returned to Newcastle at the end of his loan, but was given a free by Magpies manager Arthur Cox.

"I was ready to go to Carlisle, but Cyril Knowles, who had just taken over at Darlington, asked me to sign for them."

As a centre half, Dave didn't score many goals, but hit a memorable one from 45 yards at Chester in a 3-2 win on February 19, 1983.

The Northern Echo reported: "Chester keeper Phil Harrington was totally bemused as the ball flew under the bar."

The most unsettling trip to an away game for Dave was the journey to Plymouth for the 4th round FA Cup tie in January 1984.

Because of the distance and importance of the game, Quakers flew to Exeter, and then travelled the remaining forty miles by bus.

But Dave wasn't impressed. "We were travelling so slowly along the runway at Teesside Airport, that we were picking daffodils. It seemed to take ages to get there - we thought the pilot was following the M1.

"Before the trip back, me, Kevan Smith and Dave McLean all decided to have a few drinks, and when we were going home, I'm sure that Cyril Knowles said that we could have a couple of days off, which meant that we didn't need to be in training until the Wednesday.

"So I told Fred Barber the same thing. Unfortunately, Cyril said Tuesday when all the lads, apart from me and Fred, turned up for training. We were both fined, and I paid Fred's fine for getting him into trouble."

Quakers lost that cup tie 2-1, Plymouth scoring a late goal.

"The ball must have bobbled half a dozen times before it went into the net, and seemed to bounce away from Fred," said Dave.

Dave was skipper of Cyril Knowles' side in the 1983-84 season, the year before Quakers won promotion to the old Third Division.

"Cyril wore his heart on his sleeve," says Dave.

"He used to go ballistic if he thought we were playing badly. There was no grey area with Cyril, because deep down he cared.

"I remember one day we played at Halifax, and we were the better side in the first half, even though it was goalless at half time.

"We walked into the dressing room, and Cyril told us all to sit down. He suddenly went crackers with us all, and I asked him if he'd been watching the same game.

"John Craggs was next to me, and I could feel his knee pressing against mine. Cyril just smiled, and John told me later that it was Cyril's way of winding us up for the second half. It worked, because Alan Walsh scored twice."

Dave was forced to retire because of a knee injury, picked up in a 1-0 defeat at Bristol City on March 10th, 1984.

Robbie Blake 1994-7

League appearances	68	Goals	23
Other Games	14		

ROBBIE became a huge crowd favourite in Quakers' play off campaign in 1995-96. When Robbie scored in that season, Quakers never lost. It was just a shame that he didn't score against Plymouth at Wembley.

Strangely enough, it took him ten months to score in the first team after then manager Paul Futcher gave him his debut at Colchester in March 1995.

When David Hodgson and Jim Platt took over the following summer, he was sent to League of Ireland club Waterford on loan.

"I went over there, supposedly for a month, with Peter Kirkham.

"I came back after just a couple of weeks, because I was drinking too much. We were only playing part time over there, and we were spending too much time in the pub just round the corner from the ground.

"So I came home, and told Hodgy and Jim that I picked up a groin injury!"

Robbie was put into the side, and he finally scored his first senior goal in January 1996. "It seemed to take ages to score my first goal, but I'll always remember it - a header against Exeter City."

Robbie couldn't stop scoring after that, as Quakers played some excellent football. "I scored eleven goals in the rest of that season, plus one in the play-offs against Hereford.

"We had a good team then, and really we should have gone up. I think some of my best goals were a free kick against Colchester, and when I dribbled through to score at Doncaster."

One of the games in the run in that season was away to Preston. Quakers drew 1-1 and afterwards set off for home up the M6, then the A66 over Bowes Moor.

"Unfortunately, the snow gates were down," said Robbie.

"So the bus driver decided to take us a different route. But we got stuck, and just by chance, the supporters' bus rolled up behind us. To pass the time, we had a snowball fight."

Robbie wishes that he had scored another goal at Scunthorpe on the last day of the regular season. "We were losing 2-0 then 3-2, then we came back to 3-3. I had a chance late in the game when I just had the keeper to beat, but I hit the crossbar."

Quakers were pipped for automatic promotion by Bury that day, so instead they had to go into the play-offs against Hereford, the first leg away at Edgar Street.

"We let an early goal in, but then Sean Gregan levelled with a header. It was a great goal, but it took him about three hours to come down!"

Robbie scored the winner before half time. A few days later, Quakers won the second leg by the same score to clinch a place at Wembley

"It was a great feeling. The fans went wild that night. There was a pitch invasion, and there was a huge party afterwards."

Robbie hardly got a kick against Plymouth at Wembley.

"Their manager, Neil Warnock, did a good job on us. We'd beaten them 2-0 and 1-0 in the league, but he'd done his homework. Instead of using 4-4-2, they used a

Robbie Blake

12

3-5-2 at Wembley which stopped us from playing.

"We had a couple of early chances, one fell to Matty Appleby, but the ball went just past the post. If it went in, maybe it would have been a different story."

The next season was a disaster, and by mid-November, Jim Platt had gone, and David Hodgson returned.

Hodgson had already been in charge once, but left on principle following a second round FA Cup tie at Rochdale in December 1995.

"The lads knew that something was going on, and we weren't really surprised by what happened.

"He had problems behind the scenes. For example, we went on a pre-season tour to Ireland, and we were in youth hostels. So Hodgy hired some bungalows for us instead."

Robbie was transferred to Bradford City for £300,000 just before deadline day in March 1997, and Quakers received another £50,000 as part of a sell on clause in January 2002 when he switched to Burnley.

Phil Brumwell 1995 - 2002

League appearances	196	Goals	4
Other Games	33		

PHIL is the only Darlington player to be involved in two play off final squads. However, the former Sunderland player admits that the game at Wembley in 1996 against Plymouth provided him with the highlight of his career, but four years later the Peterborough match was one of the low points.

Phil was signed from Sunderland by David Hodgson and Jim Platt soon after they took over as joint managers in the summer of 1995.

"Our home form was good that season, and we only lost one away game, at Chester.

"We had a great squad, players like Sean Gregan, Gary Bannister, Robbie Blake and Matty Appleby.

"It was the best feeling I'd ever had when we stepped on to the Wembley pitch before the game.

"I hadn't played a lot in the team near the end of the season, so to get a place in the side was really great.

"Simon Shaw suffered a broken jaw, and that gave me the chance. I was only 20, so to be playing at Wembley was really something. I enjoyed every minute of the game, even though we lost."

Phil thought he was going to play in Quakers' next visit to Wembley in 2000 against Peterborough.

"I played in the two games against Hartlepool in the play off semi finals, but I was left out for the final. I felt very bitter about that, and that is something I'll never forget."

But he was part of the team which pulled off a shock 2-2 draw at Leeds United in the second round of the Coca Cola Cup in September 1996.

"I marked Lee Sharpe, and that was one of the highlights of my career, because I kept him so quiet, he didn't see much of the ball.

"To draw 2-2 against one of the leading teams in the Premiership, was fantastic because nobody gave us a chance.

"I really can't explain the feeling I had when Robbie Painter scored our second equaliser. We just didn't expect to get anything from the game.

"The fans that night were amazing. They were behind one goal, and made a huge amount of noise all the way through, especially when Robbie scored."

Phil didn't score many goals for Quakers, but the one the fans will remember most is his goal in the FA Cup first round in November 1995 against neighbours Hartlepool.

"Gary Bannister kept telling me to go forward, and try and get a goal. So when Steve Gaughan went down the right, Gary shouted at me to get forward, and I arrived at just the right time to score from Stan's cross.

"Gary was one of the most gifted players I played with. He had that extra bit of genius which made a big difference at our level, and he scored some great goals."

Quakers were drawn at Rochdale in the following round, and that led to a big let down for Phil.

"We drew at Rochdale, and the winners of the replay were drawn at Liverpool. Roy Evans, who was manager of Liverpool at the time, came to watch the game.

"I've been a Liverpool supporter all my life, and so was really looking forward to playing there. I came off when the score was 0-0, and they scored the winner in the last ten minutes. I was heartbroken."

13

Gordon Cattrell 1973-75

League appearances	102	Goals	6
Other Games		10	

Gordon Cattrell

GORDON, when moving from Leeds to Darlington, made one of the quickest descents in Football League history - from first place to 92nd. Leeds, under Don Revie, were a top of the league side. Gordon played in the reserves, and trained with the likes of Billy Bremner, Peter Lorimer and Allan Clarke.

. "I was surprised when Revie later quit the England job and went abroad for the money," said Gordon. "That went against his principles. He set high standards. Everything had to be right - players even had to have their hair cut to his approval."

It was a culture shock for Gordon to arrive at Feethams. "When I was released by Leeds, Darlington manager Dick Connor called, saying he would put me in the team, and I could move back home to Washington."

Gordon made his debut in a 0-0 Feethams draw with Workington, but Quakers lost their next three to slump to bottom.

Life in Quakers' midfield was very different to being with Leeds.

"When a Darlington defender got the ball, I went towards him, as I had been taught to do that and take possession.

"But the ball was launched to Colin Sinclair in attack. So I sprinted 40 yards to support him. By the time I got there he had lost it and it had been hoofed back. So I turned and ran the other way.

"Eric Young, who came from Manchester United, was coached the same way as me, so the pair of us ended up doing shuttles while the ball flew over our heads."

Gordon's first Darlington goal came at First Division Coventry in a League Cup tie, "We were 1-0 down and I equalised with a 30 yard half volley from Alan Duffy's knock down," he said. "We lost 5-1.

"My job was to cover full-back Billy Horner. I remember Colin Stein knocking the ball past Billy, who had ten yards start, and Stein still beat him to it."

Gordon was in the Darlington side that two seasons later beat Sheffield Wednesday in a League Cup penalty shoot out at Hillsborough.

Wednesday won 2-0 at Feethams, but Darlington turned the tables in the second leg. The Owls won the toss to host the replay - a 0-0 draw. Sinclair, Jimmy Cochrane, Stan Webb, Steve Holbrook and Young scored the penalties.

But the replay ought never to have been necessary. "I hit the bar in the home leg and it should have been a goal," said Gordon. "The posts were in wrong and the crossbar was too low at the side I hit!

"We had good players with character. Steve Holbrook was an excellent midfield partner, Colin Blant a reliable defender, and Colin Sinclair and Don Burluraux had pace up front."

Quakers beat Second Division Luton 2-1 at Feethams in the second round, in front of 6061 fans - officially. "To this day I think there were 10,000 in," said Gordon. Quakers lost 3-0 at West Ham in the third round.

Gordon was the star of the remarkable Paul Trevillion episode, told elsewhere. "He asked for a volunteer for his 'hat-trick' to knock a top hat off a box with one shot from 12 yards.

"I didn't know that press and television would turn up, but by then I had volunteered. I hit the box, and the hat went flying."

Gordon enjoyed playing for Dick Connor and Billy Horner, but added: "When Peter Madden took over, I got disillusioned. He typified the Fourth Division, and liked players to get up front as quickly as possible. He brought in players who I felt were no better than us."

Gordon decided to move. He had worked at a garage during the summer when he was a professional at Darlington. "It was above board. I paid my emergency code tax," he said.

He kept the job when he signed for Bishop Auckland, but was not happy when he left Darlington, as he explained: "I bumped into a Leeds scout and he said he thought I was at Watford. I learned they had bid £9,000 for me - but I had not been informed."

Watford, with Graham Taylor and Elton John at the helm, went on a roll.

Dick Connor had become manager of Grimsby and wanted Gordon to go there, but by then the player had committed himself to non league football. But he retains

14

Gary Coatsworth - Get in there...   **you beauty**   **...and the crowd go wild**

happy memories of Darlington, even putting down bibs as goalposts for training in South Park.

"There were some enthusiastic people there, especially trainer Dickie Deacon. With his work rate and banter he typified what the club was about."

Gordon believes that the move to the new stadium is a good one.

"Feethams was never inspiring," he said. "When you had to walk round the cricket field it felt second best. I'm sure the opposition turn up thinking: 'This lot cannot be up to much playing here.' "

Gary Coatsworth 1989-91

League appearances	22	Goals	3
Other Games	10		

THE name of Gary Coatsworth will live long in the memory of Darlington fans. Gary was never a regular at Feethams, indeed he played more games for his next club, Leicester City, in a higher division than he did for Quakers in the Conference and the old Fourth Division.

But his contribution was massive on a sunny day in Welling in May 1990, because it was his goal that put Quakers back into the Football League.

Gary came to Feethams after being released by Barnsley in the summer of 1989,

as new Darlington manager Brian Little rebuilt the team.

"I signed at the beginning of the season, but when I made my debut against Chorley when Les McJannet was suspended, I broke my collarbone and was out for a few weeks.

"When I came back again into the team, I then picked up a knee injury against Yeovil, so I never really had a run in the team.

"My chance came when Jim Willis broke his leg at Telford, just four games from the end of the season, and Brian told me that I would be playing at Welling.

"It was a nerve-racking day, because we were a little frightened that we could still lose the title. If we lost, Barnet would have gone up instead of us."

The 2000 or so Darlington fans in east London will never forget the goal that mattered, ten minutes from the end to break the 0-0 deadlock.

"Andy Toman crossed a free-kick towards me on the far side of the box. I just went for it with my head, and the ball looped over the keeper and into the net. It was a great feeling to score a goal like that, in front of all the Darlington fans."

(Author's note: Whilst visiting "The homes of football" in Ambleside, Cumbria, I came across a poster of Gary running towards the Darlington fans with a look of triumph on his face).

Gary was also part of the squad which lifted the Fourth Division title the following season, and played twelve games that season, nine more than the

Conference campaign.

Then, a few months after taking the Leicester job, Brian Little returned to Feethams and bought him, just as he was holding down a regular place in the team.

"I was surprised at the move, because I hadn't really been a regular at Darlington, because of the team's form, and my injuries," he said.

But it turned out to be an inspired transfer, because Gary appeared in three play off finals for Leicester, before having to retire from the professional game because of a knee injury.

Mitch Cook 1984-85, 1991-92

League appearances	70	Goals	8
Other Games	14		

Mitch had an amazing impact on almost every club he joined. He had two short spells at Darlington, winning promotion twice. He also won promotion in his first season at Blackpool, scoring in a Wembley play off penalty shoot-out.

He won trophies with Scarborough and Whitby, and probably his only failed move was to Middlesbrough - they went into liquidation shortly after he joined.

Mitch, a wide player with a sweet left foot, was aged 22 and working in a Scarborough coach works and playing part time, when Cyril Knowles snapped him up in 1984.

"For the first year at Darlington I continued working, training whenever I could. I had a well paid job, and my deal at Darlington was not all that good. It was hard work, and Cyril did pressurise me, trying to get me to hand in my notice.

"It was wonderful to play in the Football League. It took me a long time to score my first goal (22 games), and the fans gave me some stick. When I finally scored it was such a weak shot I almost had to blow the ball over the line.

"We had strong characters like Kev Smith and Fred Barber. They were vital figures in that side, as was John Craggs and Peter Johnson.

"Fred was an excellent keeper, and in that respect I was lucky, because when I came back for a second stint, we had Mark Prudhoe, also excellent and a character."

Mitch scored three goals in 31 games in his first season, as Darlington won

Mitch Cook in action (left), with team mate Frank Gray looking on

promotion. His only disappointment was that he missed the last six with a knee injury.

Early the following season Middlesbrough snapped him up, Alan Roberts and Paul Ward moving the opposite way.

"The money was better and I went full time. But I still had a knee problem. Then the club suffered liquidation. The players were given the opportunity to leave and I returned to Scarborough where we won the league in my first season."

Mitch returned to the Football League with Halifax where he became captain, and on deadline day 1991 Brian Little took him back to Darlington - just in time to win the Division Four title.

"I played in front of Frank Gray, which was brilliant because he was class," recalled Mitch, who played the last nine games of the season.

"That was a fabulous experience, especially after I had missed the end of the previous promotion year."

He remembers with affection playing alongside Smith again, as well as Jim

Willis, Gary Gill, Les McJannet, David Cork and Andy Toman.

"We played excellent football, but could also dig in. That was a testament to Brain Little. He never screamed and shouted, but you knew where you stood and what he expected.

"Cyril had been more aggressive, but not nasty. They were fine managers and I was privileged to play for them."

In the promotion push Mitch scored a fabulous goal - a far cry from his first.

"It was in a 3-0 win at Northampton, who were going well. I finished a flowing move which involved Gilly and Andy Toman, by lashing in a 20 yard volley.

"When we clinched promotion and the title in the last game of the season against Rochdale at Feethams, I remember willing the final whistle to blow, then the crowd coming on to celebrate. Even though we won the league, it was so tight we could have missed out on the top four if we'd lost."

The following season, with Little gone, Darlington struggled and Mitch left in March to go to Blackpool.

All the time he lived in Scarborough, where he is now Football in the Community Officer. Darlington holds fond memories because this is where he played in the Football League for the first time - and bizarrely had the Feethams cat named after him.

"Don't know why that was," he said. "I think it was something to do with Tommo the groundsman."

Drew Coverdale 1989-92

League appearances	30	Goals	5
Other Games	29		

DREW Coverdale was just a raw teenager when he was pushed into first team action by Brian Little for an FA Cup second round tie against Halifax in December 1989.

At that time, Quakers were in the Conference, and had already beaten Runcorn in the fourth qualifying round 4-2, and Northwich Victoria 6-2 to reach the second round stage.

And with Quakers' revival well under way, there was a good crowd of 4,041 inside Feethams that afternoon to see Drew capture the headlines against the Football League club in a 3-0 win by scoring one goal and setting up another.

Drew's display was a journalist's dream, because at the time he was studying for a physiotherapy qualification, and so the headlines and the copy wrote themselves.

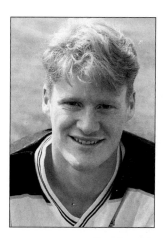

Drew Coverdale

"I was in the team because Frank Gray was out injured, and in my spare time I was studying for the FA Diploma of Management of Physiotherapy," said Drew

"The goal I scored was from a free kick, but it wasn't much. I didn't really hit it, but the ball took a deflection off the wall and went in past their keeper.

"I think it was the second goal which got everybody going. I ran from the halfway line and beat two or three defenders, and squared the ball for John Borthwick to score.

"It was a giantkilling act by us, and we were covered on Match of the Day on the evening. I had to do an interview, because it was pretty unique that a physio was called up and then put Halifax out of the Cup."

Nick Cusack 1991-92

League appearances	21	Goals	6

TO splash out a club record fee for a striker, then sell him within five months having been relegated, may not seem good business. But Nick, who arrived from Motherwell for £95,000, was a success, with both club and player benefiting.

"It was a case of returning to English football from Scotland," recalled Nick, who was one of the few Darlington players to have a press conference called on his arrival. "I didn't have a good relationship with Motherwell manager Tommy McLean. He told me Darlington had contacted him with an acceptable offer.

"What he didn't tell me was that Oxford had done the same, so it was not a decision I had to mull over. I jumped at it. I spent three years in Scotland and initially loved it.

"But there was no players' union there, and while the rule in England was that

17

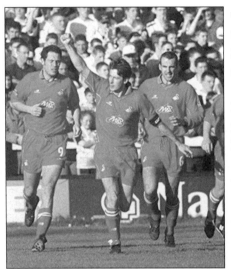

Nick Cusack (centre) celebrates a goal for Swansea against Darlington at Feethams

when your contract had expired they had to offer you more money or hand you a free transfer, in Scotland that was not the case.

"They had me over a barrel, so as English football offered a better financial environment, it was off to Darlington."

But Nick hadn't lost his rapport with the Motherwell fans. Incredibly after his arrival at Darlington, there were a few orange shirts in the crowd at both Feethams and in away games.

"For one game, at Bury, there were a lot of them. I was a cult figure at Motherwell, and to have them travel down was a great feeling.

"I made good friends at Darlington, and many of the lads I played with I'm still in touch with. I found the north east friendly."

Nick scored on his debut at Swansea in a 4-2 defeat, and at the time results were not going Quakers' way, as they struggled to establish themselves in the old Third Division.

Dick Corden was chairman, and he backed manager Frank Gray, hence the decision to sign Nick, who was 26.

But there is pressure with being the subject of the biggest ever fee for a club.

As Nick recalled: "The chairman said if it didn't work out we were in trouble. He made a big financial commitment to the club and cared deeply.

"These days it's all PLCs and big business, but I think Dick was from the same sort of mould as George Reynolds. It's a pity there are not more of them.

"We were second bottom when I joined. One thing that struck me was the distance we had to travel. That first game at Swansea was an eye opener. In Scotland every game, except Aberdeen, was a short trip."

Nick had earlier played for Peterborough. He has fond memories of a return there for he scored for Quakers in a 1-1 draw. "It's always nice to show an old club

what they are missing," he said.

Nick netted twice in his final appearance, a 5-2 win over Exeter at Feethams. By then Gray had been replaced by Ray Hankin. "Frank was cool and reserved," said Nick. "Ray was boisterous and banged heads together. I liked them both, and being at Darlington taught me to handle the pressure of a relegation battle, which later stood me in good stead."

For Swansea Nick scored an equaliser at Feethams two seasons ago, when Quakers missed out on promotion.

That 1-1 draw in March 2000 proved costly, and Nick's header did as much damage as any goal that season. "I was amazed Darlington didn't go up. They were the better side that day and we only just held on," he said. "But for me it was great. I was skipper and we won the title."

He had left Feethams for Oxford for the same fee Quakers paid. He didn't want to go, but Oxford were in a higher division, and Darlington wanted to rebuild.

So a brief but happy spell ended. "I'm pleased they got their money back. I liked Darlington, and didn't want to have cost them," said Nick.

He went on to play for Fulham before being discarded when Kevin Keegan took over with millions to spend. In came the stars and out went an intelligent, committed and good player.

Of his days at Darlington he particularly remembers getting on the end of the powerful kicks of keeper Mark Prudhoe.

"If I have any regrets it's that I didn't do better for Darlington. But I hadn't been playing at Motherwell, so it took me a while to get match fit. But I did my best. You cannot say fairer than that."

Ron Ferguson 1976-80

League appearances	114	Goals	22
Other Games	18		

RON Ferguson will be remembered for THAT goal - a thunderous 35 yarder that knocked his former club Sheffield Wednesday out of the FA Cup. But while the striker revelled in glory that night, he cringed when he saw the next day's newspapers.

"I'd just met a new girlfriend," he recalled: "Manager Peter Madden had said I looked older than I was. I remembered that, and told her I was 22. We had been together only a few days.

"Then every paper I looked at had the story of 19-year-old Ron Ferguson's wonder goal."

He still has the cuttings - and the relationship. The pair are happily married.

But while Ron bent the truth, he also bent the ball in that memorable moment.

"You couldn't plan it," he said. "The hand of God was on that goal. To draw your former club the season after moving, then score a winner like that against them was incredible. In those days it was amazing for Darlington to reach the third round of the FA Cup under any circumstances!"

The Owls dominated much of the second round Feethams clash of December 15th.

Late in the game, Ronnie moved into the Wednesday half with no team-mates near.

"I remember going past one player, and then heard Eddie Rowles shout from some distance: 'For Christ's sake hit it, and hit it well, we're all knackered.' That's what I did, but I wasn't far from the bench, and I heard them shout: 'What's he doing .... for crying out loud....he hasn't has he?' Then I remember time standing still."

The crowd of 7474 were spellbound as the ball swerved this way and that, and then dipped over keeper Chris Turner and into the top corner of the net in front of the Shed. There is no video evidence, but 35 yards is a conservative estimate.

Sadly the cup run ended in despair for Ronnie. Quakers drew Second Division Orient, complete with then wonder boy Laurie Cunningham, at Feethams.

A 2-2 draw and a 0-0 replay draw followed.

But in the second replay at White Hart Lane Ronnie was sent off in the first half of a 3-0 defeat. "Somebody tapped my ankle and I turned and swung a boot at him. It was stupid. We had outplayed Orient. It still hurts. To this day I look back and wonder why I did it."

On another occasion Ronnie was sent off against Stockport when his old Wednesday team mate Alan Thompson riled him in similar fashion. "Like a fool I had another swing. Barry Lyons was sent off shortly afterwards for the only time in his career. I felt guilty because Barry was a footballer not a fighter."

Ronnie, a robust centre forward and scorer and creator of goals, was what

Darlington needed. They had some neat and tidy players, and Ronnie complemented them.

He had played in the old Second Division as a 17-year-old and admitted: "It was too much too soon. You think you have made it, but you haven't. I got injured, and Wednesday went down.

"I was loaned to Scunthorpe, and then signed for Darlington. But I didn't get a good deal. I was young and Madden and chairman George Tait took advantage."

Only 1313 saw Ron's debut against Torquay at Feethams. He scored the only goal. "The ball hit my chest, bounced down and I hit it," he recalled.

Darlington were scrapping to avoid having to apply for re-election. Colin Sinclair hit a purple patch of 12 goals in 12 games, several created by Ron, who scored in the second last game of the season, at home to Bournemouth which Quakers won 2-0.

Ron Ferguson celebrates 'that' goal

They got the point they needed in the final game, and Ron said: "Madden respected me for what I did towards the end of that season. I have mixed feelings about him because my contract was so poor, but he was fair to me, and gave me another chance when I was ready to quit the game."

He has vivid memories of the way Madden left him out of the side for the cup tie at Everton in 1978.

"We stopped at motorway services, as always, for a pre-match meal. It was steaks all round. Then Peter said to me: 'You can have chips with yours.' I knew straight away I wasn't playing."

Ron laughs at the time tough midfielder Dave Crosson was in trouble with the manager. In a game against Huddersfield Crosson stamped all over winger Lloyd Maitland, who later played for Darlington.

19

Crosson claimed it was an accident. But videos had just come out and Madden sat the players down to watch it.

It soon became clear that the violence was deliberate, and all the players gave Crosson some stick.

Tragedy was not far from Ron when he played in Belgium. He was with a Brussels club that trained at Heysel stadium, and on the night of the ill-fated European Cup final, was watching on television in his top floor flat not a mile from the ground.

"I could see over the city, stadium included. I remember helicopters flying low over the flat on their way to help. Parts of the ground were used as a makeshift mortuary.

"It was awful. The nucleus of our side had been together six years and we were great mates, but after that the Belgians were a bit strange towards me. I was English and they were appalled at the Liverpool fans who behaved like animals."

Ronnie had gone to Belgium after Darlington boss Billy Elliott made it clear he was no longer wanted at Feethams, Ronnie being out of the side for a year before he left.

He now works for a printing company in Lincoln.

FOOTNOTE: Andrew Wilkinson spoke to Hartlepool boss Chris Turner the day after talking to Ron, saying "I spoke to an old mate of yours - Ronnie Ferguson - last night." Turner, who has not seen his Wednesday team-mate since that night, said instantly: "I bet I know what you were talking about, and yes, it was every bit as good a goal as Ronnie will have told you. It was so good you could hardly exaggerate it."

Mark Forster 1984-85

League appearances	38	Goals	16
Other Games	7		

MARK Forster didn't have second thoughts about signing for Darlington - but his mother did.

Mark was born in Teesside, and the chance to come to Darlington on loan arose when he was at Leicester City. "I was really homesick at the time, and when Cyril Knowles asked to take me on loan, I was delighted. I told my mother about it, and she sent me a cutting from the Northern Echo about Darlington's away trip to Bristol City, when the fans had to pay for the team bus. She wrote on it: "Do you really want to sign for them?"

"I made my debut at Chester, but we lost 2-1 against a team which at the time was well adrift of the bottom of the table. Cyril wasn't too happy with the performance and he ordered us to play for the reserve team against Seaham Red Star in the Northern League Second Division the following Tuesday."

After he was signed permanently by Knowles at the end of that season, Mark was offered the chance to play in Sweden during the summer.

"Brian Honour and I were both asked if we wanted to play in Sweden. Cyril, really, wanted to save money on the wage bill.

"Brian saw Cyril first, but he wouldn't go, so Cyril told Brian that he was released. Brian told me what had happened outside the office, so when I went in and Cyril asked me the same question, I said yes!"

Mark returned in early October 1984 and played his first Fourth Division game of the season against Colchester. "I got a bit of a shock when I went on the field, because here was Willie Young, an ex Scottish international, in the same team as me. I thought things had changed quite a bit since I'd gone away!" It didn't do Mark much harm - he scored twice in a 4-0 win.

Mark was on the bench for the two FA Cup games against his old club, Middlesbrough in the same season.

"In a way, it wasn't a bad thing, especially for the replay considering all the crowd trouble that night. There was also a lot of stick towards the ex Boro players at the time, Garry MacDonald in particular got a lot of abuse, which wasn't very pleasant at all."

Quakers were then drawn against non league Telford in the next round. "I was sub that night, and I had to go on the field early in the game after Kevan Smith hurt his shoulder. I scored our goal in a 1-1 draw.

"We weren't in the replay at all and were beaten out of sight. They were the much better team on the night – they scored two in the first half and another just after half time, all from long range."

Quakers won promotion that season, but Mark felt that there was tension between the players and the manager.

"We lost an away game at Northampton by 2-1 one day, and Cyril brought us in

20

for a rollicking the next morning. Cyril pointed to me, and said that I was the best player at the club – but I was only on the bench for the Northampton game! He said that if I had pace, I would be in the First Division, but that made me wonder why I wasn't playing in the first team if he thought I had the skill.

"The players decided afterwards that we would get promotion for ourselves and the fans. There was a Paul McCartney song around at the time - the Frog Song which went "Sink or Swim" – and we adopted it. We decided that we would "stand together", as the words in the song went, as a team."

Mark picked up an ankle injury early the following season which led to his retirement. "Even though it was promotion year, times were hard. We had all taken pay cuts, and the club tried to do me out of £200 from the insurance. They offered me £800 and I wanted £1000. I discovered later that the club got close to £10,000 as an insurance settlement."

Ken Furphy 1953-62

League appearances	316	Goals	8
Other Games	33		

KEN joined the club in December 1953 after finishing his National Service, and stayed until the end of season 1961-62, after playing 349 games in all competitions. Ken was a key player in one of the most successful periods in the club's history.

"I was called up for National Service when Everton were interested in me, and when I was posted to the north east, I wrote to all the clubs asking for a trial, but only Darlington replied. I had a trial when Bobby Gurney was manager, but he didn't ask me to come back. I spoke to the chief scout at the time, a chap called Collins, and he told me that he and Bobby thought I didn't have the stamina.

"I told him I was second in the Durham cross country championships once, and could I have a retrial in a probables v possibles game.

"They printed the names of the players in the papers in those days, and I wasn't included. But on the day of the game, a telegram arrived at my house at 12.30 asking me to come, because a chap called Brown had dropped out.

"The problem was, I was at full back, and I'd never played there in my life, because I was a midfield player. I must have done all right, because they took me

on at £1 per week, and £3 per match."

Ken played at right back for three months, until he was switched to right half.

He never missed an FA Cup tie during his years at Feethams, and was part of the side that reached the fifth round in 1958.

"We played Rochdale in the first round, and I marked a chap who used to play for Everton. I tackled him really hard, it was maybe a little over-zealous, and I knocked him over the advert hoarding into the crowd. He had to go off injured.

"At the end of the game, a spectator ran on to the field and kicked me, so my dad ran on and whacked the spectator!"

Because of the injury picked up in that incident, Ken was going to miss the next two league games, so manager Dickie Duckworth had a job in mind for him ahead of the next cup tie against Boston. "He told me that he wanted me to go and beat Boston for him. I was a qualified coach by then, so I took my dad with me, and we went and had a look. We beat them 5-2, and maybe my trip did some good."

It was Norwich away in the next round. "Norwich really fancied their chances, because they had reached the semi finals of the cup the previous year. When we ran on to the pitch, the PA announcer said: "I'm sure you'll be wishing us luck in the next round." That really got us going, and we beat them 2-1."

Mighty Chelsea awaited in the fourth round, but Ken wasn't too sure of his place in the team.

"I thought Dickie didn't like me much," Ken says.

"I had a feeling I might not be playing at Stamford Bridge. When he read the team out, he said that at right half, he was going to play Billy Rutherford, so I thought that I was out of the team.

"Then Dickie said to me that I was going to play at left half to mark Jimmy Greaves who he called a flash in the pan."

Quakers led 2-0 at half time at Stamford Bridge. "Ronnie Harbertson, who had a powerful right foot, scored one of the goals. When we came off at half time, Joe Turner, our goalkeeper, said that we only had to hold on for another 45 minutes. I replied that we could kill this lot off."

Quakers very nearly did. They stretched the lead to 3-0, and missed a good chance for a fourth. "Dave Carr dribbled around the keeper, turned to look at us, and then backheeled the ball towards the net, but the ball stuck in the mud. That would have made it 4-0."

Chelsea hit back to draw 3-3, but for the replay four days later, Greaves was omitted. "Chelsea said that he wasn't used to the hustle and bustle."

Quakers won that game 4-1, but went out in the next round at Wolves, by 6-1.

Ken actually helped to build part of Feethams one summer - the terracing along the West side.

"The supporters club managed to get a lottery going, and they suggested doing a few jobs at the ground, because the club's money went on to the team.

"So Keith Morton and I helped the supporters by lifting a few bricks and mixing some cement."

Keith was one of Ken's closest friends in the team, and in one derby game against Hartlepool, he was badly injured.

"One of their players knocked Keith down on the halfway line, and stood on his neck.

"Keith said immediately that his neck was broken, and that he had pins and needles in both his arms. I told Dickie Deacon, our trainer, who helped him to his feet and took him off the field, which isn't the sort of thing they would do these days.

"At the final whistle, Keith was sitting in our dressing room on a concrete base, with a blanket around him and a cigarette dangling from his mouth. His eyes were gone, and I told Dickie Deacon to call an ambulance.

"But the manager, Dickie Duckworth told him not to, and to have a shower instead. I was really annoyed and Dickie and I squared up to each other. The players separated us, and I took Keith to hospital, where they diagnosed a broken neck, and he had a very serious operation."

Ken carved out a very successful career as a manager after leaving Feethams, taking charge of Workington, Watford, and Sheffield United.

"I had no aspirations for the Darlington job. I applied to become a physio, but the FA advised against it.

"I had a chance of a job outside football with my uncle, so Eddie Carr, the manager, agreed to knock £2 off my wages so I could go part time.

"Then one day, Eddie said that he wanted somebody younger to do my job, even though I was only 32 and had fought off possible replacements. Workington wanted me to go to them as player-manager, so they interviewed me, and sent me a letter offering me the job.

"The board weren't too happy, and told me that I wasn't going to Workington. I went on holiday, and when I came back, Eddie said that Darlington wanted £1500 for me. Workington agreed to pay it, and I asked for £500 of it, which I spent on a car for my new job."

Allan Gauden 1968-72

League appearances	127	Goals	43
Other Games	13		

ALLAN was training on the pitch at Sunderland's Roker Park when he found out that he was on the way to Darlington.

"I was halfway through a training session, and Allan Brown, the manager, told me that Darlington wanted to speak to me. After talking with the manager, I agreed to sign."

Quakers paid £6000 for him, and he rewarded them with 15 goals in his first

Smiles all round as Allan Gauden (front) and team mates limber up

season as they pushed for promotion.

"We beat Workington 6-2 just after I signed, and I scored two of the goals. The fans carried me shoulder high off the pitch.

"We thought that we were going to win the league. When we were beating Southend 2-0 at half time, we thought that we were home and dry and lost our heads a little bit.

"We lost 3-2. And in the last match of the season against Bradford City, I thought we lost our momentum after we had to go off the field because of crowd trouble."

The goals dried up in his second season. "I played for around two months with a cartilage problem. In those days if you had cartilage trouble, you knew that you would be out of the team for ages, so I kept on playing. In the end though, I had to have the operation."

Allan scored 16 goals in season 70-71, and another seven at the start of the following season.

"One day, the manager Frank Brennan and chairman George Tait called me into the office, and told me that Lawrie McMenemy, who was at Grimsby at the time, wanted to sign me.

"I told them that I didn't want to go, and that I was happy. George said that the club was struggling, and in the end, I agreed to meet Lawrie after a game at Sunderland.

"I agreed to sign, and Lawrie told me that I was the only player that Darlington could sell for money."

McMenemy was to play another financial part in Quakers' later history, when he brought his Southampton team to Darlington for the appeal game in 1982 which helped save the club from financial ruin.

Steve Gaughan 1992-96, 1997-99

League appearances	218	Goals	19
Other Games	34		

STEVE reckons he left Darlington too soon. "Manager David Hodgson told me he was going to sign more players and I might be on the fringe. I opted to join Halifax, which was a mistake," reflected Steve.

Mark Dobie takes to the air during training at Catterick. Steve Gaughan (fourth right) looks on

"Hodgy told Peter Duffield the same thing, yet Peter became a key figure in the team that got to Wembley for a second time, and I might have been a regular too. If I had stayed I think I would still have been playing league football now.

"Halifax is a rugby town and the fans have nowhere near the passion of Darlington supporters. I never felt down at Darlington, even when the team was struggling.

"Of all my clubs (Doncaster, Chesterfield, Halifax and Sunderland) Darlington is the one I look back on with most affection."

He arrived from Sunderland, where he didn't make the first team, when Quakers were struggling in the old Division Three, making his debut in a 4-2 defeat at Swansea. "I have never won there in my career. It was a freezing night.

"But under every manager I played for, Darlington played an attractive game, never the kick and rush stereotype for which the division is known.

Billy McEwan

24

"I had a good rapport with older players such as Mark Prudhoe and Kev Smith. They were daft as a brush, but committed. Kev's telescopic legs were unbelievable. Sadly things didn't work out for the manager Frank Gray.

"Darlington had won promotion in successive years, progressing too far too quickly. Frank was a smashing bloke, as was assistant Tony McAndrew.

"Ray Hankin took over, and I took to him. He was straightforward, and knew how to get the best out of players. And he was a big man who had a presence. If he had kept the job he would have done well."

However he couldn't save Darlington from the drop, and by the time Steve had been at the club six months he was on his third manager, Billy McEwan.

"He was the first manager I had who understood modern fitness methods," said Steve. "He knew about eating properly, and was disciplined. He realised the dangers of the drinking culture that was prevalent in football.

"Training was enjoyable, though he sometimes pushed us too hard. At Catterick army camp one day we were up at 6am working with medicine balls under the eye of a typical army coach complete with vest.

"When we got in the car to come back on the Friday afternoon three of us were asleep before we left the camp. We were soon 3-0 down the next day. I could hardly run.

"But we had some good wins. It wasn't until David Hodgson arrived some time later that we had the next manager who understood sports science. With him we had Jaffa cakes, and stopped training every 20 minutes to drink water."

When Alan Murray took over from McEwan, Darlington immediately beat Colchester 7-3 at Feethams.

"I was in bed with flu," said Steve. "I had such a fever that when I put saw the result on teletext, I almost phoned the club doctor. I thought I was hallucinating!"

The best years were under Hodgson and Jim Platt. "Hodgy got us believing in ourselves, and we played fabulous football. Gary Bannister was quality on the pitch and in the dressing room.

"Sean Gregan came good; Robbie Painter was scoring goals, and wing backs Simon Shaw and Mark Barnard were great going forward.

"It took me a while to win a regular place, and then things snowballed. Once we got past Christmas, even though Hodgy had left, we believed we could beat anybody.

"Jim Platt made Robbie Blake a regular and he started scoring. I remember one at Doncaster when it was 1-1 and we were under pressure in driving rain. I had the ball by the corner flag at the end we were defending, and sent Blakey racing away.

"He left two defenders for dead and from a tight angle rifled the ball into the top corner. It was a brilliant goal out of nothing. We won 2-1.

"I remember travelling up to train when the Yorkshire lads would play against the rest in five a side games. We used to plan tactics in the car and often won, even though the others had the better players."

Steve, a strong midfielder, scored his best Darlington goal that season - against Hartlepool at Feethams. "We battered them, but it was 0-0 with about 10 minutes left. I picked up the ball in defence, beat a couple of players and gave it to Paul Olsson.

"He returned it to me. I cut inside and was about 25 yards from goal when the ball sat up. I hit it with my left foot and it flew into the top corner. I had also scored at Hartlepool in the FA Cup that season when we won 4-2."

So Steve played a key role in Quakers reaching Wembley and remembers a great night after Hereford were beaten in the play-off semi-final.

"The players went to the cricket club and a lot of fans were there. To see them celebrating was fantastic. I was out until around 3am and stayed at Sean Gregan's house.

"I felt sorry for Paul Olsson, who had by then suffered the knee injury that ended his career. He had played well, but what impressed me most was how upbeat he was with us, even though he could not play at Wembley.

"I later had a similar experience at Chesterfield, being injured when we reached the FA Cup semi-final against Middlesbrough at Old Trafford. I felt on the outside looking in, and found it hard to handle. Yet Paul was with us all the way and that's a reflection of what a great bloke he is."

Nerves got the better of Steve and he didn't sleep the night before Wembley. "I was up at 6.15 in the hotel and had breakfast on my own," he said. "The day was a blur, but I remember the guy on duty in the changing room. He did all the England games and had got the autographs of just about all the top stars in the world.

"I was jelly legged in the first 10 minutes of the game. We paid for one lapse.

"I felt sorry for Matt Carmichael, one of our subs, who had scored a couple of crucial goals, but only got two minutes' action when he replaced me."

That was the final game for Steve in his first stint at the club.

"I would have stayed if we had gone up. I had been to Chesterfield for talks when Alan Murray was Darlington manager. When they came in again I felt it was time to move."

Steve had injury problems at Chesterfield, who were in Division Two, and didn't play many games. Hodgy, now back in charge, phoned him and asked if he fancied coming back to Darlington.

"They say you should never go back, but I didn't regret it," said Steve. "But one of the things I remember from my Chesterfield days was when we played against Plymouth. Ronnie Mauge who had scored the Wembley winner said Darlington were head and shoulders above the rest of the division and he couldn't believe we didn't go up. I could tell he meant it.

"Initially when I returned to Darlington I was a regular. Then I was in and out. And we didn't always get our wages on time. It's not as if we were Premiership stars where one week's wages would last months.

"One game that stands out, was when we beat Sheffield United 2-0 at Feethams over 90 minutes in the second leg of the Worthington Cup, only for them to win in extra time.

"We had Glenn Naylor sent off early on, yet hammered a First Division side. My shot led to the first goal, though it was credited as an own goal. I remember the Sheffield fans going so crazy that none of their players wanted the ball.

"But I was never happy to be out of a side and that's why I left. I watched the play-off final against Peterborough while on holiday in Marbella.

"It was the same story - should have won but didn't. I was gutted for Michael Oliver, who is a good mate, and the other lads who were at Darlington when I was there. It was a pleasure to play in the same side as the likes of Marco Gabbiadini.

"I remember meeting Martin Deans after my debut. I used to tell people that we had a fan who travelled to every game from London. To me Martin was a star. What he does is incredible. But that sums up the passion that Darlington generates.

"I was proud to have played for Darlington. I suppose that after relegation to the Conference, when times were so grim they must have been frightening, the ten years that followed could not be so bad whatever happened.

"And the crowds are bigger now. Maybe when people almost lose their club they realise how important it is to them. Now that I'm out of the league (playing for Barrow at the time of writing), I appreciate how happy I was at Darlington."

Martin Gray 1999-2001

League appearances	69	Goals	0
Other Games	12		

MARTIN arrived at Darlington in the summer of 1999, just after new owner George Reynolds took over the club.

"Before the first game at Halifax that season, I spoke to another new signing, Neil Aspin, and we still didn't know how the season would go.

"Marco Gabbiadini scored the only goal of the game, and it was the start of a fantastic season.

"In fifteen years in the game at places like Sunderland and Oxford, I'd never played under so much pressure. It was such a roller-coaster season, full of ups and downs. We were the Manchester United of the Third Division with all the hype.

"I had the feeling that it was starting to go wrong near the end of the season, when I was brought off at Carlisle. We'd had so many opportunities to wrap up promotion, but from a personal point of view, I achieved my dream of playing at Wembley against Peterborough.

"I'd never had such a bad result as that in all my career especially after the way we performed in the first hour. Peterborough were no great shakes, but we just couldn't score.

"We'd beaten them earlier in the season, when we had a run of six consecutive wins. We didn't become complacent. We were a sensible bunch of lads.

"You couldn't blame the management. It was the players, because we lost our form at a crucial time."

At least Martin got his hands on the FA Cup that season.

"When we were the Lucky Losers, the cup was brought to Feethams for a press conference. I suppose it could only happen to our chairman. He just had that little bit of luck.

"On the day at Aston Villa, I had one or two tussles on the field, and my shirt was torn. I gave it away to one of the young supporters after the game."

Martin was involved in probably one of the fastest ever sendings off in history at Swansea.

"The game was stopped because of a free kick, and one of their players received treatment.

"When that was going on, Swansea made a substitution, and a lad called Walter Boyd came on the field.

"He came and stood in front of me, and I gave him a dig in the ribs. He turned round and looked at me, and I gave him another dig in the ribs. This time, he turned round, whacked me and knocked me over.

"The linesman saw what happened, told the referee, who sent him off - and the match hadn't even restarted from the free kick."

Martin also remembers coming back from an away game in 1999.

"We were near Nottingham, when Derek the bus driver said that we were getting low on fuel.

"He had a fuel card with him, but it could only be used at certain service areas. He knew we wouldn't have enough fuel to get to the service area he wanted, so we looked at a map, and headed towards a garage in Sheffield.

"When we got there, it was all boarded up!

"So we had a whip-round amongst the players, but all we got was £10!"

Martin had to retire from playing because of a back injury at the start of season 2001-02, and was appointed youth team coach.

26

Ron Greener 1955-67

League appearances	439	Goals	6
Other Games	51		

RON, affectionately nicknamed "The Man Mountain", played in 490 games for Quakers – more than 500 if the Durham Senior Cup is taken into account – until he was ignominiously given a free transfer, in the back of a car, by manager Jimmy Greenhalgh in 1967.

Ron started his professional career at Newcastle United, where he played three first team games in the same team as Joe Harvey and Jimmy Scoular, and he played in one of the first experimental games under floodlights, for Newcastle away to Falkirk. "I was very upset when I was told that I was no longer required," Ron says.

"But within a week or two, there were several clubs asking about me, and because I lived at Shotton Colliery, I decided to join Darlington because they were one of the clubs near to where I lived."

Later in that first season, he made a swift return to St James Park with Quakers, when 34,257 saw them win their FA cup first round second replay against Carlisle - one of the first FA cup ties under floodlights.

"We were told that the official gate was over 30,000, but we thought that there were more in the ground than that. Newcastle fans were very keen, and when I was there, it wasn't unusual for thousands to turn up and watch us train."

After a 5-4 defeat at Rochdale on September 11 1957 - Quakers led 4-1 at one point and conceded two very late goals. Bobby Gurney, who had helped Sunderland to the FA Cup in 1937, was sacked as manager, and was replaced by Dickie Duckworth.

"Bobby was a nice man, and I was sad to see him go. Dickie replaced him, and always seemed to be on tenterhooks and under pressure to get results."

Quakers probably had their most famous FA Cup run in 1957-58 (told elsewhere), although their feat at the time didn't generate as much national publicity as maybe it would now.

"When we arrived in Norwich for the third round, their local press weren't thinking of whether Norwich would win or not, but instead by how many goals they would score." says Ron.

"That really got us going, especially when we got together to do exercises in Dickie Duckworth's hotel room the night before the game.

"In the match itself, we were going off the field at half-time, and suddenly the public address announcer said to the crowd 'come on, get behind our players' and that really got our backs up.

"He did the same again in the second half while play was going on, but we still won. It really annoyed us." Ron Harbertson and Tommy Moran scored the goals.

Under the headline "Darlington confound critics with a confident victory" The Northern Echo reporter, Darneton wrote: "The Darlington side were full of fight, and were never prepared to surrender."

Reflecting on the 3-3 draw at Chelsea, Ron recalled: "When we got back into the changing room, we were very disappointed that we hadn't won after leading 3-0, but Dickie Duckworth said that we should be very proud of ourselves and it was still a good result. Only the week before, Chelsea had beaten Newcastle 4-0 at Stamford Bridge, so I suppose we didn't do too bad."

Mobbed on his way off the pitch after the 4-1 win over Chelsea in the Feethams replay, a spectator called Ron over to him, and handed him a brown envelope.

"I knew who it was from. Inside, there was £25 for each of the players – much more than a week's wages for each of us."

Every Darlington player was a hero, and Duckworth asked them all to come to the ground the following day. "Dickie just wanted to see us, because he couldn't believe that we'd won. We didn't do any training or anything like that, he just wanted to speak to us."

In the next round at Wolves, before the game, Ron met Wanderers skipper Billy Wright, who was capped 105 times by England. "When I shook hands with him, he was shaking like a leaf - they were really worried about us. We held them for half an hour, but once they went in front, that was it." Quakers lost 6-1.

Ron was one of the team which was nicknamed "The Invincibles" for a short spell in season 1960-61, when Quakers carried all before them in league and league cup for a four month spell.

Again, they were handed the mantle of giantkillers. They put Crystal Palace, their Fourth Division colleagues, out of the Football League Cup by 2-0 at Feethams on October 12, and in the next round West Ham United came to town complete with big name players John Bond and Bobby Moore.

Quakers won 3-2, but the London press weren't exactly complimentary. "They wrote that we had kicked them off the park, which wasn't true at all. They just didn't fancy it," recalled Ron.

"In the next round Bolton Wanderers had a strong side out – I was up against Nat Lofthouse. I got to the ball before him early in the game, and he growled at me and told me not to do that again.

"I thought we should have won, instead of losing 2-1. Our keeper let in a daft goal. He thought a shot was going wide, but instead it beat him at the near post."

Ron Greener (left), breaks the appearance record of Brian Henderson in 1966. It was his 489th league game

That same season, Quakers became involved in a five game epic against Hull City in the second round of the FA Cup, Hull finally winning.

Quakers were back in the FA Cup limelight in season 1964-65. After beating Scunthorpe and then Hartlepool in a second round replay, Quakers were handed a home tie against Arsenal, but they lost 2-0.

"Lol Morgan, our manager, told us to go out and play football like he normally did, but I think that was a mistake. It played into their hands. A lad called Joe Baker, an England international, played up front for them, and I couldn't get near him. I've never run around so much in my life and not seen the ball. George Armstrong and George Eastham were superb that day," said Ron.

The 1965-66 season saw Quakers' first promotion since their early days in the Football League.

They clinched it on the last day of the season with a 0-0 draw against Torquay in front of a jubilant crowd of 16,469, but it was against the Gulls earlier that season when Quakers produced their best performance in a 4-0 win at Plainmoor.

"We played some of our best football of the season there. It wasn't a case of just scoring four goals, we played some very good possession football, and Bobby

Cummings scored a hat trick."

Quakers went straight back down to the Fourth, but there was bad news for Ron.

"One day after the season had ended, I was working at Neashams, and Jimmy Greenhalgh walked across the yard and said he wanted a word with me.

"He put his arm around me, we got into a car in the yard, and he told me that my Darlington career was over. Jimmy told me that he wanted to tell me personally, rather than me find out through a letter."

It was an undignified end to his Darlington career as many fans wanted the chance to say farewell to their hero.

Ron Harbertson 1957-58 and January to April 1961

League appearances	63	**Goals**	30
Other Games	6		

STRIKER Ron was a crowd hero in his first spell at Feethams, after arriving in January 1957.

Ron made club history in season 1957-58 by scoring in each of their five FA Cup ties before Quakers lost 6-1 at Wolves in the FA Cup fifth round.

He scored both goals in the 2-0 win at Rochdale in the first round.

The Northern Echo reported that Ron "was carried shoulder-high from the field by a band of happy Darlington supporters…his brilliant control and trickery was something not often seen from Darlington players."

In the next round he scored two against Southern League Boston in the 5-3 win.

Norwich City came next. "We were branded as no-hopers. But we were really worked up, especially the skipper, Brian Henderson. I scored one of my rare headed goals when we won there, and it gave everybody a lot of pleasure."

The Northern Echo's headline read "Darlington confound critics with a confident victory." Ron scored with a right foot shot after 20 minutes, then he headed the winner just six minutes from time.

Ron also scored in the fourth round at Stamford Bridge, the fighting 3-3 draw at Chelsea after the players enjoyed a seaside break in the days before the game.

"We went down to Brighton, and for me it was a real experience being away from home, because I'd never done that before. It took away a lot of the tension, which would have been there if we'd stayed at home."

"We should have won the game at Chelsea – they took it for granted that it was going to be a stroll.

"I scored one of my best ever goals there. We got a throw in just on the halfway line, and Ken Furphy threw the ball into the inside forward position, and I hit a right foot shot from thirty yards. The ball flew into the top corner of the net.

"We all got some stick in that game. We were pulled back and hacked down while we were ahead, because Chelsea got desperate."

Ron also scored in the replay at Feethams, which Quakers won 4-1 in extra time.

"I'd been off the field with a shoulder injury, because their keeper collided with me, but I came back and played up front. One of their players missed a good chance near the end of the ninety minutes, but in extra time we paralysed them. I scored when Tommy Moran put the ball across the 18 yard box, and I hit the ball into the corner. Jimmy Greaves played in the first game, but he didn't play in the second because Ken Furphy didn't let him get a kick."

Ron had a marathon working day. "I worked a shift down the pit, from midnight until eight in the morning. I travelled forty miles down the A1 to play for Darlington, got home at 9.30, and then went back down the pit for another shift at midnight."

It was a different story in the next round at Wolves, and Quakers lost 6-1.

When Ron was transferred to Lincoln City, Darlington refused him permission to retrieve his boots from the dressing room.

"The manager, Dickie Duckworth, had the keys of the dressing room, but not the main gate. I wanted to climb over the wall to get into the ground, but Dickie wouldn't let me. So he climbed in, got my boots, and I set off down to Liverpool, where I played the next day for Lincoln."

Paul Heckingbottom 1999-2002

League appearances	100	**Goals**	5
Other Games	15		

PAUL suffered the agony of limping off injured in the 2000 play off final, and watched helplessly from the sidelines as Peterborough scored the winner.

Paul had problems with a groin injury throughout most of the 1999-2000 season, but managed to keep playing.

Paul Heckingbottom

And there were no signs of problems when Quakers reached the play off semi finals against Hartlepool, against whom he'd scored in the league just a few games before.

"The first game set it all up for us," he said. "Craig Liddle headed the first goal, but then Craig Midgley missed a sitter for them from just a yard or so out.

"We broke away, and Glenn Naylor was brought down for a penalty, which Marco Gabbiadini scored.

"It was a great feeling to get to Wembley, but we should have already been up through automatic promotion. The Hartlepool games got us buzzing again."

On a wet night at Wembley, Quakers missed several chances to go in the lead.

"When it was goalless at half time, we should have been at least one goal up, maybe two, because we played some very good football.

"But after 70 minutes, my groin ripped apart when I stretched for a tackle.

"I sat on the bench, and the enormity of the game suddenly sank in. Peterborough scored after I went off injured, and maybe if I'd been on the field, then I could have done something about it."

Paul thinks that were a couple of turning points that season.

"Against Northampton near the end of the season, we needed a draw or a win to keep them out of reach. Peter Duffield scored early on in that game, but the goal was disallowed, then Northampton went on to win.

"When we played at Leyton Orient, we were drawing 1-1 when I went off injured, and Gary Himsworth replaced me at left back

"They got a free kick, but Gary didn't know the offside routine and he played their forwards onside, and they scored a late winner.

"It was a tough season, because we were the team everybody wanted to beat. We had to be up for every game."

Paul was part of the team which were the Lucky Losers in the 1999-2000 FA Cup. Manchester United controversially withdrew from the competition, so the Football Association decreed that one of the sides losing in the second round would be re-admitted.

Quakers lost at Gillingham in the second round, and were put in the Lucky Losers draw with all the other second round losers.

Paul was training with the rest of the Darlington squad when the draw was made one morning.

"We'd all been laughing and joking that we'd be pulled out of the draw, but we thought no more of it.

"Then John Murray, our physio, dashed on to the training field and shouted that we were going to play at Aston Villa in the third round of the Cup.

"We thought that it was a wind up of some sort at first, but then we realised it was true.

"We did well at Villa Park. Benito Carbone scored a great goal for them, and David James, the Aston Villa keeper, pulled off two great saves from Peter Duffield and Martin Gray.

"Even when we went 2-0 down, the lads didn't give up and we got a penalty when Peter Duffield was brought down. David James saved Peter's penalty and then Craig Liddle and I fought over the ball to put it over the line. Craig shouted "Time" to me and I thought mainly of getting a touch to put the ball over the line.

"It was a great feeling to score, but then the stadium public address said that Neil Heaney got the goal!"

Paul, now fully recovered from his groin trouble, decided to move on to Norwich at the end of the 2001/2 season, though added:

"I will always think of Darlington as my first club, because that is where I first played regularly. I have had some great teammates and the fans have been really good to me. I hope for their sake that Darlington go on to have a successful future in the new stadium."

Brian Henderson 1952-64

League appearances	423	Goals	3
Other Games	3		

BRIAN stands second to Ron Greener in the list of most Darlington appearances. But it is a wonder he played at all, considering the polio-like illness that afflicted him.

He recalled: "When I was four I was paralysed. We lived in Hexham, and a

29

specialist said it was too low lying, and we should move into the hills, so the family ran a smallholding in Allendale. While he worked my father took me in a wheelchair. He laid me down one day.

"When he returned, I had climbed a tree! That was how remarkable my recovery was. But ever since my left leg has been for standing on - football was played with my right."

Brian became a right back, initially with Newcastle, then Carlisle. It was his appearance at Wembley for the 1952 FA Cup Final that earned him a move to Darlington - though he didn't set foot on the hallowed turf.

"Bob Stokoe, best man at my wedding, promised me a ticket. Newcastle were to play Arsenal and I was thrilled," said Brian.

"I asked the Carlisle manager - I think it was Fred Emery - who said I could go. The semi-final was six weeks before the final, but come the time, our reserves were to play West Stanley. Fred said I must play, but I went to the final."

Brian was given a free transfer, and Darlington manager Bob Gurney signed him. Brian's Darlington debut, on September 8, 1952, was at Feethams - against Carlisle. Some tigerish tackling from him was the only memorable feature of a 0-0 draw.

He was to take part in some of the club's most amazing games, before retiring after breaking his leg against Stockport at Feethams on January 4, 1964.

He scored only three goals, for the sole responsibility of full backs was to stop the opposition winger.

He could recall only one of his goals, in a 5-1 defeat at Barnsley. "I was getting skinned by the winger, and they won a free kick. Taken by Tommy Lumley, the ball smacked me in the face.

"I said I had double vision, and went onto the wing. Although my vision was a bit blurred I really wanted to get away from that winger.

"Ken Furphy had to go to full back and the winger gave him the same treatment. I think we were five down when I scored. I caught the ball on the volley, and it was still rising as it crashed into the top corner from 20 yards.

"Everyone was impressed - except Ken. He realised then that there wasn't much wrong with me."

Brian's other goals came in a 5-1 win over Stockport at Feethams in March 1963, and in a 3-1 defeat at Barrow the following October.

He recalls laying into the referee after a draw at Elland Road, when Quakers were playing Hull City in an FA Cup replay. Brian was skipper and on a quagmire Quakers looked liked winning.

But the referee decided the pitch was not fit for extra time. "I went crackers," said Brian. "We ended up drawing four times and when I shook hands with the Hull skipper, before the final game, he said: 'you again. I'm even dreaming about you." Hull won 3-0.

Brian also played against Chelsea in Darlington's victory, and against West Ham, including Bobby Moore.

The Darlington squad included six part timers, so sometimes the full squad saw each other only on match days. Training was running and five a side - no tactical work.

"We played five a side in the car park behind the East Stand. There were so many injuries we referred to it as the Scar Park! My pre-match warm up was a cold shower, which made me tingle and warmed the blood."

Brian once played on for six weeks after breaking an ankle. He stuffed cotton wool inside the bandages to deaden the pain.

His enthusiasm never waned, and even when the lengthy coach journeys became a fortnightly bind after the introduction of the Third and Fourth Divisions, he didn't mind. "We had longer card games," he recalled.

His career ended in a clash with Stockport's Tony France (who also played for Quakers) at Feethams. "The ball bounced in the corner of the pitch and I connected so well that it flew out of play on the opposite side. As my leg went up, his came down on mine. You could hear the crack all over the ground. I was still angry with him decades later," said Brian.

What followed was like a scene from Laurel and Hardy. Bobby Whitehead had already been taken off on the only stretcher, so not only were Quakers down to nine men (no substitutes then) but Brian was placed on an unrolled joiner's bag.

"My leg slipped off it and was agony," he recalled. "Then they caught it on the tunnel wall. After I had gone to hospital and had it set, I had to go home with my shorts still on and my other leg still covered in mud."

He was in plaster for 26 weeks, partly because the leg had to be re-broken and set after a month. Thereafter he managed only a few games for Northallerton.

He worked as a farmer, gardener, and car salesman for Quakers' chairman John

Neasham, before getting his own garage. He lived in Darlington, occasionally visiting Feethams, until his death last year.

Brian Honour 1981-84

League appearances	74	Goals	7
Other Games	12		

BRIAN was one of the first players to be offered a YTS place at Darlington when he signed in 1981.

"We were the pioneers of the Youth Training Scheme, and we were given the opportunity to go to college and learn other skills.

"I spent two years in the Northern Intermediate League, and then I played for the reserves in the Northern League," he said.

"I was also called in to the first team while I was still an apprentice, and I played quite a few times.

"We had a good set up. There was Jimmy Shoulder and Richie Pitt, and it was the first time that Darlington had ever introduced a youth policy."

However, the youngsters were also involved in other jobs, apart from football.

"We had to do a lot of work on the ground during the summer. For example, we dug the foundations for the floodlights, refurbished the dressing rooms, cut the grass and did all sorts. It was slave labour, really.

"One day, though, the club's attitude changed. Gavin Liddle learned how to drive one of the dumpers, and one day went too fast around a corner. He jumped off into a fence, but the edge of the dumper caught him on the back of his calf, and he was badly hurt. It was light duties after that."

Brian hardly missed a game in season 1983-84, before he was freed by Cyril Knowles.

"Cyril called me into his office one day, and asked me if I fancied playing in Sweden during the summer. He offered me a three month contract out there, but I asked him if there would be a contract waiting for me at Darlington when I came back. "He couldn't offer anything. I asked what the point of stopping was, so he freed me.

"Mark Forster was the next player in to the office. He went to Sweden and returned to Darlington, because he had more of a contract offer than me."

Brian joined Hartlepool, and later in his career, Knowles took over as manager, but the relationship was much more cordial, and Brian went on to become one of Pool's most popular ever players, before having a spell as caretaker manager - which included a 3-2 defeat by Darlington at Victoria Park.

Despite the rivalry between the clubs, Darlington fans were pleased he went on to enjoy a long career, as his commitment at Feethams won the admiration of the Quaker fans.

Brian Keeble 1965-69

League appearances	154	Goals	2
Other Games	22		

BRIAN was one of the new signings brought to the club by Lol Morgan at the start of season 65-66.

However, the initial move didn't quite go to plan. "I moved house to Darlington from Cleethorpes, but on the day we were due to move, the removal van didn't show up," he said.

"We had a baby, who was only six months old, so Lol said we could stay at his house while it was all sorted out!"

Brian was an ever-present in the league that season, and played a key part in the shock 2-1 win at Blackpool in the third round of the Football League Cup on October 13th 1965.

"Blackpool had a full strength side out that night, and included players like Alan Ball and Jimmy Armfield. I put in one crunching tackle on Alan Ball - he was expecting me to pull out of it.

"Jimmy Armfield was a real gentleman. After the game, he came into our dressing room and congratulated us. There was a big celebration that night."

In those days, it wasn't unusual to play teams home and away over holiday periods, and Quakers played Doncaster on Good Friday and Easter Saturday.

They beat Doncaster at Feethams by 3-2, and the following day travelled to Belle Vue.

"Lol was delayed on his way to the game, and missed the start of it. We got off to a really bad start and by the time he got there, we were 3-0 down. I think he believed that we would do all right until he arrived!" Quakers lost the game 6-3.

32

Lol Morgan with Bill Hopper, Eric Johnstone, Tony Moor, Joe Jacques and Brian Keeble (right) in 1965-66

Brian only scored one goal that season, but it was a crucial one, the decider at Colchester six games from the end of the season.

"Both teams were going well at the time - I think they were just above us in the league.

"We were pushed on the defensive for most of the game, but when we had a corner, I was caught a little bit upfield.

"Colchester broke to our end, and they had a shot which Tony Moor saved. He threw it to me about midway inside our half, and I just ran towards their box and whacked the ball into the top corner.

"I was surprised at half time, because Lol gave me a ticking off for being so far upfield when I was expecting a few words of congratulation instead!"

Quakers were on the cup trail two years later, when they played Derby at the Baseball Ground.

"We put all the pressure on Derby in the first half, but the pitch was terrible. We led 1-0 at half time, but they scored with a couple of deflected goals in the second half, and they led 5-2.

"We pulled two more back, and maybe with another quarter of an hour, we might have won it."

Gavin Liddle 1981-83

League appearances	31	Goals	0

GAVIN spent two seasons at Feethams, after he was signed from Hartlepool United as an 18 year old.

His biggest memory of his stay was when he was part of the team which faced Sheffield United in the penultimate game of the 1981-82 season, when the Yorkshire side needed three points to win the Fourth Division title.

"There were United fans everywhere, and to this day I've never seen anything like it. There were over 11,000 of them inside Feethams, not just on the terracing, but on the pylons, on the stand roof even on top of the dugouts.

"In fact, one fan came through the dugout roof and brushed George Herd with his foot and Bob Farrelly, our physio, was going to chin him!

"There was a mass of orange and yellow shirts. At the end of the game, the fans wanted a souvenir of any sort, so they stripped one of our players, Alan Kamara, of his shirt and shorts. Billy Elliott wasn't too pleased because it meant that the club had to pay for another set!"

Financially, times were hard at Feethams in those days when Liddle was an apprentice making his way in the football world.

"We used to go training in South Park, and when there were bright and sunny days, especially during the school holidays, it wasn't unusual for us to be dribbling around families having picnics!

"Financially, as a kid, I thought I didn't get looked after.

"When pay day came along, some players didn't get paid at all. At the age of eighteen, I was on £100 per week, with £20 appearance, and £30 for a win. We didn't win many games, so I was never taking much home."

Just like every youngster, Gavin wanted to move higher up the league ladder, but those hopes were dashed after a game at Tranmere in October 1982.

Gavin Liddle challenges the Sheffield United goalkeeper in 1982 in front of the massive away support at Feethams

"I didn't play particularly well in the first half, but I'd been feeling unwell before the game.

"The manager, Billy Elliott, came up to me at half time, and told me that I'd "well and truly messed my chances up there." Obviously, he was referring to the fact that a couple of scouts were watching me.

"I felt bad for ages after that, and I wish that Billy had put his arm around me and told me a little gentler."

He still earned some good reviews for his performances.

"Before I was taken on at Darlington, I was training to be a butcher, so the occasional headline would be along the lines of "mincing up strikers" or "making mincemeat out of the opposition"

Gavin's contract was up for renewal at the end of the 1982-83 season, and he went into negotiations with the new manager, Cyril Knowles.

"I was offered the same money by Cyril, and two or three players in the dressing room told me that I should hold out for more. I called the club's bluff, and in the

meantime, Bishop Auckland offered me a deal and a part time job offer came along. I couldn't afford to stay at Darlington - financially I was better off playing part time."

Phil Lloyd 1983-86

League appearances	127	Goals	5
Other Games	23		

PHIL had one moment in a Darlington shirt that he will particularly treasure - the second goal against Middlesbrough, the club that released him, in the FA Cup third round win of 1985.

A stylish and committed central defender, that goal in front of the Shed End was hardly a classic. It was a typical muddy January goalmouth scramble.

"I remember Micky Angus winning a tackle, the ball ran loose, there were legs flying in from all angles, and I prodded the ball past keeper Kelham O'Hanlon," recalled Phil. "It put us 2-0 up and then there was a pitch invasion.

"While we were off the pitch I remember the ref telling Cyril that the game would finish, even if the ground had to be cleared first. When we went back on Tony McAndrew pulled one back, but we hung on.

"For Darlington to beat Boro was fabulous, and that goal would have been special whoever scored it. But having been discarded by Boro it was extra sweet for me. We had drawn at Ayresome, and I remember thinking as I went into the first game, that there was no way I would let them past.

"When they released me I felt I was no worse than other players there. I had England youth trials with Boro coach Harold Shepherdson. But when Malcolm Allison took over at Ayresome, he bombed out several of us even though we had been promised six month contracts. "

Cyril Knowles had been Boro coach and Phil obviously impressed him, for Cyril had no hesitation in bringing him to Feethams.

Phil had gone from Boro to Barnsley on a non-contract basis, when Cyril phoned.

"I was on the scrap heap and would have taken any offer. I made my league debut at Chester and gave away a penalty, from which they scored and we lost 2-1. I was not used to the pace of the Fourth Division.

33

Farewell to Feethams | a collection of Darlington FC memories

Phil Lloyd

"After the game I trudged into the dressing room, and Cyril had a go at every player except me."

Phil kept his place, and the following year Darlington won promotion as well as beating Boro.

"We signed good players. John Craggs was one of the best, and Carl Airey banged in the goals. I had played against him in the Northern Intermediate League and we drove to Darlington from Yorkshire each day. Garry MacDonald arrived from Boro. As an apprentice I had cleaned his boots. And Micky Angus and Colin Ross were former Boro lads as well. I also cleaned Dave Hodgson's boots, and when, years later, he was Darlington manager and recognised me when I was watching a game at Torquay, I was delighted.

"Cyril had no budget, but his strength was motivating players. Lower division

management suited him. I'm not sure whether his style would have worked higher up the ladder."

When Phil needed a cartilage operation - complete with five inch scar and not the keyhole surgery they have now - Gary Pallister was brought in on loan.

The story goes that Cyril could have signed Pally for £10,000, but Darlington couldn't afford it. "As soon as I was fit I was back in and he returned to Boro," said Phil. "Two or three years down the line he was playing for England and I was finished. But I can always say that I took Gary Pallister's place.

"We won 2-0 at Reading in my comeback game, to two own goals. I later played against Gary Bennett. Cyril used to refer to him as 'Psycho' and I had a few scraps with him."

Phil created such an impression that he was included in an all-time best Darlington team in one newspaper. "When you think of all the players the club had in living memory, that's a great honour."

Phil's Darlington career came to an end when he fell out of favour after Cyril left and Dave Booth took over. But in came Cyril again, this time to take Phil to Torquay, and he still lives in the area.

"Cyril began to lose his way at Darlington," said Phil. "When I was out injured we lost a game 7-0 at York and I remember thinking that such a defeat should never happen to one of Cyril's teams.

"But I had no hesitation in following him to Torquay. I played at Wembley in the play-off final, when we lost 4-1 to Bolton after being one-up. But how we got to Wembley was typical of the spirit Cyril instilled.

"We lost at home to Wolves 2-1 in the first leg of the semi-final. They had Steve Bull in their team, and for the second leg, they had printed Wembley mugs and T-shirts, and included directions to Wembley in the match programme. We beat them 2-0."

Phil played 200 consecutive games for Torquay, and was twelve off the club record when his leg snapped in two places. He had to hang up his boots or finish up in a wheelchair.

But he retains fond memories of Darlington and Cyril, who was incredibly committed. "When Darlington lost at Telford in the FA Cup fourth round after beating Boro, you could hear a pin drop," said Phil.

"Then through the flimsy dressing room walls we heard their players singing

'Nice One Cyril.' That was more than Cyril could bear and he ended up kicking furniture around."

As for Cyril, he not only took Darlington to promotion and Torquay to Wembley, but was on the verge of winning promotion with Hartlepool when his fatal illness struck, Alan Murray completing the job.

That's a treble that may never be matched, and Phil is proud to have been part of two of those achievements. And like most Darlington players - he probably never wanted to play for Pool anyway!

Barry Lyons 1976-79

League appearances	97	Goals 12
Other Games		17

Barry Lyons

BARRY had played as a winger and inside right for Nottingham Forest at the highest level, and admitted he questioned whether he had made the right move before his first game for Darlington at Swansea.

"I went into the bathroom and two players had their heads over the sink. They were putting contact lenses in. One was skipper Bobby Noble and the other one was Alan Ogley, our goalkeeper. At that point I wondered what I had let myself in for! But my fears were misplaced. Bobby was a leader, and Alan an excellent keeper."

Barry was more cultured than many of those around him, but Darlington had a reasonable team, so he settled in, and he was happy to continue a career that seemed to have ended when he was released by York because of a back injury.

"I'd played alongside Peter Madden at Rotherham, and I think it was Dennis Wann who told him I was out of a job, so Peter signed me, and switched me to central midfield."

Barry was a regular for three seasons, becoming skipper. He scored the penalty at Feethams that beat Second Division Fulham in the League Cup.

"I can't remember that penalty. But I'll have sent it high to the keeper's left. I always aimed at the post, but with a bit of curl on the ball, so that it swung inside."

When Madden left, Barry was disappointed.

"He was a good manager. He protected players from the problems of the boardroom, and tried to get us a pay rise whenever he could. I know there was a fair bit of friction between him and the board, but he acted as a barrier so that it didn't filter down to the players.

"I was older than the other lads and was aware that things were not running too smoothly, but Peter wanted his players to concentrate on playing.

"By then we should have been in a higher division. We had a good enough side to go up, and in my first season it looked possible. I remember Clive Nattress got up and down the flanks to good effect. Then there were lads I had played with at York, plus Derek Craig and Colin Sinclair, who was a very good striker."

Barry was mild mannered, but in one game when he tried to diffuse a situation with a bit of humour, it backfired. He was sent off in just his fourth game for the club - his first ever early bath. In fact he had hardly ever been booked until then.

"We had already had Ron Ferguson sent off. Every decision was going against us, and I let my frustration get the better of me."

The referee had finally given Darlington a free kick, and the fans cheered sarcastically. Barry not only joined in, but waved his arms to encourage the crowd further. The ref didn't see the funny side (do they ever!). Stockport won 2-0 as Darlington finished with nine men. Even hardened professionals, who think they have seen it all before, discover new frustrations at Feethams.

One training session has stuck in Barry's memory.

The squad went to the gym at Teesside airport to try and escape heavy snow. "We had just started training when the Middlesbrough squad arrived and said they had booked the hanger where all the equipment was. They kicked us out. While they did weights and circuits, we played five a side in six inches of snow!"

Once Madden had left, Barry helped Len Walker, the caretaker boss, by doubling up as his assistant. Then an offer came in from York to be youth team coach. "I said to Len that as I still lived there and my playing days were just about over, it made sense for me to go. So my final games of a good career were played for Darlington."

Barry later managed York, and now owns a small hotel in the town.

35

Dave McLean scores against Hartlepool's ex-Darlington 'keeper Martin Burleigh

Dave McLean 1979-86

League appearances	294	**Goals**	52
Other Games	44		

36

THE livewire Geordie was inspirational in a side which rose from perennial strugglers to promotion winners under Cyril Knowles. "After struggling you appreciate the good times," said Dave. "Though even when things were not going well, I was happy at Darlington. They were easily the best years of my career."

He played a few games for Newcastle, until Bill McGarry became manager.

"I was injured," recalled Dave. "But McGarry said he knew what I could do, and encouraged me to get fit. Then within a week I was on my way to Carlisle. That was my first lesson in not believing everything I was told."

Dave hankered after a return to the north east.

"Billy Elliott was Darlington manager, and signed me after a trial. He had quirky ideas, but was a former international and had coached abroad, and I respected that.

"Jimmy Shoulder, an honest and hard working guy, was coach. They made me want to play for them. Money was tight, and we ended up with a side full of players

other clubs didn't want. But we forged a good spirit.

"Billy left out of the blue, and I hoped the next guy would be as good." It was Cyril, and Dave quickly learnt that what the manager wanted, he got.

"There were no grey areas. You were told something, and you did it! He brought in John Craggs as player coach. He was class, and suddenly we had a talented, though small squad.

"We stuck together and played through injuries. I was captain, and to win promotion was fantastic after we had finished third from bottom in my first season, and struggled in others.

"I had a few run ins with Cyril, but none lasted more that a couple of minutes. I had a reputation as a fiery character - maybe because of my red hair - but I never saw myself that way.

"The Fourth Division toughened me. I was all pace and skill as a winger in my young days, but in midfielder in the lower leagues you must look after yourself."

Dave was penalty taker, and recalls smashing one over the bar, but that was the only time he missed the target.

His commitment was summed up by the very few games he missed. An injury towards the end of his first season restricted him to 36 league appearances. The following year it was 41, then for two seasons he was ever present, before making 43, 44, and 38 appearances.

A model of consistency, he started as an attacking midfielder then gradually assumed an anchor role.

The final game of the promotion season when Torquay were beaten 1-0 in an incessant storm that left the pitch standing in water remains in his memory.

"We had a trialist goalkeeper that night (Rocha Kaara, a Tunisian). What a character he was. It's funny that I played all those games yet can't remember many, yet he played only once and I recall him vividly."

Dave also remembers the 2-2 draw with Crewe when Quakers clinched promotion. "We'd got the jitters and hadn't won for five games. But ten minutes before the end of the Crewe game we knew a draw would see us promoted, and we were jubilant, coasting home."

Dave left a big impression on the fans, none more than Neil Maddison.

"He was a Darlington fan before becoming a professional," recalled Dave. "When he was at Southampton, a magazine did a profile on him. It was after I had finished playing. When asked his favourite player, he replied: 'Dave McLean.' I was really proud of that."

In Dave's time Darlington took some hidings, but had famous victories, including a 6-1 win at Aldershot. "We were all good players - but so inconsistent. When it clicked we looked world beaters. But often we were awful."

Among the players he remembers well was Alan Walsh. "What a hammer of a left foot he had," said Dave. "He scored some incredibly powerful goals - mind you, his right foot was not much use.

"David Speedie was unbelievable in the air for one so short, and a right little bugger on the training ground, always up to tricks. Kev Smith was the local boy made good. He was raw, but had a huge heart."

Dave left in regrettable circumstances after Darlington's first season in the old Third Division.

"My contract was up, but I wanted to stay. We were a division higher and I wanted a pay rise. Cyril and chairman Ken Warne offered me the bare minimum. I felt let down. I had worked so hard and was captain. Cyril and I had discussed a lot together.

"Freedom of contract was coming in, and the phone didn't stop. Even a Belgian club came in but I went to Scunthorpe because my old mate Bill Green was there.

"Then I found out that Scunthorpe had tried to buy me for £30,000. Darlington had never told me, which I felt bad about after all my service."

Dave had offered to stay at Darlington for very little more money, as long as he got a testimonial in three years' time after completing ten years. The answer was no.

He played in the last game at the Old Show Ground before Scunthorpe moved to Glanford Park. "It was the second leg of the play-offs and we lost to Torquay," he recalled. "That was my last game."

He played at Wembley for Brigg Town when they won the FA Vase in 1996, ironically the year that Quakers first played there in the play-off final.

"We beat Billingham on the way," said Dave. "Kev Smith was in their side."

Dave still coaches Brigg, and works in Sheffield as a production manager for a company that makes three piece suites. He's still got the shirt from the soaking night against Torquay, when Darlington won promotion.

"It's just about dried out," he laughed.

Tony Moor 1965-71

League appearances	239
Other Games	7

Tony Moor

TONY was Darlington keeper for six years, during which time he helped Quakers to their first promotion in nearly forty years, when they finished second in season 1965-66.

He played part time for Darlington, after starting his career at York. "I was full time at York for three years, but I thought that there wasn't a lot of future in it because of the money, and left.

"So I opened up a sports business in my home town, Scarborough. Lol Morgan, was looking for a keeper, but he wanted me to go full time again.

"I refused, and I heard nothing else for a while. He eventually came back to me, and said he would sign me, if I would train a couple of mornings per week. I felt I could manage that, so I signed on."

In fact, Moor cost Quakers £100, after Lol and chief scout Jack Watson watched him playing for York Reserves at South Shields.

Moor stepped straight into a promotion chasing side, and was an ever-present on their way to glory.

"We had a very good team that season. One of our best performances was a 4-0 win at Torquay. They were top of the table, and we were just below them.

"They had some good pressure, but every time we attacked them, we seemed to score. We played some good football that night. We had another good performance at Colchester near the end of the season. They were near the top, like us, and we won 1-0, Brian Keeble scoring.

"The last game of that season was against Torquay. We drew 0-0 with them to win promotion, but they scored a blistering goal from about 35 yards out which I didn't see at all. It was disallowed for some reason, fortunately."

Unfortunately, Lol quit that summer for Norwich City. "Lol was very good at man-management. He knew how to get the best out of his players. He worked a lot with the ball, and liked to use different tactics.

37

"When Jimmy Greenhalgh took over, he had us running a lot, and that year, we seemed to get a lot of injuries which meant we lost our rhythm."

Jimmy made his mark early on. "Usually after away games with Lol, we would go into a restaurant and order from the a la carte menu.

"We did this after an away game at Swindon, and after we got back on the bus, Jimmy told us to get off again. He closed the bus door, and shouted; "This isn't blooming Barcelona. When you go into a restaurant again, order from the menu, and not a la carte." By the end of that season, we weren't going into restaurants - we were using transport cafes!"

Quakers came straight back down from the third division, but in season 1967-68, they reached the last sixteen of the Football League Cup.

"We had two very good wins against Second Division clubs Portsmouth and Millwall.

"We played Derby at the Baseball Ground on a horrible pitch in the fifth round. We played quite well in the first half, and Bobby Cummings gave us the lead, and at half time we fancied our chances.

"But in the second half, I was beaten by two deflections. I went one way, and the ball went the other - nothing I could do about them."

Ray Yeoman took over from Jimmy Greenhalgh in March 1968. "We went to Port Vale for an away game. Before the game, Ray laid into me, and told me that I was too soft when I was coming out for the ball. He reckoned I should hit players instead.

"So when the first ball came into the box, I charged out with my feet flying, and I knocked a couple of people over. It was only when I turned round, that I saw John Peverell and Brian Keeble, both my full backs, flat out. I didn't do it again, and Ray never mentioned it either."

The 1968-69 season saw Quakers mount another promotion challenge.

They started the season with an unbeaten run of fourteen matches, Exeter City ending the sequence with a 2-1 win at Feethams at the end of October.

"I had ten clean sheets in that run, seven of them in a row. We played at Doncaster on a Friday night in October, and there were 22,000 people in the ground. When we walked on to the pitch, John Peverell said to me "We're all right for a crowd bonus tonight". We won 1-0 with a goal from Harry Kirk."

Quakers had a mini slump, but they were back in the running for promotion thanks to a run of four wins in six games, but some bad results meant they had to beat Bradford City in the last game of the season to win the last promotion place.

"We scored early in the game, but then the barrier collapsed behind my goal. Although I didn't think there was any crowd trouble, we had to go off the field.

"Bradford won the game 3-1. They got one goal at a corner, when one of their players stood in front of me, and as the ball was hit towards him, stuck his backside into me and I could only push the ball into my own net."

Tony decided he was going to retire when he suffered a kidney injury against Everton in the second round of the League Cup in season 1969-70.

"I ended up in hospital after that game. Everton were one of the favourites for the league at the time, and they fielded their strongest team at Feethams. We held them to a goalless draw in the first half, and in the second half, I came out for the ball, and Joe Royle came in sideways, and kneed me in the kidneys.

"I had treatment for a few minutes, and stayed on the field (There were no substitute keepers in those days). Five minutes later, Alan Ball scored the only goal of the game.

"After the game finished, I rushed straight to hospital, and the doctors told me that I had internal bleeding. In fact, they were frightened that my kidneys might rupture. So it was at that point when I decided to retire."

Ironically, on the day we interviewed Tony for this book, Joe Royle was sacked as manager of Premiership club Manchester City.

It took Tony another eighteen months to finally hang up his boots, at the end of season 1970-71, although he came back and played twice more in an emergency the following season. He was widely regarded as one of Darlington's best ever keepers, and some fans say he was the best the club has ever had.

Lol Morgan Player-Manager June 1964-June 1966

League appearances	31	Goals	0
Other Games	3		

LOL was the first manager to guide Quakers to promotion in almost forty years in 1966 and became a firm crowd favourite. He was appointed player-manager in June 1964 - but for the first month of his reign he shared an office with his predecessor, Eddie Carr.

38

"Eddie had been told by the board that he wouldn't be staying on as manager, and when I arrived, he still had a month to go on his contract and the board wouldn't pay him up.

"So instead of staying away from the ground, he continued to come to work. He didn't have anything to do, but just sat behind a desk in the same office as me. There was no bad feeling between us, and he didn't bother me at all. Some days he wouldn't even come into work."

Lol's first season didn't see Quakers doing much in the league, but instead they had a good run in the FA Cup. After winning 2-1 at Scunthorpe, Quakers' next opponents were the old enemy - Hartlepool, at the Victoria Ground.

And unusually, Quakers decided to stay overnight, at a hotel in Seaton Carew.

"I wanted the players to be at their best the following day. Their manager, Brian Clough, tried to take the mickey out of me in his interviews on the television and in the papers, but it didn't work."

Quakers drew 0-0, then four days later completed the job with a 4-1 replay win in front of 14,466 at Feethams, a victory which earned them a home tie with Arsenal in the third round.

"Because Ray Yeoman was injured at the time, I asked him to go and watch Arsenal play. He watched them the Saturday before we were due to play them, and when I spoke to him a day later, he told me: "This is the worst Arsenal team I've ever seen."

"On the same day, I had a conversation with a journalist from the Daily Mail. I told him what Ray had said, and the next morning, I picked up the paper and here it was word for word.

"We never got to grips with Arsenal on the day, and we lost 2-0.

"The team spirit around then was tremendous. We didn't have many players, so I couldn't rotate them like managers do nowadays. The players knew very well that if they had a bad day, they would still be playing the next week. Everybody gave their best."

Lol worked very hard in the summer of 1965 looking for new players, and he and chief scout Jack Watson brought in Tony Moor, Joe Jacques and Brian Keeble.

They started the 1965-66 season slowly with four wins from the first eleven matches but the turning point came at a league Cup tie at Blackpool on October 13th 1965.

Lol Morgan with the Mayor and Mayoress

Blackpool, with several stars in their side, were still a First Division side then, but Quakers won 2-1 with goals from Billy Hopper and George McGeachie.

"We all went out for a beer afterwards to Blackpool Tower.

"A few days before the game, I had been instructed by the board not to let a certain player on the coach because he had been in jail all night as he'd been involved in a fracas.

"I told him that he would probably be suspended, and if he was, then he would never play for the club again. He didn't like that, and sure enough when the board met, he was suspended.

"After the Blackpool game, we were all having a few beers, and this particular player came over to me and I feared the worst.

"But instead, he shook my hand, and told me that it was the best he'd ever seen Darlington play."

The last game of that season was against Torquay United on May 21st. Quakers needed a point to guarantee a promotion place, a victory for the title.

They had to settle for a 0-0 draw, but Lol says: "I thought we'd lost it. Torquay scored a goal from well out, and I thought we were 1-0 down. But Dickie Deacon,

39

the trainer, said: "Look, Lol, the linesman's got his flag up for offside." The player who was offside was well out on the wing, and he wasn't interfering with play.

"It was my happiest moment in football when we were promoted. One of the lads even threw his shirt into the crowd. I played hell with him, as we hadn't the money to buy any more."

However, on that famous day, there was a big question mark hanging over Lol's future.

"I came to Darlington on a player's contract, for less money than I was earning at Rotherham. I played part time there, and I had a job outside football, just like a lot of players.

"I was on £30 per week then, which wasn't a lot of money. The chairman, Harry Robinson, offered me an extra £10 per week, and I told the chairman if that was all I was worth, I was packing in at the end of the season."

The story broke in the Northern Echo on April 22nd 1966, and under the headline "Morgan quits the Quakers" Bob James wrote: "Lol Morgan resigned yesterday - because he doesn't want to be the poorest paid manager in the Third Division next season."

He commented further: "Darlington's directors will find themselves facing a barrage of criticism over Lol's departure from Feethams - and it is a storm of their own making. In two years he has wrought a great transformation but not until a week ago did the directors offer him a contract, or even a pay rise."

The fans weren't too happy, and chanted his name at subsequent games, both at home and away. After the 1-0 win over Luton, there was a twist in the tale, when it was announced over the tannoy that Lol had signed a new contract.

"I wasn't offered a new deal at all," said Lol. "The board never came back with anything more."

When it was becoming even more and more clear that Lol wouldn't be staying, Norwich contacted him. "It was a so-called secret phone call. When I wasn't offered a new deal, they asked me to become their new manager."

Lol had three years at Carrow Road, but then he had a chance to come back to Darlington in the summer of 1970. "I got a phone call from the chairman at the time. They'd just sacked somebody, and asked if I was interested in coming back.

"I told them that I wouldn't mind, but I wouldn't move up there, because my wife and I had just moved back to Rotherham. I told them that I was quite happy

to do the job and live in a flat in the town. At a meeting, the chairman said that he wanted me to live up here, but I repeated what I'd told him earlier, and that we'd wasted each other's time.

"The chairman replied that if I'd gone up there to meet them, I might change my mind about moving. I wouldn't, so it all fell through. My wife cried, because she wanted to come back to Darlington."

Keith Morton 1955-61

| League appearances | 171 | Goals | 55 |
| Other Games | 24 | | |

Keith Morton

KEITH was featured on the front cover of a best selling football book called "The Hotbed of Soccer" by north east journalist Arthur Appleton.

"It was in our best season when we played at Chelsea in the fourth round of the FA Cup in January 1958.

"We were winning 2-0, and I scored the third goal, and there's a picture of me turning away after I scored.

"It was a disgraceful pitch, but the conditions suited us. It was greasy on top, but underneath it was still hard.

"I twisted my ankle in that game, and it was the most painful journey home I ever had. I went to the ground next day for treatment, but I couldn't make it in time for the replay."

Keith joined the club two years earlier, in season 1955-56 after Sunderland freed him. "We had two very speedy wingers in those days. On the left, we had Tommy Reynolds, and on the right there was Johnny Spuhler. They used to do the running, and put the ball into the middle for me." Keith scored 14 goals in his first season thanks to those two.

He broke his wrist in one of the first ever floodlit FA Cup ties against Carlisle, "I had to keep on playing, because there were no subs in those days. After the game I had it plastered, and a soft bandage put over it. Dickie Duckworth told me to wrap an ordinary bandage around it, and to tell the referee I'd only sprained it."

He also suffered concussion in a game at Bradford Park Avenue.

"The dressing rooms at Bradford were at the top of the stand, through the crowd. I remember jumping up for the ball with their centre half, and that was it - I couldn't remember anything else.

"Apparently, I'd walked all the way across the pitch, up to the top of the stand, and eventually I came round on a bench, with John Neesham, the chairman at the time, asking me if I was all right.

"John was a great friend of mine. He started me off in business.

"He ran a car showroom (it's now Skippers), and Brian Henderson worked for him. I bought a filling station in Consett, and I started selling cars. John used to send cars though to me on a sale or return basis, and I used to give players like Joe Turner ten bob to run it through to Consett."

Keith had a much more serious injury against Hartlepool in December 1958, soon after he'd scored one of the goals in a 3-1 victory.

"I dislocated my cervical and it touched my spinal cord. At the hospital, they stuck my head back as far as it would go, and they bandaged me up like a penguin. I didn't play again until the following September."

Clive Nattress 1972-80 and 1985

League appearances	303	Goals	15
Other Games	43		

CLIVE'S first season with the club was 1972-73 after he joined from Blackpool, who were then in the old Second Division - and it was a real eye-opener for him.

When Clive arrived the manager was former Blyth boss Allan Jones, but Quakers had a torrid start to the season. They had won just three league games before they went to Wrexham for a first round FA Cup replay in November, after drawing the first game 0-0 against the Third Division side at Feethams.

"At the team meeting before the game, Allan said his piece, and about how we were going to play against Wrexham. He left the meeting, but then George Tait, the chairman at the time, came into the room.

"He changed a few things around, and then said to Peter Carr; 'Peter, you're

Clive Nattress keeps his eyes on the ball as he sends it goalwards

41

giving away too many corners'. Nothing at all about the way he was playing, or should play.

"I couldn't believe it. When I was at Blackpool, I never even saw the chairman or the directors."

Not long after that, Clive and several other players were invited to George Tait's house in Gateshead.

"There was me, Colin Sinclair, Alan Sproates and a couple of others invited to his house, and we couldn't understand why.

"He gave us all a drink and a cigar, sat us down at a table, and asked 'what are we going to do?'

"We were all sat there, wondering what he meant. He asked me what I thought, but I'd only been there six months and couldn't really speak with any authority.

"I told him that we needed more players, because at that time we had a very small squad, and if we had some injuries, then we would really struggle.

"The others said a few other things, and shortly after that, Allan Jones left."

Shortly afterwards David Frost visited Feethams for a documentary on life at the bottom of the Football League.

Fortunes improved for Quakers after that season - they finished 19th, 21st and 20th in the following seasons.

In 1975-76, they had a good run in the Football League Cup.

"In the third round, we were at West Ham, who had won the FA Cup only the season before, and had Billy Bonds and Alan Taylor in their side.

"The referee was Alan Kirkpatrick from Bolton, and he disallowed what was a perfectly good goal for us.

"I got involved in a run down the left, and when I got to the deadball line, I crossed into the middle, and Eric Young scored. But the referee disallowed it for offside, even though we protested that I'd pulled the ball back. They scored a second soon after, and the game was over."

Clive was part of the team which was drawn at First Division Everton in the third round of the league cup in October 1978 after they beat Fulham in a second round replay.

"We were very unfortunate not to win that night," says Clive. "Peter Madden was manager then, and just as we were about to go on the field before the game, he told us all to sit down. He opened the door, and Bill Shankly walked into the dressing room. Apparently Peter had bumped into him outside, and asked him to come in and have a few words with us.

"What a surprise - we just couldn't believe it. Shanks told us that we could win the game, and we very nearly did. Everton had beaten Wimbledon 9-0 in the previous round, and they only beat us 1-0. Shanks was an inspiration."

Phil Owers 1972-75 and 1976-80

League appearances 114	Other appearances 11

PHIL was three months short of his 18th birthday and still an apprentice, when he was called up for what turned out to be an unforgettable debut against Southport on January 6th 1972.

He had been part of the first team squad from the start of that season, when Ralph Brand was manager.

The season went downhill after a good win at Cambridge on the opening day,

Hard at work: Phil Owers (right) training with David Frost, who was filming a documentary about Darlington FC

and by the time Quakers went to Bradford City on December 23rd, they had won just three league games.

"Bradford won 7-0, and Ralph Brand said after the game 'That will never happen again.'"

The games at Christmas and New Year were postponed because of the weather, but there was also a flu epidemic at the time.

"Ernie Adams, the keeper, had flu, and I was told an hour before the kick off that I'd be making my debut against Southport. It turned into a day I'll never forget."

The promotion contenders hammered Quakers 7-0. "Jim Fryatt, their centre forward, kept heading them in." Phil was the only Darlington player to come out of the game with any credit.

David Lewis, writing in the Northern Echo under the headline "Darlington could fold before the end of the season", said; "Peter Graham met Phil Owers on the pitch and consoled the youngster. The crowd knew that he (Phil) was in no way to blame for the disgraceful shambles. He made several first class saves, and if it wasn't for him, then the club's record defeat of 10-0 would surely have been beaten."

Phil kept his place in the team for the next four matches - when David Frost (now Sir David) arrived to film a documentary on the club for ITV.

"Ralph Brand told me that he wasn't going to put me on television, in case it affected me, so Ernie Adams was recalled. Ernie had a nightmare. We lost 5-0 at Chester, and then drew 3-3 with Cambridge at our place. (The Northern Echo wrote that Ernie had a severe attack of stage fright, and presented Cambridge with three gift goals.)

"David Frost came to show what life was like at the bottom of the Football League, and he wanted to speak to me because I was the Great White Hope at the club. The cameras followed me all over. They filmed me walking up Church Street in Shildon to catch the bus, and they actually jumped off the bus in Redworth to drive ahead and film me getting off the bus again in the Market Place in Darlington.

"They did an interview with me and my parents at our house in Shildon. David Frost turned up in an entourage of six cars, to the astonishment of the neighbours. They re-arranged the furniture in the living room so we could do an interview. When they finished with me, they went on to Newton Aycliffe to interview Steve Holbrook and Colin Sinclair.

"The programme itself didn't paint a bad picture, even though it was a little derogatory in places."

Phil actually received a vote for Footballer of the Year at the end of that season. "I never found out who voted for me," he said.

Billy Horner, who brought in Graeme Richardson to replace Phil, freed him at the end of season 1974-75.

"Billy was sacked a fortnight after I went, and Peter Madden, who replaced him, wanted me to re-sign, but I'd already gone to Gillingham.

"The daft thing was, at the end of the 1976-77 season when I was back at Darlington, Billy wanted me to sign for him at Hartlepool!"

Billy Elliott became manager in 1979. "Billy told us all that he was going to sack us all at the end of the season, and he was true to his word - even though I played 42 games that year."

Robbie Painter 1993-1996

League appearances	115	Goals	33
Other Games	21		

Robbie Painter

LIVEWIRE Robbie was one of Darlington's most popular strikers in recent seasons. He started with a bang and finished with a flourish, scoring his first Quakers' goal at Hartlepool, and his last against Leeds at Elland Road.

"That first goal set me up with the fans. I loved playing for them and they seemed to take to me. I didn't realise then the significance of playing against Hartlepool," said Robbie.

"It was an Autoglass Trophy game. It's always a good feeling to get off the mark for your new club."

There were only 1454 fans in the Victoria Ground, but Robbie scored his final Darlington goal in front of 15,711 in the Coca Cola Cup. Two games later he joined Rochdale.

"I was on the bench at Leeds," recalled Robbie. "I replaced Robbie Blake when we were 2-1 down and I saw the disappointment etched on his face. I raced clean through, Nigel Martyn came out, making my mind up for me. I went round him to my left and rolled the ball into the net. I ran round in a semi-circle then straight to the fans behind that goal. There were a couple of thousand of them, and it was a great moment, especially as I had not been a regular."

The goal came after 72 minutes - as related elsewhere - and it was fitting that Robbie should score. He was a hero to many fans, and that goal meant his name was written in indelible ink in the club's list of great moments.

But his final appearance in front of the Darlington fans was less glamorous. It came four seasons later when playing for Halifax. He missed a sitter in front of the travelling supporters at The Shay.

Robbie, just a couple of yards out, had a tap in at the far post. "I fell as I hit it - deliberately to make sure I steered it in. But the ball bounced up and hit my backside - so there I was, in a heap in front of the fans who meant so much to me. That was my last league game."

43

It was not the first time the striker lay prostrate in the goalmouth. The most famous occasion was against Crewe at Feethams in his first season at Darlington.

He was involved in the quickest sending off in Football League history, when Crewe keeper Dean Smith was dismissed 18 seconds after kick-off.

Robbie went down as he rounded Smith. A few days earlier a high profile Premiership keeper had escaped red after a similar challenge and referees were ordered to clamp down.

"The keeper came across me and I went down. A dive or a foul? Well, I'll admit now that I made a bit of a meal of it, though there was contact," said Robbie.

"I was penalty taker and it seemed to take for ever for Crewe to decide who to take off to bring the sub keeper on. But I scored what turned out to be the only goal."

All the sympathy went to the keeper, but there was another Crewe victim. They took off a young lad who was making his debut, and he was substituted without having had a kick!

Robbie arrived at Darlington on loan from Burnley early in the 1993/4 season. Manager Billy McEwan was coming to the end of his reign, as the team was without a win.

The fans were crying out for a goalscorer and Robbie fitted the bill.

"I had to look on the map to see where Darlington was, and at the league table," said Robbie. "But I wasn't a regular at Burnley, so was pleased to come.

"Billy left while I was on loan, but new boss Alan Murray signed me."

Robbie's first league goals for the club came in the incredible 7-3 win over Colchester. In the next home game against Mansfield he had to play as a central defender and did the job admirably, before reverting back up front where he scored 14 goals in his first season.

"I still speak to Alan Murray. He was a good talker who the players could relate to."

The following season, which was more successful, Robbie scored nine goals, but was hampered by a double hernia, and Murray's departure. "It happened so quickly and there was a bit of uproar. Most of the players didn't want to see him go."

Robbie needed operations that summer, so missed the start of the club's Wembley season. He sat out the first eight league games, and scored just once before the turn of the year.

But he then added another seven. "I scored an important one in a 1-0 win at Plymouth. I scuffed it, but it crept in. Then in the last home game, I scored one of my favourite goals.

"It came against my old club, Chester. Their keeper Billy Stewart sent a clearance to me. The ball sat up and I cracked a half volley over Billy from 30 yards.

"In the previous home game I had scored twice as we beat Bury 4-0 yet they pipped us for promotion. In the 3-3 draw with Scunthorpe on the final day when we needed to win to go up, they had nothing to play for, but their players bust a gut to try and beat us. Our fans were magnificent that day."

Robbie scored the opener at Feethams in the play-off win over Hereford.

"Gary Bannister whacked in a shot and I chested it over the line. That was a wonderful night. I remember going up into the East Stand afterwards, and the fans gave us a fantastic reception.

"I phoned my parents and they were so proud that I was going to play at Wembley. I had been to Wembley the year before to see Liverpool beat Bolton in the Coca Cola Cup, but we made a mistake in not going to look round the night before we played there. The Plymouth players did and perhaps we were overawed.

"But I could have equalised. Stevie Gaughan sent a cross agonisingly over my head as I moved in at the far post. He wanted me to pull into space, and if I had done I would have scored."

For Rochdale, Robbie scored even more goals than for Darlington, including a couple against Quakers in a 5-0 mauling at Spotland.

"Darlington was my favourite club, because of the fans and the highs like Wembley and Leeds. And I met my wife there.

"I had talks with David Hodgson when he returned to the club, but he was looking for first division players, and signed Lee Nogan. I would have walked back to sign for them again.

"I have kept cuttings and videos. I sometimes watch them, but I have never looked at the Wembley highlights.

"One of the Darlington fans bought me a plaque, and said it was because I was his favourite player. What a lovely thing to do. I can honestly say in reply to that, that Darlington supporters are my favourite fans," said Robbie.

John Peverell 1961-72

League appearances	419	**Goals**	14
Other Games	46		

John Peverell

John was all set to leave for Spurs until Quakers persuaded him to stay in his home town when chairman John Neesham arranged an apprenticeship at Darlington Forge.

One of John's first games for Quakers was against Second Division Rotherham in the League Cup in season 1961-62, and it wasn't exactly one to remember for him, just two days after making his full debut at home to Colchester.

"Their left winger got away, and I went into the middle to cover. The ball went across goal at 100 mph, but it bounced off my chest and went past our keeper. I didn't play much more that season!"

John once had the distinction – if it can be called that – of scoring two own goals in a game.

"It was at Chesterfield. I was playing centre half that day. One of their defenders made a long clearance down the middle, and I was between the 18 yard line and the centre circle. I backheaded the ball, but our keeper had wandered off his line and the ball went over his head into the net.

"For the second goal, the ball went across the goalmouth, hit the post, and rebounded off me into the net."

Bob James of the Northern Echo wrote of the first goal: "Darlington have given away an alarming number of goals this season, and this was one of the worst."

John, perhaps fortunately for him, wasn't directly involved in one of the most comical own goals Quakers have ever conceded on February 7th 1964, after just fifteen seconds - a record maybe.

"We played at Southport, and kicked off. The ball was played back to Doug Robson by one of our forwards, and he turned round and hit it back to our keeper. Unfortunately, the ball went straight past our keeper, Eric Oliver, into the net. Southport scored without touching the ball!".

Oliver, who was an amateur keeper, came out with the standard goalkeeping excuse, and said: "I was stranded, and couldn't see the ball for the glaring sun."

After one particularly good Quakers performance - a 3-1 win at Brentford in February 1963 – the Londoners made an enquiry about buying John.

"The rumour was that three of us were going to be transferred to Brentford – me, Lance Robson and Jimmy Lawton. But nothing really came of it, and besides that, I wouldn't have gone.

"Lance certainly wouldn't have. With his outside job as a dentist, he was reckoned to be one of the best paid players in the game. He had an E type Jag, which was quite a luxury in those days."

Quakers had a great away win at Swindon in the early stages of the League Cup in September 1965.

"I had to mark Don Rogers, who was an excellent winger. I couldn't get near him that night, he turned me inside out, and I was dizzy at the end of the game. I was sick of having to pick myself up off the ground.

"After that game, Jimmy Lawton, who scored one of the goals, was transferred to Swindon, and we got Alan Sproates."

John appeared in Quakers' record defeat, their 10-0 thrashing at Doncaster in January 1964.

"Every shot at goal they had, went in. But it could have been different, because George McGeachie missed two good chances early in the game.

"Afterwards, when we were looking at the scores on the television, instead of them printing the scoring as simply 10-0, they printed "ten" in brackets after the numbers, which made it worse for us."

John scored what is reckoned to be one of Quakers' best ever goals, one of the rare highlights of their Third Division relegation season in 1966-67.

"We were playing Peterborough at our place, and I got the ball just inside their half. I shaped to shoot, and Joe Jacques, who was playing alongside me, said "You're not going to shoot from there, are you?"

"But I did. I gave the ball a huge whack, and it flew into the top corner. I used to score a couple of goals a season - two in their end and two in ours."

John played under several managers. One of them was Ray Yeoman, who took over from Jimmy Greenhalgh in March 1968.

"Just after Ray took over, we played an away game on a Friday night at

45

Southend. We were losing 2-1, and Ray had gone up the tunnel towards the dressing rooms ready for the half time team talk.

"When his back was turned, I scored from a Joe Jacques header. Ray came dashing back down the tunnel, and in his haste, kicked a bucket of water over and soaked the first four rows of fans."

Another was Lol Morgan, who led the team to promotion in 1966.

"When we won promotion that year in the last game, we were in the directors' box, throwing our shirts into the crowd.

"When Eric Johnstone threw his into the crowd, it was thrown back at him!"

John can remember one of his first training sessions with Lol.

"Usually, Dickie Deacon took us for a run. We used to go down the Croft Road, turn left at the bridge, go down to Hurworth and back to town.

"On Lol's first day, we went down the Croft Road as usual with him in the lead, and we all started heading towards Hurworth as usual. But instead of turning left at the bridge, Lol turned right and he led us past the Croft Spa Hotel, and then up past Newton le Willows and the A1 before we turned for home. We must have done an extra five miles.

"Dickie was a great character. He used to go out with us on his bike, and told us not to run too fast, because he couldn't keep up."

Mark Prudhoe 1988-93

League appearances	185	Other Games	27

MARK admits that he hadn't really achieved anything in the game until he came to Darlington - but he did so well at Feethams that he was voted Player of the Decade.

Mark was one of Brian Little's first signings soon after the new manager took over in the middle of March 1989.

"I was at Carlisle, and Alan Ashman, the manager, said that Darlington were looking for a keeper, and would I be interested in joining them.

"I definitely was, because I was desperate to get back to the north east and my family. Stockport were also interested, but I thought that it was time to go home.

"Unfortunately, I was a disaster in my first few games. Brian told me that I was trying too hard, and instead should concentrate on just being a keeper. Brian was a big influence on me."

Unfortunately, Mark couldn't prevent Quakers going down to the Conference.

"The pressure on the team then, was the heaviest which I'd ever experienced. We used to go into games, and maybe not enjoy them, and it was very difficult for Brian to motivate us.

"It was a terrible day when we were relegated, but we always felt that we had a very good chance of coming straight back up.

"We all gelled together. We were like a bunch of crooks and pirates. Virtually all of us were mavericks - we'd played for a lot of clubs, without winning anything.

Mark Prudhoe (right) with Kevan Smith

"Most of the lads hadn't been successful, and in the Conference, it was probably the first time most of us had a bonus in our pockets."

There were one or two hairy moments in the Conference, including the so-called Battle of Northwich on a Monday night in March.

"I was nearly sliced in half at Northwich," said Mark. "A blood vessel burst in my thigh and my leg really swelled up. It was a naughty game that one, to say the least."

Happily, Mark recovered quickly, and regained his place in the side for the run in to the Conference title.

"The game at Welling was always on a knife edge. They had a couple of chances, but I don't think they ever really troubled us.

"But when Gary Coatsworth scored, all hell broke loose. It was a massive relief more than anything else to know that we were back in the Football League."

Quakers kept the momentum going the following season.

"We never ever thought that we wouldn't get promoted again. The Fourth Division championship was a bonus, but it never entered our minds that we could have finished up in the play-offs. All we were thinking about was finishing in the top three.

"We had that little bit of extra belief, which we never had before the Conference.

"We all gelled together at just the right time, and the team spirit was very good. Brian signed only Mick Tait after we were promoted from the Conference. Mick had a great season, and was voted Player of the Year."

Unfortunately, it all went wrong the following season.

"In a way, some of us felt a little let down when Brian left, because he never came and said goodbye to us - but he had his own career to think of.

"Maybe he felt that he'd taken the club as far as he could, but the players were confident of making it three out of three. Brian was never replaced, and it was a tough act for Frank Gray to follow."

The financial problems worsened in season 1991-92. "We didn't get paid for five weeks, and we held a players' meeting one day. David Cork said "No pay, No play," but Tom Hughes, the chief executive, promised that we would be paid.

"The following day, we went to Bradford City, and won 1-0!"

Mark was one of the club's most saleable assets, and the club sold him to Stoke City.

"I was gutted, because I didn't want to leave. I played for the club for four years, and they said they wanted to keep me, but they didn't offer me anything extra.

"I don't regret going to Stoke, but it left a bad taste in my mouth. Darlington eventually got £120,000 for me." Mark was voted Player of the Decade by supporters in 1999, and he returned briefly for a month on loan the season after, but didn't play.

Jimmy Seal 1976-79

League appearances	122	Goals 22	
Other Games		18	

TELEVISION personality Richard Whiteley had a role in striker Jimmy's move to Feethams from York City.

The presenter, who went on to host Countdown, was a newsreader on local television - and he was not as good with figures as his future assistant Carol Vorderman!

Jimmy explained: "I wanted to leave York, and had spoken to the Grimsby manager. He asked how much I wanted, but we couldn't agree terms.

Jimmy Seal

"It came on the local news - read by Mr Whiteley - that Grimsby wouldn't sign me because I had asked for a £5,000 signing on fee. That was rubbish, but I turned to my wife and said I'd better find a club outside Yorkshire, as no club inside the county would pay that now."

Jimmy had done well at York, but fell out with new boss Wilf McGuinness, who wanted a clearout so he could bring in players from his former club, Manchester United.

Darlington boss Peter Madden snapped up Jimmy for a fee of around £10,000.

"I was told Barry Lyons, who had moved to Darlington from York shortly before me, had recommended me. I thought he had told the manager I was a good player, but on my first day of training with Darlington, we had a 10 mile cross country run.

"Eric Young was cross country champion at the club, but I beat him by 100 yards. However I was brought back down to earth, because Barry said to Peter Madden: 'I told you he could run. But he can't play!'"

But Jimmy soon took to Madden, recalling: "He was the most honest manager I played for. Whatever he promised me, financial or tactical, he delivered. He was a laugh too. When I left Darlington I joined up with him at Rochdale.

"Darlington was a good club, but the football was not the same standard as at York where we had finished fifth in the old second division. I noticed the step down when I went to Darlington, but had some good times."

Cup games especially stick in his memory. "I scored twice against Orient at Feethams in a 2-2 draw, and they were two divisions above us.

"We also drew the away game 0-0, but lost the toss for the third game, which was held at White Hart Lane, but would, I think, have been at Newcastle, had the coin landed right. We played well enough, but Orient got the breaks and won 3-0."

That was an FA Cup third round game, and Jimmy had also scored in the first round when, along with an Eddie Rowles' hat-trick, they beat Scarborough 4-1. In the second round Quakers saw off Sheffield Wednesday at Feethams.

When Ronnie Ferguson scored the winner, a wonder goal against his old club,

47

what happened next is etched on Jimmy's memory.

"He ran straight over to their dugout and stuck two fingers up. It wasn't quite the thing to do, but I remember thinking at the time, "Well done Ronnie!""

And the moment left such an impression on Jimmy, he almost did something similar the following season.

"We played at York, for the first time since I left. Me and Eddie Rowles, another former York boy, scored in our 2-1 win. The adrenalin was flowing because I wanted to show McGuinness what I could do.

"When I scored I ran past him, and was tempted to do what Ronnie had done. But I stopped myself. I had a lot of affection for York and I didn't want their fans to see me do that."

Jimmy had bad moments too, none more agonising than when Darlington lost 1-0 at Everton. At 0-0 he missed what he still admits was a sitter.

"Dennis Wann sent the ball over, Derek Craig nodded it down to me from the far post and I was unmarked six yards out. It came to my left foot which was my stronger, but I caught it on the top of my boot, like a wedge shot in golf, and it floated into keeper George Wood's arms."

Jimmy fondly remembers Feethams as a 'strange little ground with a character of its own.' Sometimes the team would train at Feethams, sometimes at South Park. "When the wind got up on the park, it spoiled training. And as I recall, the wind always got up," he said. "I got on fine with Len Walker when Peter Madden left, and it was Billy Elliott who sold me.

"To begin with he wanted me, but then things went a little sour. He said he had got me some bonuses but it then turned out that Len had arranged them before he left.

"Billy had a trainer working with him, but while training was well organised, the fun went out of it. Also I got the impression that things said by one player to another on the training ground, were getting back to the manager.

"The young lads maybe didn't notice, or mind, but by then I was a senior professional, and you suss these things out. I was pleased to join Rochdale.

"But I still look for Darlington's results. They were good days. I'm in the decorating business now, but if I could have my football career again, I'd jump at it."

48

Simon Shaw 1990-98

League appearances	176	Goals	14
Other Games	23		

MOST players who visit Wembley have a memento in the form of a medal. Simon has a metallic reminder that will stay with him for life - three plates and 16 screws in his jaw.

He missed Quakers' first ever Wembley appearance in 1996 after being punched outside a nightclub. He travelled to the game, and even hit the net, but his dream of playing was as shattered as his jaw.

"I borrowed Matty Appleby's boots before the game and went on the famous turf, whacking a few balls into the net. But not being able to play was agony, more painful than the punch.

"We stayed in a hotel in Watford the night before Wembley, and me and Paul Olsson, who was also injured, went out for the evening. It didn't feel right to stay with the lads."

Simon sustained the injury hours after Darlington had earned their play-off place with a draw at Scunthorpe.

The players had returned to Darlington and gone for a night out. "We were the worse for wear," said Simon. "We had been around the pubs and had got to the Mardi Gras nightclub. I had a bottle in my hand, so was not allowed in. I went to put it in a bin.

"Beside the bin was a girl crying. I asked her what the matter was, and she advised me to leave. The next thing I knew, some bloke, presumably her boyfriend, had punched me.

"I told everybody I took the punch well, but a security camera caught the incident, which was shown on Crimestoppers on television.

"I went down like a sack of spuds, but the pictures were blurred and the person responsible was never prosecuted.

"When I told manager Jim Platt he was shocked, but not angry. He knew I was not the sort to deliberately cause trouble."

Simon was convinced it was not going to be Darlington's day at Wembley. "There was a problem with the kit, and the lads didn't get the track suits until late on the Friday night. They were delivered to the hotel, with the squad already in bed. They looked more scruffy than those of the Plymouth players on the walk down the tunnel."

Simon had joined Darlington straight from school, when the club was in the GM Vauxhall Conference. Because of that the youth team couldn't enter the Intermediate League.

"Instead we played in the Teesside Junior League, and won easily," recalled Simon. "But there were some grudge matches, because we played against some of the lads we had been at school with."

Simon, an attacking, wide midfielder, later converted to full-back, made his debut as a substitute at Bury two seasons after joining. It was the penultimate game of the season in the old Third Division and Darlington were already relegated.

That summer Billy McEwan took over as manager, and under him Simon's career blossomed.

"I became a fixture in the side. He was a disciplinarian, but knew the game inside out. He rated me, filled me with confidence, and I like to think I repaid him."

In Simon's second start in the 1992/3 season, he scored the opening goal in a 3-0 win at Colchester. Later he scored some tremendous goals - but this wasn't one of them.

A defensive lapse left him on the edge of the penalty area with an open goal. "It was a tentative effort, but the keeper was absolutely stranded. The ball just about stopped between the goal line and the net."

Towards the end of the season he cracked in three beauties, including the best of his career, a 25 yarder at Scunthorpe - minus his boot.

"It came off in a tackle. But I was so confident that I decided to whack the ball anyway, and it flew into the corner," said Simon.

"That was a reflection of the confidence Billy had given me. Everything I touched seemed to turn to gold."

But the following season Quakers were second bottom and when they lost to bottom club Northampton, McEwan left.

"I was very disappointed," said Simon. "The previous season there had been talk of bigger clubs being in for me. I now regret that I was so naive.

"I was young so was earning just £90 a week. Billy offered me a new deal of £130

a week. Like a fool I signed instead of waiting to see what offers came in from elsewhere."

New boss Alan Murray dropped him, and he played only a handful of games, but scored again at Colchester in a 2-1 win.

"I got the impression that assistant manager Eddie Kyle rated me, but Alan didn't. To be fair results improved under Alan. The following season I didn't play at all until the end of December. I came off the bench and scored in a 4-1 win over Northampton. But I was left out again.

"When Paul Futcher took over results nose-dived, but I was back in favour. It didn't work out for Futch which is a shame because he was a nice guy - very well spoken.

Alan Murray

"When he rollicked us, it sounded out of character. In his last training session he worked us really hard. That afternoon he left. He must have known it was coming."

Kyle took temporary charge, and Darlington promptly won 4-0 against Rochdale. That summer, 1995, David Hodgson and Jim Platt took the helm and the upturn in fortunes culminated at Wembley.

Simon played 41 games that season. "Until then it had been a constant battle to stay away from the bottom, but Hodgy changed that. By the time he left the team was virtually picking itself, and under Jim we kept up the head of steam.

"We didn't realise at the time how good that team was. If we were guilty of mistakes, it was to settle for away draws when we could have won. We lost only one away game, and went into every match feeling we were not going to lose."

The following season after the Wembley defeat, Simon suffered another shattering blow. He was left out of the team that drew at Leeds.

"Again I was left to stroll on a famous ground knowing I was not going to play."

Simon scored in the penalty shoot out at Solihull in the year Quakers went on to play Wolves at Feethams.

"That was another one I miss-hit. It went straight into the middle of goal, the

49

keeper diving out of the way. If he'd stood up, he could have thrown his cap on it!

"I would rather have played Wolves away. We lost 4-0 but should have been two up. The scoreline flattered them.

"That was the season when the East Stand had been demolished. There was no atmosphere at Feethams with no fans on one side."

It was to be Simon's last season. By now David Hodgson was back in charge, and Simon recalled, "Cardiff were interested in me. They said they could easily match my wages, but instead signed Mark Delaney, who went on to play for Aston Villa. In the end Doncaster came in for me so I went. They were in the Conference, but it was the only firm offer I had."

Simon has only ever once returned to Feethams to watch a game. Now, at 28, he is working outside the game while playing for Barrow.

"I don't regret signing professional. But if I had my time again, I would not have signed the £130 deal."

He would probably have gone straight home after the Scunthorpe game as well.

Colin Sinclair 1971-76

League appearances	203	Goals	65
Other Games	20		

THE high pitched tone of Barry Davies was unmistakable. It was October 18, 1975, and the BBC man, who later provided the commentary when Darlington visited Altrincham in November 2001, was completing his round up on Match Of The Day. Torquay played on Saturday evenings in those days, and Davies reported: "There's one Division Four result to bring you: Torquay United 2 Darlington 4 - and Sinclair scored all four!"

His voice rose almost to glass-shattering pitch as he completed the sentence, and no doubt all over Darlington, fans danced in the living rooms.

Having won the first three games of the season to go top, Quakers had failed to score in their next seven matches until Colin's night to remember.

"They were quality goals," he recalled. "But for the first one I brought the ball down with my hand. Another came from a throw in we had worked on, and I turned and hit the ball into the top corner. We stayed in Torquay because we were to play at Swansea two days later.

"We were in a night club that Saturday and Match Of The Day was on in the club. I remember little else - except that Clive Nattress and I ended up in Exeter!"

The Torquay blitz was Colin's only hat-trick.

He loved Darlington with a passion that still exists, and is an occasional visitor, still referring to the team as 'we.'

"It was my favourite club in my career. A family club, with no cliques. Trainer Dickie Deacon was a great character, and if it had been up to me I wouldn't have left."

A natural goalscorer, Colin arrived for a small fee from Raith Rovers. How small depends on whether you believe the accounts, or Colin's version. The fee was either around £5,000 - or £3,000.

"The deal was done at Newcastle Railway station, and there were a few brown envelopes handed about. One came my way with £500 in it," he said.

He had made a name for himself at Raith, scoring against Rangers on his debut, then Celtic.

A change of manager led to his departure. "He left me out, though I was top scorer. Darlington chairman George Tait had connections with Ronnie Simpson, a big name in Scottish football. Darlington came in for me and I went."

Len Richley was Quakers manager, though he didn't last long, and Colin was to play under eight bosses at Feethams.

At first the young striker struggled, and despite making his debut on the opening day of the 1971/2 season (a 3-0 defeat at Southend) he was in and out of the side and didn't score until February.

"There was time in the Scottish First Division, but not in the English Fourth, where the play was hard and fast. But I clicked, and from then on I loved every minute."

After barren months he scored twice in one game, against Aldershot, and finished the season with eight goals. The goals flowed, his best tally being 22 in the season he sunk Torquay. Towards the end of the campaign he scored in seven successive league games.*

"I remember scoring against Mansfield in a 1-0 win. The opposing manager used to pick a Man of the Match. He gave it to me, saying that I never did much, but always scored against them.

"One of my favourite goals was against Bradford. They had a full back called

50

Cec Podd, a hero with their fans. I kicked lumps out of him and got some stick from the terraces.

"A corner came over and it stotted up in front of me, so I lifted the ball over a defender's head and volleyed it into the top corner where it stuck in the stanchion. The goal was featured on television."

Colin also recalls a game at Hartlepool where Quakers trailed 2-0, only to score three times, Colin heading the winner - eventually!

"John Hope was Pool's keeper, and in the first half I was unmarked and tried to be smart and let the ball run through my legs before flicking it into the net. But I missed, and got a rollicking from manager Peter Madden at half time, so you can imagine how pleased I was when I scored the winner.

"We had a good record against Pool. Their manager was Len Ashurst and I later played for him at Newport. I kept reminding him of our wins over Pool - maybe that's why he got rid of me."

Darlington struggled for most of Colin's time. Chairman Tait was quick to wield the axe and none of the managers had time to produce a winning side. Colin recalls with a shudder the feeling of helplessness when the Football League meetings took place which would determine whether Quakers were re-elected.

He considers Dick Connor the best Darlington manager he played under. "He was strict, but fair, and you wanted to play for him."

He signed big Bill Atkins, and the wily striker brought Colin on no end. "I liked playing under Billy Horner too," said Colin. "Don Burluraux was class and a good mate, so was Clive Nattress.

"But I felt I would score loads of goals if I was playing for a better side. My ambition was to play in the first division, and my only regret was that when Sheffield United (managed by Darlington old boy Ken Furphy) offered £25,000 plus John Hope for me, Tait turned it down."

Colin scored in the famous penalty shootout at Sheffield Wednesday. Quakers beat Luton 2-1 in the next round of the League Cup, before bowing out 3-0 at West Ham.

"We were robbed. As I recall, Clive Nattress got to the byeline and pulled the ball back for Eric Young to score, but the linesman flagged for offside. It couldn't have been and we were fuming."

Colin was at Boro's Riverside Stadium to see Darlington beat Burnley 3-2 in

1999, and watched the Feethams game against Manchester City in the next round of the FA Cup.

"Darlington were denied a clear cut penalty when Glenn Naylor was pushed over with the score at 1-1. Man City's Paul Dickov is a mate of mine, but I was supporting Darlington."

Colin has fond memories of training at South Park, Longfield School, Durham University, and pre-season on the beach.

"We were running up and down sand dunes, and were knackered. Then a group of people in wheelchairs was pushed past us. Manager Peter Madden said: 'That should make you feel better.' He was right. Being young and fit is wonderful.

Colin Sinclair (right) wins an aerial duel

"We got all sorts of things free - including tickets for the Odeon cinema. We used to go after training and have a good sleep!"

Colin is still amazed by the time Paul Trevillion came into the club. The story is documented in this book elsewhere, but Colin adds an additional tale.

"Paul was standing in the dressing room when suddenly he threw a golf ball to one of the lads, who caught it with ease. Then he produced a crystal vase that he said was worth £20,000. He threw that too, and the player it went to suddenly turned into a nervous wreck.

"He was making a point about dealing with pressure, I suppose."

Colin was playing at the time Quakers were featured on the David Frost show and he recalled. "The crew was filming when the manager saw our defensive wall dive out of the way at a Cambridge free kick, and the ball flew into the net.

"He called us f....ing cowards. Frost assured him that bit would be cut.

"But when the boss was sitting with his family watching it, his language was heard loud and clear. His kids were shocked and said: 'Daddy how could you!' "

Colin has coached a Scottish non-league side for 10 years, and admits: "Sometimes I dream I'm managing Darlington."

He's back in Scotland these days and doing well in the hotel trade. "That's thanks to Darlington too. Ralph Brand, another of the managers at Darlington, reminded us that it was a short career and urged us to save something every week. I did, and finished up with enough to buy my first pub.

"If I was a multi-millionaire I would have bought the club. I really do love it that much."

* JIMMY Lawton scored in nine consecutive league games - a club record run in league football - in the 1962-3 season. Sinclair apart, the only other players to score in seven successive games are Ken Allison, 1964, and David Brown, 1924.

Kevan Smith 1979-85, 1989-93

League appearances	396	Goals	22
Other Games	44		

DARLINGTON have won promotion only five times, and on three of those occasions Kev Smith was in the side - a reflection of his ability, attitude and leadership. He played over 400 games for the club, and is perhaps the most influential player to pull on a Quakers shirt.

He had wonderful highs and awful lows, and throughout wore his heart on his sleeve in a manner that earned the respect of a generation of fans.

He first appeared on trial under Lennie Walker. After a wet winter the reserves had several fixtures outstanding, and central defender Kev was drafted in: "The Skerne was so high the rats have never had so much swimming to do," recalled Kev, who saw many a rodent in the old East Stand - and allegedly once pulled along a folded sock on a piece of string to frighten the life out of physio Bob Farrelly, who was scared of rats.

"I played in a trial against the club's professionals, and after half an hour Lennie asked me to switch sides. I made my Darlington debut for the reserves against Barnsley."

Summer came, Lennie left, but Kev was invited back by new boss Billy Elliott.

"My name was up on the reserves teamsheet at left back. He wanted to see if I was adaptable. I scored, created a goal, hit the bar and we won, I think 4-1.

"When I went into the dressing room, everything went quiet. Coach Ian Larnach and Elliott were whispering in a corner. Striker Ronnie Ferguson nudged me and said they were about to sign me.

"My face lit up like the lights at Piccadilly Circus. I was earning £75 a week, and even though I was only 19 was in charge of people older than me at the factory where I was a welder.

"I was so keen that I would have signed for a Mars bar. Elliott knew that and mugged me. He said those never to be forgotten words: 'How would you like to be a professional footballer?'

"He asked me how much I was earning. He offered me a three year deal at £65 a week. He said the bonus was £40 for a win and £20 for a draw.

"While I was trying to work out how much I could earn, Billy and his shifty looking secretary Andy Rowell were standing together peering at me. It looked like a scene out of Oliver Twist.

"In the years to come I saw lads arrive in rusty minis and leave in a Rolls Royce. But Billy was only doing his job with me. He was there to save the club money.

"He asked if I could start the next day, and I said I would have to give a week's notice as the company had been good to me. He said he admired loyalty.

"But my boss Harold Ingledew told me to join straight away. He was so pleased he was almost in tears.

"I was showing a new girl the ropes, when the boss said there was a phone call for me from Billy. I was asked to look at the back page of the Northern Echo and it said I was playing at Torquay. Billy had phoned to see whether I could travel the next day.

"On the coach I was told: "You're a footballer now son, not a yob, take that earring out." I have never worn it since.

"It wasn't a dream debut, as we lost 4-0. Clive Nattress called me 'Smudger' that day. It has always stuck.

"In training every time I kicked the ball with the outside of my foot, George Herd, who had become trainer, got me to do five press ups. I had to work out why.

"I didn't like his booming voice, but I had come straight from the Stockton District League into professional football, working with players a lot better than me.

"I couldn't believe I was a pro. I had no magic. But I was brave, honest and hard working. I took a lot of stick for own goals over the years, but I laughed about it. You cannot escape it.

"A couple stand out. The ball came to me at the far post. I decided to pop it back to keeper Pat Cuff. He was ambling along like a tortoise, and the ball went in. He blasted me for not heading it away. He was right.

"Another time I arrowed a cross straight into the net. Fortunately I scored an identical one in the right end in the same match. Next day the paper said: "Smith gets a brace." I was so naive. I thought a brace was something to do with pheasants.

"I was an out and out stopper, and always used to pride myself on getting in the way. I remember in one game, when attacking I chested the ball between two defenders, before blasting it goalwards. The ball smashed into the keeper's hand and stayed out. Cyril Knowles, the manager, asked why I didn't place it.

"Because I'm a centre half," I said. "There's no answer to that," he replied."

Kev was at the hub of much of the laughter and micky taking. But David Speedie was just as much a joker, though he didn't see the funny side on one occasion.

"Speedie and I were both sent off, though mine was a case of mistaken identity, not that anybody looked much like me," said Kev. "Speedie was hauled in first by Elliott and fined £50. As Dave came out, he told me I was being fined the same amount. I told Billy that he knew I wasn't guilty. He let me off, but said on no account was I to tell Dave.

"Billy stood no nonsense. I once went to his office to ask for a bonus, because the word was that Alan Walsh had been awarded a bonus for each goal.

"Billy said: 'Pick your window, because the one you pick you're going through if you are not out of my office in five seconds.' I left in a hurry, but as I went, said: 'What about a bonus for clean sheets?' I didn't wait to find the answer."

Kev admits that he improved immensely under new boss Knowles. "He said he couldn't believe I was a footballer, but added that I was his hardest working player. During training I once saw Carl Airey get booted five feet in the air by Cyril because he wasn't getting stuck in.

"Cyril got really angry at times and demanded 100 per cent. He didn't suffer cheats and fools.

"When we lost in the Cup 3-0 to Telford, I played despite a dislocated shoulder. The medical people were not happy, but I didn't want to let Cyril down.

"We had an inquest and Cyril went for me. By then the players looked at me for

It's ours! Kev Smith with the fourth division title trophy. The sign on the Quaker Sports Centre had been repaired by then

leadership. He told me I was to blame for the goals. I was about to have a go back, when one of the players whispered to me not to. Cyril was just trying to spark us off. He was upset and angry that we had lost.

"When Cyril died I was devastated. I had sent a card to the hospital thanking him for what he had done for me, and hoping he would battle through his illness. His family didn't want to turn his funeral into a circus. They said family only, so I stayed away. I later heard that other players had gone, and was upset about that. Cyril had lost a son and then he died too young himself.

"After I had left for Rotherham, his secretary Irene told me she had heard Cyril say that he should never have let me go. I was touched.

"Many of my managers had played for their country. Cyril, Billy, Brian Little, John Sillett, Frank Gray and Norman Hunter. It's a compliment that they all rated me."

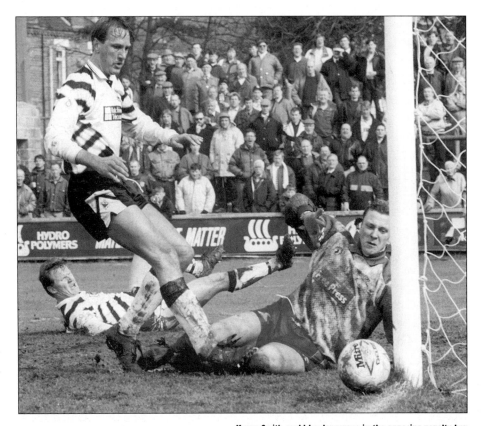

Kevan Smith could be dangerous in the opposing penalty box

54

Magaluf, and Ray went with them. There were some tremendous laughs, often after a bout of celebrating. Dave McLean (allegedly) threw a chair off a sixth floor veranda, while Micky Angus, who was immensely proud of his Tom Selleck style moustache 'lost' it while asleep in the bath. Gary Macdonald was allegedly the culprit with the razor. The players were told they would be kicked out of the hotel.

After negotiating with a ranting manager, it was agreed that if the four main trouble makers went, the rest could stay. Airey, Kevin Todd and Phil Lloyd, plus one other who escapes Kev's memory were packed off - and much to the jealousy of the rest, found better accommodation.

Before the start of the following season, 1985/6, Kev had left for Rotherham. "Cyril asked me not to go. I said I had worked hard for six years, and had just been voted player of the year. I wanted a £50 rise and Cyril offered me £25. Then Ken Warne, the chairman offered me the £50. I said it was too late. I added that it was not about money, but about the manager not rating me enough."

Kev later moved to Coventry for £65,000, but broke his leg and although he played top flight football, and was there when Coventry won the FA Cup, he opted for York City and regular first team football. But it didn't work out. Hartlepool and Quakers wanted him, which was no contest.

"I spoke to Brian Little who told me his plans for Darlington. I told him if he got me a signing on fee from York, and as well as a fee for joining Darlington, I would sign.

"He phoned York boss John Bird straight away, and I could hear Birdy refusing to pay. So I told Brian to tell John I'd see him for pre-season training. That swung it. John agreed to pay a percentage.

"I signed. Two days later Coventry mates Speedie and Cyrille Regis phoned to say I was crazy to have dropped from the top flight to the Conference in under a year. I told them it would be an adventure, and the best move I could have made."

And Kev was spot on. What followed is part of Quaker legend - successive promotions.

"They were the best years of my career. I loved the jet set life style at Coventry, flying out to play golf in Spain. But what happened at Darlington surpassed all that.

"Brian was extremely professional - there were rules such as no eating in the dressing room, no stubble unless you were growing a beard. Somebody once threw me an apple knowing that Brian was coming. I had just taken a bite when he walked

Quakers reached the FA Cup fourth round in successive years under Cyril. The second run, in 1985 was ended by Telford, but the previous year Plymouth had put Darlington out. Kev remembers the mode of transport better than the game itself.

"I was terrified of flying. There was loads of snow on the ground too. I had to lift an air hostess up for a photo on the runway. I was shaking with fear. And the plane took ages to take off. I had hardly slept the night before.

"The flight back was all right because we had a few beers. We lost 2-1 and Plymouth went to the semi-final that year. Some fans made the trip with us to help offset the cost, and one of them, Ray Hebdon became a friend.

"We were home by 8 o'clock and suddenly flying didn't seem so bad."

At the end of the following season after Quakers won promotion they went to into the dressing room. I was fined a fiver, but you could laugh about things like that. The spirit was brilliant.

"In the Conference everybody was out to beat the new boys from the league. There were allegations of underhand stuff from Barnet, trying to make sure that all other teams had an incentive to beat us.

"But there was an invincibility about us. I remember one game at Feethams where I tripped a player by the corner flag. Three times I picked him up, and deliberately tripped him again as he got to his feet. Somehow the ref missed it, but the fans were laughing.

"Then there was the time my clearance knocked a letter off the Quaker Sports Centre. It wobbled and fell, almost in slow motion. There was a roar from the crowd as if we'd scored.

"It was brilliant to win the title, but I didn't think we would win the Fourth Division. We went from strength to strength."

But Kev's world fell apart when Little left. "I was so close to him and admired him so much. I would run through walls for him. He improved my game. All the training was with the ball," said Kev.

"He pulled me to one side, and said he was joining Leicester. I was the first person to be told, and I begged him not to go. I said if he did, everything would collapse.

"He said he had recommended me for the job. I was shocked. I had never even considered management. I needed a hernia operation and was up straight after it to go back to the club - even though I was in agony - to ask Frank Gray to take the job for the sake of continuity. I tried to be as loyal to him as I was to Brian.

"But things went badly in the higher division, and there were rumours of me taking over. Frank called me in and asked me about it. I said I was doing no such thing, and reminded him I had crawled out of my sick bed to ask him to take the job.

"I told him everybody was 100 per cent behind him. And I added that I was hurt by his comments. He dropped me."

Kev felt he had been too young to take the manager's job, but when Gray left, Kev applied, only for the job to be handed to Ray Hankin on a temporary basis.

"I got on well with him, but had a beast of a game at Hartlepool. I scored an own goal. I felt I should have been left on to rectify it, but he subbed me.

"I didn't deserve it, but then Hank didn't deserve such a bad display from me.

"I hoped to get the job after Hank left, and wrote a dossier on all the players, who we could sell, and what we needed to do to go forward. And I had a good interview with John and Sean Brockbank."

Alan Noble, a director and friend of Kev's, stayed out of the interview, but later phoned Kev asking to take him for a meal. "I knew straight away I hadn't got it. He said it was very close, but they had gone for Billy McEwan.

"The story goes that Alex Ferguson phoned to recommend him. And Billy had a file full of players he could bring to the club."

Kev Smith in uncompromising mood

Kev's relationship with Billy was at best rocky, and at worst virtually unbearable. Kev needed a big operation that summer (1992) which involved cutting and drilling the bone to encourage new growth. He was told there was a ten week recovery programme, but he hobbled back after nine, only to be told that Billy wanted a new centre half.

"He sat me in the middle of his office. He pointed out we had conceded 70 goals the previous season. He said I was skipper and it was my fault. I said it was a team game, but I held my hand up to some of the goals.

"I congratulated him on getting the job and told him I was willing to help with coaching or scouting. He said 'OK' but after that he tried to isolate me."

Kev claimed he was given a hard time, and on his first day back after his layoff, the players were running round South Park.

"We had to do six circuits. The other lads had built up their fitness, and couldn't believe I managed it. On the last lap I cut inside one of the poles that marked the circuit.

"Tim Parkin, player coach, who had taken my place in the team said: 'Well done

55

Smudge, but Billy wanted you to run round the pole.' You can imagine how I felt."

The season's first game was at Cardiff, and to my surprise I was picked. But I broke my nose in training. There was even a problem getting authority from the club for the operation.

"I went back to Feethams two days later with a mask on. Billy said I couldn't travel. He didn't want injured players on the bus. But I wanted to look keen so I hired a car for £60 and drove. You should have seen his face when I walked into the dressing room."

Later the manager said he was handing the player a free transfer, but Kev was close to a testimonial and refused to go.

The atmosphere between the pair worsened, and Kev ended up training on his own. "The lads used to leave me notes, saying: "Smudge, we're alive, are you!"

Eventually Billy called Kev into the dressing room and said he was playing, and after that results were much better - though to be fair to the manager, there had been some impressive wins that season, including three goal home wins over Torquay and Crewe, and a 3-0 success at Colchester.

Kev played 13 of the last 14 games, and the side lost just four of them. Though there was more animosity.

"We were drawing 0-0 at Carlisle at half time," recalled Kev. "I had held the defence together, and had particularly helped our young left back Alan Dowson. He was a good player, but a lot of their attacks were coming down that flank, and I helped stem them.

"Billy said he was taking me off because other players had been doing my job. I was furious and threw my boots down. There was nothing I could do about it. It was terrible for my last ever season at Darlington to be like that.

"But the fanzine Mission Impossible backed me, and I think the public knew what had gone on. I went to Hereford to play for my old mate Greg Downs, but am very proud to be part of Darlington's history.

"The statistics show what I did there and I served 10 years for a club that will always be part of me. We had some great teams and managers, and only one bad year personally.

"When I left football, I realised the outside world was not for me, and was pleased to come back to Darlington to work for Football in the Community."

From there Brian Little took Kev to be his assistant at Hull City. "He's a one-off," said Kev. "I had a marvellous career and he was a big part of it. I'm so pleased we worked together again."

Perhaps the team spirit that always revolved around Kev was best summed up by an incident in his first season.

Quakers had travelled for a New Year's Day clash at Huddersfield. Snow and ice had made any hope of play the next day remote, so, it being New Year's Eve the players sneaked out to the pub.

"I was feeling really rough next day, when we were told the game was on," recalled Kev. "None of us could believe it. I was marking Steve Kindon and he sent me crashing into the advertising boards. Somehow I carried on, and shortly afterwards during a break in play, and out of sight of the referee, our centre half, Derek Craig, punched Kindo, who had to be carried off. Derek came up to me and summed it up in one word 'Sorted!' he said."

David Speedie 1980-82

League appearances	88	Goals	22
Other Games	7		

DAVID was transformed by the Quakers into a rising star who was to go on to score top flight goals and play for Scotland.

He arrived at Feethams for £5,000 from Barnsley as a 20-year-old midfielder. In 23 league games he had never scored for the Tykes, but by the time he left Darlington for Chelsea for £65,000 two years later, he had hit the goal trail in style.

A hard tackling, fiery player, just 5ft 7in tall, he admitted that coming to Darlington was the turning point in his career. He notched 17 in the second season after being converted into a forward.

"I made my name at Darlington so it will always have a place in my heart. I'm grateful to Billy Elliott for signing me, and to George Herd, who was coach in my second season. He taught me so much about my own game, and awareness of people around me.

"I didn't know Kev Smith before I arrived, but we struck up a friendship and to this day he is my best mate.

"I was impressed by a lot of the lads, including Pat Cuff, Peter Skipper, Alan Walsh, John Stalker and Alan Kamara. I still see some of them."

56

Former England star Bobby Charlton - who supported the Evening Despatch appeal to save the club - with David Speedie

marvellous cross field pass to Dave McLean.

McLean crossed first time, and Speedie rose to bullet home a header.

But it wasn't league or cup goals that earned him a move to Chelsea. "I scored a hat-trick against a Southampton team that included Kevin Keegan, in a fund raising game at Feethams," he recalled.

"Chelsea boss John Neal was in the crowd. Darlington had stood me in good stead. Even the training with Billy Elliott and George Herd was good. Sometimes we went to Barnard Castle, and sometimes to South Park - complete with all the dog dirt!"

David found out one day just how much Elliott rated him.

"He was late for training, so I mimicked him by stuffing a football up my top (Billy had a slightly hunched back), and started giving the lads a lecture in Billy's voice.

"He sneaked in behind me, saying: 'You think you're funny, eh. Well you're dropped for the next game.'

"But he didn't follow up his threat, so I suppose I must have been important to his team."

David is proof that coming to Darlington can be the start of a glittering career.

David made his debut in a 1-0 home win over Northampton, and scored his first goal in a 4-4 draw with Rochdale at Feethams. His second goal came in another high scoring draw, 3-3 at Bournemouth. "I can't remember much about individual games, though I do remember that we were a decent side. The club had twice applied for re-election in the seasons before I joined, but we finished eighth in my first year. With a couple more players we could have won promotion. I wish there had been play-offs in those days.

"I was a left sided midfielder but Billy Elliott stuck me up front. He saw something in me that nobody else did.

"I had always been a good header of a ball despite being short. It's down to timing. Alan Walsh had a great cross, as well as being able to score from anywhere, and that helped me."

David's one cup goal was a gem in a 2-2 home draw with Carlisle in the FA Cup first round. Walsh had the ball wide on the right around the halfway line, and hit a

George Switzer 1993-94

League appearances	14	Goals 0
Other Games	4	

GEORGE arrived at Feethams as a 19-year-old having played alongside such stars as Ryan Giggs and David Beckham. But whereas his former Manchester United teammates went on to earn fortunes, left-back George slipped out of Feethams into non-league obscurity after just a handful of games. To make matters worse he claims he was owed several hundred pounds.

His final game was against Bury, and Darlington were in danger of finishing bottom of the League. The players were promised a lump sum if they won, and they did 1-0 courtesy of a Bernie Slaven volley.

But George was released, and never got his money.

His time at Feethams holds mixed memories. He appeared to be heading for a wonderful career when in the United youth team. But when Darlington manager

57

George Switzer

Billy McEwan spoke to Alex Ferguson, George was allowed to join Darlington.

"I couldn't understand what Fergie was saying, and Billy's accent was even stronger," said George. "But Alex told me that Billy was genuine and would look after me - and he did.

"The third division was much more physical than youth team games. But I relished a battle, and was happy to face any winger.

"But the team had a terrible start to the season, and I was used to winning. We lost 5-1 to Bradford in the Coca-Cola Cup but I was named man of the match and got a trophy and a watch. I was proud of that."

Even though Darlington lost the second leg 6-0, and went 12 league games without a win, George was knuckling down.

Then McEwan left and in came Alan Murray. Some players were pleased, but not George. "When Billy left I hated Darlington. Money was tight and the club struggled to scrape enough together to sign Robbie Painter.

"But I'm pleased they did, because he was from Lancashire and I'd get a lift home from him after games. I loved the Darlington fans. Sometimes I would stay over with Tommo, the groundsman. When we went out the fans loved talking to me. I even got invited to weddings.

"Tommo and his family were great, and there were plenty of pizzas in whenever I went round.

"Apart from that I was unhappy. I asked if I could go home on loan to Macclesfield, who wanted me. Darlington said that if I wanted to go on loan I must go to Gateshead. By then I was in the reserves and the football was dire. I was living with a family, who were fine, but I didn't have enough privacy."

He won back his place, playing in the last five games of the season.

"I enjoyed those games but knew I wouldn't be staying as by then Murray had brought his own players in.

"I went back to Manchester to sign for Hyde and I soon realised I had been further let down by Darlington. Hyde manager Mike McKenzie had phoned some time before trying to sign me, but I had never been told."

By a quirk of fate, Darlington visited Hyde in the FA Cup the following season. "That was a game I really wanted to win," said George. "Darlington didn't fancy our plastic pitch and we went 1-0 up. But they settled and won 3-1."

However, he doesn't look on the black side, and added: "I made some good friends at Darlington, and played league football, which nobody can take from me.

"You take the good memories. Likewise I have no regrets about not making it with United.

"I wasn't quite good enough. I occasionally see Giggsy and one or two of the others. But I'm not jealous.

"I've seen players leave Man United who cannot stand watching them on television, because they get bitter and angry that they didn't make it. I've never felt like that."

George is now working at opticians Dolland and Aitchison, so his life is in focus!

Kevin Stonehouse 1987-89

League appearances	72	Goals	24
Other Games	15		

KEVIN made Darlington the last stop in his professional career. His first manager at Darlington was Dave Booth, and in his first season, the squad decided to go out for a drink after training.

"We all went to the North Briton in Newton Aycliffe, and were there for quite a while. The next day, Dave went crazy with us in the dressing room, because he'd found out that we had all been out drinking.

"He told us all to sit down, and he asked us one by one, whether we wanted to play for the club. Each one of us in turn said yes, until he came to Peter Robinson.

"Dave said: "Do you want to play for this club?" to which Peter replied: "No I don't."

"We all fell over laughing, apart from Dave, who was gobsmacked. Peter then said: "I don't think I can offer any more than I am at the moment."

Kevin was also the cause of the full first team squad being sent home one day from training.

"I was injured, and I missed an away game at Colchester. Gary MacDonald and

58

Paul Ward were also injured, so we went out for a few drinks. In fact, the few drinks lasted the weekend, and when I went into training on the Monday, Dave Booth said I looked awful.

"So he called all the players together, and said that because I had flu, he was cancelling training. He didn't want the other players to catch it."

Mick Tait 1990-92, assistant manager March 2001 to the present

League appearances	79	Goals	2
Other Games	12		

MICK arrived at Feethams from Portsmouth in the summer after Quakers lifted the Vauxhall Conference title in 1990, and he became a key figure in Quakers' charge to the old Fourth Division title under Brian Little in season 1990-91.

"Most of the teams who come up from the Conference seem to struggle, but in that season, we just went from strength to strength," says Mick.

"I was the only signing that summer, but everything seemed to go well for the team."

Mick's debut for Quakers was in their first game of the season at Gillingham in August 1990, but he finished on the losing side to a penalty after Les McJannet handled.

"I played in midfield at Gillingham – and that was the first and last time that season. After that, I played in the middle of the back three with Kevan Smith and Jim Willis.

"It didn't take us long to realise that we weren't a bad side, even though we'd just come up from the Conference. We all had a bit of ability. We picked up from the defeat at Gillingham and got better.

"We just seemed to be a great bunch of lads, who hit it off with each other. That doesn't seem to happen very often, but it did with us. There were no splinter groups in the dressing room, everyone was together, and the manager knew that was one of our strengths."

Mick is credited with what some fans think is one of the best goals at Feethams – a 35 yarder against Walsall.

"They hit a long ball up the middle. I intercepted it, and ran into their half.

Nobody came to challenge me, so I thought that I'd better hit it, and the ball flew into the goal at the Tin Shed end."

Just like the rest of the players towards the end of that championship winning season of 1990-91, Mick knew that there was a good chance manager Little would leave Feethams for pastures new further up the league.

"We all had the feeling that it was inevitable he would leave for somewhere like Leicester. If he didn't move on, then it was clear he wasn't ambitious.

"He did really well at Darlington in two years, taking them from the Conference to the old Third Division."

Mick Tait with supporters' club official Karen Davies

Unfortunately, it all went wrong the following season. Frank Gray took over from Little, and for various reasons Quakers struggled at the bottom of the league.

"The club didn't have enough money to do things, and maybe Brian knew that when he went.

"Frank tried to bring young lads through, but it was difficult to do that in the Third Division at places like Birmingham and Bolton.

"We needed to invest in the team, and we didn't, so we struggled. If season 1990-91 was very enjoyable, then season 1991-92 was equally as hard, although I enjoyed helping the young lads along when they came into the team."

Mick left Feethams in the summer of 1992 - "the board had to cut the wages" – and he joined neighbours Hartlepool as a player, and then manager, before he eventually returned to Feethams as assistant manager to Gary Bennett in March 2001, and when Bennett resigned in October 2001, he stayed on as assistant manager to Tommy Taylor.

Farewell to Feethams | a collection of Darlington FC memories

Kevin Todd 1983-85

League appearances	102	Goals	26
Other Games	18		

NOT many players turned their backs on the Newcastle glory days when Kevin Keegan finished his career there as a player, but that's what Kevin Todd did.

Kevin was signed on loan by Darlington manager Billy Elliott at the same time as Dave Barton, and at the end of the 1982-83 season, he decided to make the move permanent. He stayed at Feethams for two seasons, helping the club to promotion in season 1984-85.

"After I'd been on loan at Darlington, I went back to Newcastle, and they offered me a two year contract.

"But I didn't think that I would get first team football, because at the time, they had Kevin Keegan, Imre Varadi, Chris Waddle and Peter Beardsley in their side.

"Cyril Knowles phoned me up and offered first team football, and so I decided to move on. It didn't bother me leaving St James' Park.

"I got on well with Cyril, just like most of us did, as long as we worked hard.

"He made a big difference to the club. He was very professional, and made sure we were fit. He turned the club around.

"After we won promotion, I was released because the club was losing money, and Cyril admitted to me later that letting me go was one of his biggest mistakes, because it cost him a fortune to sign Steve Carney."

Andy Toman 1989-93

League appearances	155	Goals	22
Other Games	28		

ANDY was signed by manager Brian Little, and is one of the few players who have successfully made the switch from neighbours Hartlepool to Feethams.

"I met Brian twice before I signed. I was worried about dropping down into the Conference, but he offered me a good package.

"He made me that confident we would win promotion, I had thought before about having a clause put in my contract about getting a free transfer if we failed

A job well done: Andy Toman (centre) celebrating Darlington's promotion at Welling

to win promotion from the Conference, but I just took his word for it.

"I thought Brian was a great manager, who got the best out of his players. I have never played with a manager who had so much enthusiasm. We never knew what to expect from a training session, because every day was different."

Like everybody else, Andy has plenty of happy memories of the Conference season, but one sour note was the game at Northwich - or as it was nicknamed "the battle of Northwich."

"I was sent off in that game. We got a little worried when the referee called all the Northwich players by their first names. When I told him that he couldn't do that, he told me to "f... off"

"Mark Prudhoe was carried off in that game because of a terrible tackle, but nothing happened to the player that did it. We got home really late that night, because Mark was in hospital. There was something in the air that night."

The crucial game of that season was the away game at title challengers Barnet.

"It was a turning point for us, because if we lost that game, then they would have

60

gone quite a few points clear of us. On the day, Brian put me at right back. He told everybody that he had picked his best eleven against their best team, and to go out and prove ourselves. His tactic put me against Eddie Stein, and I came out on top."

Andy, remarkably, couldn't remember taking the free kick that led to Gary Coatsworth's memorable promotion clinching goal at Welling.

"It wasn't until I watched a video of the game ten years later that I realised I took the free kick. The game quickly passed me by that day. The pitch was bone hard, and we didn't expect much football to be played.

"There were plenty of fans there that day, and the families of the lads. But what I remember most was Brian in tears, because it was a real weight off his shoulders."

The players' celebrations on the way home turned into an anti climax.

"We didn't get home until around 5am because the bus broke down – fortunately outside a pub. But we still didn't have a really good drink, because the driver wouldn't allow us to celebrate on the bus."

The one let down that season was the defeat at Leek Town in the quarter final of the FA Trophy.

"Losing that game was one of the biggest disappointments of my career, because I didn't get to play at Wembley *. I was unlucky in the opening few minutes, when I headed the ball from five yards out, and the keeper pushed it over the bar. From that moment, I knew it was going to be one of those days.

"The goal they scored was from a ricochet, and the ball trickled over the line.

"The lads were gutted. Some of the fans said that we wouldn't have won the league if we stayed in the Trophy, but Brian had a squad of twenty, and everybody would have been involved."

Andy once scored a hat trick for Quakers in a Leyland DAF Trophy tie against Grimsby - who had two men sent off for fighting between themselves.

"They'd been arguing with each other since the start of the game, and the referee had a word with them. Midway through the first half, one walked past the other and slapped him, and the other one grabbed his shirt and they started fighting.

"I used my hat trick as a quiz question when I became a Football in the Community Officer."

Quakers won their second successive title that season when they lifted the Fourth Division crown.

"The team spirit was fantastic, and the atmosphere was probably the best I've ever known in a dressing room. We won together, and we lost together. Brian told us that if anybody was having a bad time on the field, then other people should help him. I felt that I could always turn round to Mick Tait and Kevan Smith to keep me going."

Andy was probably one of the first people to get an inkling that Little would leave.

"After the end of the season, Brian had me in his office to negotiate a three year contract and his parting words to me were "you're the last one to get signed up before I go."

The Third Division season was a disaster.

"The season was very flat. We didn't really strengthen the team, and maybe some of the lads who had been there for two years had been there too long.

"Frank Gray, the manager, didn't have the same appetite as Brian Little, and was too laid back."

Ray Hankin temporarily replaced Gray, before Billy McEwan came along.

"I was in Hong Kong when Billy got the job. My mother phoned me to say that somebody called Billy McEwan had been on the phone, and was desperate to speak to me. I phoned him from Hong Kong, and I told him that I would be back the following week. Billy replied, "We can't afford to pay you to go to Hong Kong every summer."

"When I arrived home, he took me into his office, and asked me to take a pay cut. I said no. He asked me again on another occasion, and he went mad when I said no, and he kicked me out of his office."

It was a war of nerves between Andy and McEwan.

"I had my car stolen one week, and I arrived for training in an old Escort and parked it outside Billy's office. You couldn't see into his office from the outside through the net curtains, but he could see out.

"That day we were training in South Park, and McEwan said to us all that you could always tell by the cars in the car park what sort of players he had - obviously referring to me and my old Escort. The following week, the insurance paid up, and I bought a brand new car and parked it outside his office.

"I was told later that Billy went mad when he saw me getting out of the car."

Andy is still a regular at Feethams, but never sets foot on the pitch. Instead he watches games from the press box as he is involved in media work.

Andy fulfilled his dream of playing at Wembley when he appeared there for Whitby in the 1997 FA Vase final.

Bill Tulip | 1956-58

League appearances	44	Goals	36
Other Games	2		

Bill holds the post war scoring record for Darlington, with 32 goals in 38 league games in season 1956-57.

In one particular spell from New Year's Day 1957 to the middle of March in that year, he scored hat tricks in four out of five home league games. His scoring sequence in games played was like this: 3, 2, 0, 4, 3, 1, 2, 0, 3, 1.

One of those hat tricks was against Hartlepool, so no wonder he was given a standing ovation at the end of that derby game on March 2nd. "Hartlepool were top of the league when we played them, and it was the biggest gate at Darlington for a long time.

"Hartlepool must have brought around 5000 supporters with them, and they had a lot of good players. They said that they were going to turn us over, but we made sure they didn't."

The Northern Echo reported: "When (Bill) Tulip completed his hat trick, his colleagues overwhelmed him with congratulations, and the crowd gave him the sort of ovation that is reserved only for big occasions. The Hartlepool fans sportingly joined in the applause."

Bill scored four against Quakers' other local rivals, Gateshead on January 19th, the first time two Darlington players scored hat tricks in the same game - Charlie Wayman also on target.

"Gateshead had wanted to sign me when I left Newcastle, and I had a letter from the Gateshead chairman which started "dear namesake" – he was a cousin of my grandfather. I signed for Darlington because of Ron Greener – he fixed it up for me."

Bill's most memorable Darlington game wasn't in the league or FA Cup, but the Durham Senior Cup.

"We played Sunderland at Feethams, and won 8-1. I scored three, and Ronnie Harbertson scored four. It was a tremendous night. Sunderland had eight first teamers in their side, including players like Don Revie."

Sadly, Bill's Darlington career ended prematurely. "I had a back injury, but we couldn't find out exactly what it was.

"I went to see lots of specialists in London and Brighton, and one day Stanley Matthews put me in touch with a specialist in Manchester, who discovered what the problem was. I was put in plaster for six months, and had to learn to walk again, basically. I got fit again, but only for the reserves, not the first team."

Bill was full time up to then, and when he stopped playing, he worked for a Ford dealer in Newcastle until he retired.

Steve Tutill | 1998-2000

League appearances	70	Goals	1
Other Games	12		

STEVE joined Darlington from York - and as with many before him, the Quakers gain was City's loss. He had been a good servant to York, playing in their League Cup win over Manchester United, but there's no sentiment in football.

"York wanted rid of me, and the first offer came from Darlington. I took it and never looked back," he said. "I had heard about manager David Hodgson from Gary Himsworth. Himo told me he looked after his players and was hard but fair. That's how I found him.

"I had a long term problem with my patella (kneecap) tendon at York. But the surgeon at Darlington did it and it was fine straight away."

Steve made his debut (along with Craig Liddle) on loan from the Minstermen, in a 4-0 thrashing at Mansfield. A 2-0 win at Doncaster the next game started a revival, and Steve went on to be everything a club looked for in a captain.

He was quick, brave, talented, and a good talker on and off the pitch.

As an uncompromising central defender, he took knocks, but played on whenever possible, and returned from injury as committed as ever.

"I had a few bad ones," he recalled. "I remember the physio John Murray's face when I broke my cheekbone at Chester in a clash with Luke Beckett, who became a teammate at Chesterfield.

Steve Tutill (centre) battles with old foes Hartlepool

"When the physio turns pale, you know it's bad. My cheek had caved in. But it didn't hurt as much as the dead leg I got in one pre-season game at Scarborough. My leg doubled in size, the pain was unbelievable, and I couldn't play for weeks."

But when Steve was fit he was a vital part of a good team. Arriving when Feethams looked like a bomb site, the east stand having been demolished, he finished his Darlington days with a heartbreaking defeat to Peterborough at Wembley.

"I had already had a memorable day at Wembley for York in the play off final. We were 1-0 up to Crewe and I went on as substitute with two minutes to go. I handled, Crewe scored from the penalty, but we won in extra time, and it was a glorious day."

His visit with Darlington could not have been more different. The pitch was a quagmire in pouring rain, the Friday night atmosphere was strange, and the journey a nightmare.

"We travelled on the day, and while I understood the manager's thinking in trying to treat it like a normal away game, it didn't work," said Steve. "The train got held up - at Peterborough of all places. It took a couple of hours to get across London to the hotel, and we had only about 40 minutes to rest in bed before throwing our pre-match meal down our necks.

"Then it took another one and a half hours to get to Wembley. All the time the pressure was building. In the second half we ran out of steam. For the last 20 minute my legs felt like lead."

Even so, Steve almost equalised with a flying header. "After we should have

gone up automatically, it was such an anti-climax. We had good players, and respect for the manager, but hit a bad patch at the wrong time."

But Darlington had a terrific season, with many more high points than low, especially the goals of Marco Gabbiadini, another York old-boy.

"He was brilliant," said Steve. "As a defender it makes life so much easier if you can get the ball to a player who can bang in goals. He did well in his first season when we just missed out on the play-offs, but the next year he was even better.

"It was tremendous to be in the top three nearly all season, and we also had the FA Cup game at Aston Villa."

Steve scored his one goal for the club at the start of the cup run, putting Darlington 1-0 up with a header against Southport.

It was a header from a corner that beat Darlington at Villa Park. "Dion Dublin scored it. I was marking him, but he lost me in a blur," said Steve, who had earlier predicted that Darlington would get the famous 'wild card' place, following Manchester United's withdrawal.

There were other memorable cup games, such as coming from 2-0 down to beat Burnley 3-2 at Middlesbrough's Riverside. "I went on a run up field, lost the ball, and Andy Payton scored for Burnley. I thought we were dead and buried," said Steve.

"We did well against Manchester City in the next round, but one of the games that meant most to me was beating Hartlepool in the play-offs. We tore them apart at their place in a brilliant performance."

Steve left in the summer after the play-off final. He had an option on his contract that entitled him to £10,000, but Darlington were reluctant to pay.

"I asked for a free transfer, and they said 'no.' So I said the matter should go to a tribunal," said Steve. "Then Darlington changed their minds and gave me a free. Chesterfield paid me the £10,000.

"But I was sorry to leave. The fans were great, while my wife Rachael is from Aycliffe. I would willingly come back to Darlington. I was even happy in the first year when the wages were sometimes paid late.

"That was before George Reynolds took over. When we were having similar problems at Chesterfield, he asked me to return to Darlington for £1 a week. It's better than getting nothing like you are at the moment, he pointed out!"

Sadly, Steve has since had to retire through injury.

63

Alan Walsh 1978-84

League appearances	251	Goals	100
Other Games	28		

ALAN'S League goal tally is a club record, and including cup goals, he totalled exactly 100. He went on to give similar service to Bristol City (99 goals) and has an extraordinary record of having reached double figures of League goals in 10 consecutive seasons, five for Quakers, followed by five for City. From the age of 22 to 32 he hit 10 or more every campaign. Then he had a spell in Turkey and banged them in there as well!

Throughout it all Alan remained modest. "I had no idea I was heading for Darlington's record," he said. "One day manager Billy Elliott said: 'Walshy, are you going for that record?' I didn't know what he meant. I thought he wanted me to pick up an LP after training."

To make his wonderful contribution to Quakers' history more special for the Feethams faithful, their goal hero was a Hartlepool fan, and had the Victoria Ground outfit scraped together the £15,000 that Middlesbrough wanted for him, he would have joined Pool.

As it turned out he scored his only League hat-trick for Quakers against the old enemy when he hit four in a 5-2 Feethams win.

So how did such a scorer come to play for Darlington?

"I played only three games as a substitute for Boro," said Horden-born Alan. "Jack Charlton had signed me 18 months earlier.

"John Neal took over and I never got a chance, even though I had scored 16 goals for the reserves, playing on the left of midfield. David Armstrong held that position and I couldn't oust him. Boro turned down an offer for me from Blackpool.

"But two weeks later when Darlington came in I was allowed to join them. I learned later that Pool had asked before Darlington, but couldn't raise the money.

"I would have gone to Hartlepool. I used to watch them. When I scored four against them, there was an article in the Hartlepool Mail asking why Pool had allowed me to join Darlington."

Alan made his Darlington debut in a 2-1 defeat at Rochdale, two days after

'Stop that' says Alan Walsh. As usual, the 'keeper couldn't

joining. But manager Peter Madden was sacked after the defeat. It was a strange decision so soon after the board had let him spend £15,000. If only the directors had realised that their manager had signed a player who was to re-write the history books.

Len Walker took over and Darlington walloped Port Vale 4-0 the following Saturday, Alan scoring one and creating two. "My goal came early and settled me," recalled Alan.

"I went from being dejected one Saturday, to elated the next."

He scored nine in his first season, being an ever present from the day he signed until the last game of the season, when he was on the bench. He finished equal top scorer with John Stone, but Darlington finished fourth bottom.

Even though he notched 15 League goals the next season, missing only three games, Quakers finished third bottom.

"I was playing out wide, and was pleased to score so many goals from there. I preferred to play up front, but you did what you were told."

A young Scottish striker, John Stalker, had arrived, and he notched 12 goals in 30 games to add to Alan's 15. A partnership was formed that would be prolific in the following campaign.

"By then Billy Elliott was manager and the club was on the up," recalled Alan. "His football knowledge and man management turned it round - and he bought David Speedie.

"John Stalker and I became the second most effective striking partnership in the country that season (1980/1) behind Tottenham pair, Garth Crooks and Steve Archibald. We had good players such as Dave Hawker, Ian Hamilton and Dave McLean and created a lot of chances."

Alan scored 22 league goals and Stalker 17, as Quakers finished eighth.

The following season Alan was pipped as top scorer for the only time at Darlington. He hit 13, four fewer than Speedie.

Darlington finished 13th, but Alan retains two important memories. On April 12, 1982, came his four goal blast against Pool.

"We went two down after quarter of an hour or so, but Dave McLean pulled one back before half time. Then in the second half everything I hit went in - except a penalty. Former Darlington keeper Martin Burleigh saved it, but the referee ordered a re-take and I scored. One goal was from around 30 yards, and I knew from the second I hit it, it was going into the top corner."

The penultimate home game that season - in which Alan missed only one game - was remarkable. Sheffield United were visitors and needed to win to be Fourth Division champions.

A crowd of 12,557 flocked into Feethams, and well over 11,000 of them were Sheffield fans, many in fancy dress. They filled all four sides of the ground, but for little pockets of Quaker fans.

"Financially it was marvellous for the club, but was weird for the players," said Alan. "The fans were packed onto the grass behind the goals and down the touchline. We wouldn't have dared score!

"We lost 2-0, but at 0-0 I got to the byeline and crossed. A fan dived out of the crowd and pulled the ball back. The referee gave a goal-kick. He had no choice."

The following season Alan rattled in 18 goals, including a double against Bristol City.

There was no stopping him, and other clubs were casting a jealous eye. But he

Alan Walsh scores with a flying header

was hardly living the jet set life.

"I remember getting up at 3.30am to travel to Aldershot on match day. That was around the time the club was facing a financial crisis.

"The players attended several fund raising functions a week. People were generous and we were saved. A great camaraderie grew from that."

In Alan's last season at the club, under Cyril Knowles, he was handed a goalscoring bonus, once he had reached 15. Every one after that was worth £50 to him.

He had already played through the pain barrier when Cyril insisted he couldn't get a team out without Alan, who defied ankle ligament damage by playing with his foot strapped as tightly as physiotherapist Bob Farrelly could manage.

Having reached 18 goals, he was hit by flu, and climbed out of his sick bed to play, after another plea from the manager.

"I stretched for a ball and felt a tear. I was out for weeks. I was in bed for four or five more days with flu, and my injury was agony every time I moved."

Alan was never to score another goal for Darlington. His last two were in a 5-3 home win over Northampton on February 28, 1984. Only 1278 fans attended.

"I went to hospital to see a specialist about the groin. I told him I had done it playing football.

"He didn't know who I was and told me I must pack in playing. I was 27. I told the club, and was ordered to go back to the specialist the next day. He apologised and said he had no idea I was a professional."

By the time he was fit, Alan's contract had expired. "I've scored 100 goals and given you six years. What will you offer me," I said. "No more," was the answer. "I had three children, but they wouldn't give me a fiver more.

"Ken Warne was chairman, and I had nothing against him. He was a businessman looking after the club."

Alan had no desire to leave, but matters came to a head while he was on holiday that summer. Not in some foreign resort of sun and sand.

"No, my mother in law's caravan at Thirsk. The site owner said there was a call for me on the public phone. It was Cyril. He said Plymouth had offered £30,000 for me."

An offer of £50,000 from Colchester had already been rejected, but Cyril asked Alan to come into Feethams for a chat. The player pointed out that he was on holiday, but Cyril's persuasive ways won.

"Ken and Cyril were waiting, and told me that they had turned Plymouth down. I thought that they were about to offer me more money. They didn't. I was angry because they could have told me that on the phone.

"I said all I wanted was a car to get from my home at Hartlepool. They said if they gave me one every player would want one. Ken left the meeting and Cyril said he was trying his best for me.

"An hour later the phone rang. It was Terry Cooper, manager of Bristol City, who had been with me at Boro. He said he had seen me score twice at Halifax, and he offered me this and that to join them."

City had plummeted from the first division to the fourth, but Alan was interested if the deal was right. Cooper was told Quakers wanted £80,000. He offered £5,000.

Two days later Ken Warne phoned and said he had got a car for Alan. But it was too late and the matter went to a transfer tribunal at Maine Road, Manchester.

"I went with my wife. When we got there, at the top of the steps were two groups of three. On one side was Cyril, Ken and Darlington secretary David Thorne. On the other side was Terry, his secretary and chairman. As I walked up the steps I didn't know who to greet first," said Alan.

"Tommy Docherty was there, trying to sign John Burridge (who later played for Darlington). Doc took Coops aside and Terry told him what he had offered and what Darlington wanted. "Tommy's advice was: 'Tell the tribunal you want to buy the player, not the club."

Alan, who felt stuck in the middle, was called in and asked why he wanted to leave Darlington. He told them he didn't but hadn't been offered a rise.

Then the two clubs went in, came out, had a general discussion, and after around an hour everyone was called back in to face the panel which included Gordon Taylor and Graham Kelly.

The fee was set at £18,000. Cooper was delighted. Any more and he would have had to back out. Alan was unfazed, explaining: "Darlington had already turned down more than Bristol would pay, so I knew I would be going somewhere and didn't mind where.

"But I was sad to leave. I never let Darlington down."

That must rank as one of the great understatements in the club's history. The fans were fuming at the panel's decision. How could they let such a great player part for a pittance?

But by the sort of irony that football throws up, Darlington won promotion the following season - without their greatest ever goalscorer.

Alan's reaction? "I was delighted. The nucleus was there when I left. It was a team on the up."

A season later Walshy whacked a free kick past Fred Barber to give City victory over the Quakers at Ashton Gate.

"I'm very lucky," said Alan. "Lucky to have played for Darlington, and to have been a professional for 18 or 19 years. I earned as much in two years in Turkey as I could in eight in England, where I never made much.

"But I'm very proud to be Darlington's top scorer. I don't know if anybody will beat it, because if you score a few goals these days another club snaps you up. But if somebody does, I'll be pleased for them," said Alan, now a youth coach at Bristol City.

"David Brown was all time top scorer before me, and when I beat his record, his

66

son wrote to congratulate me. That was a lovely thing to do.

"Some of my goals will always be in my memory. That one against Hartlepool, my home debut goal, and one at Altrincham in the Cup. We were told they had never lost at home to a League side. Everybody wrote us off after we drew at Feethams, but we won the replay. And there was one goal on a foggy night at Feethams when I sent in a cross from the touchline and it flew over the keeper and in."

A rare fluke. There weren't many among 100 fabulous goals.

Dennis Wann 1976-79

League appearances	121	Goals	15
Other Games	20		

DENNIS was just eight minutes from a move to top flight Sheffield United, when the course of a promising career changed dramatically. The left winger was playing for York at Oldham, a move to Bramall Lane having been agreed. But he suffered such a badly broken leg close to the end of the match that he was ruled out for 15 months.

When he was fit again not only had the glamour move gone, but York didn't want him either. He agreed a move to Darlington, and such was his recovery that he missed only 13 league games in three happy years with the Quakers.

"I have nothing but good memories of the place," he said. "After that long out with what in those days was a career threatening injury, I was pleased to be playing. You are no use to anybody when you're in a pot."

Settling at Feethams was easy for Dennis, who started his career at his home town club Blackpool before joining York. Darlington manager Peter Madden engineered an exodus of players up the A1 from Bootham Crescent.

At around the same time as Dennis made the move, so did Jimmy Seal, Barry Lyons, John Stone and Eddie Rowles.

Darlington had endured years of struggle and re-election applications in the preceding seasons, and the influx of the York boys showed that Quakers could attract quality players, who could breathe new life into the club.

"York had won promotion shortly before to the old second division, and had good players who were wanted by bigger clubs. A few of us got injuries, and when

Peter Madden - gentle giant

Wilf McGuiness came in as manager he got rid of several who had helped the club go up.

"Me and Eddie Rowles were the best of mates. I used to commute home to Blackpool when I could and when I stayed in Darlington it was with Fred and Peggy Wealands who were great.

"What struck us was what a nice town Darlington was. I thought about buying a house there, and was looking at the Coniscliffe Road area, but had business interests in Blackpool.

"I got on well with the fans, and we played good football. The likes of me and Barry Lyons had a bit more to offer than some of the cloggers in the Fourth Division!

"I scored a few goals, and made many more for Jimmy, Eddie and a powerful young striker we had - Ronnie Ferguson.

"And I got on well with Madden. He was a gentle giant, but let you know if he was not happy with you. I swore at him once, so he picked me up right off the ground with one hand. After that I kept quiet.

"The club was hard up and Peter was manager, trainer, physio. He was a good judge of a player.

"The game I remember most was the League Cup third round visit to Everton. They beat us 1-0 but we gave them an almighty fright. It's easy to say it looking back 25 years, but we could have won 4-1.

"Their players admitted they were terrified at the prospect of having to play us at Feethams in a replay. But we didn't recapture that form in the league.

"As a left sided player with pace and an accurate cross I would have been worth a fortune these days," said Dennis.

Quakers finished a creditable 11th in his first season, a relief for fans who had endured five successive nailbiting seasons when they hadn't finished higher than 19th.

67

They failed to build on it, finishing 19th (again) the next season. Then under Len Walker Dennis was ever-present, but they finished fourth from bottom.

By then he was having to play on the right which didn't suit him. A certain youngster - Alan Walsh - with a deadly left foot had joined the club.

Dennis had the pleasure of scoring at his old club York, but Darlington lost 5-2.

Dennis has no recollection of his first Darlington goal, a last minute winner, which took a wicked deflection, against Torquay. "If it's in the record books, I must have claimed it," he laughed.

The arrival of Billy Elliott as manager marked the end of Dennis' days with the club.

"He didn't want players travelling from other parts of the country, and by then my hotel was doing well in Blackpool and I wasn't prepared to move north. So I joined Rochdale where Peter Madden had become manager. I think Darlington got around £10,000."

Dennis ended his career where he started it, at Blackpool. He now runs a newsagent's shop, which he has owned for almost 20 years.

"I was recently in the cricket club in St Anne's when a chap said to me 'you used to cross a great ball'. He was a Darlington fan and I was amazed he recognised me, because I have lost much of the hair I had in those days.

"Moments like that are nice. I did my best for Darlington and loved it there. Football is fleeting. You have to make the most of it."

Paul Ward 1985-88

League appearances	124	Goals	11
Other Games	19		

PAUL was the youngest ever manager in not only Darlington's history but also in Football League history, when he replaced Cyril Knowles, who was sacked in March 1987.

Paul came to Feethams as a player as part of the deal which took Mitch Cook to Ayresome Park in September 1985.

"Middlesbrough were desperate to sign Mitch," says Paul. "Once Boro boss Willie Maddren approached Cyril, a deal was put together with me and Alan Roberts coming to Feethams.

"I was in the Boro first team at the time. On a Tuesday night, I played for Boro against Mansfield in the Second Division; the next day Willie told me that Darlington wanted me.

"I was interested in going to Darlington, because it was obvious from what Willie had said that I didn't figure in his plans.

"Cyril spoke to me, and told me that I would be regularly in his team, and without hesitation I signed."

Paul had heard some of the stories about Cyril's man management and training techniques, and he had a quick introduction on his first day in training as they prepared to play Wigan on September 14th.

"We were playing a five-a-side game outside. (In Cyril's time, they also played five-a-side inside, but that was nickname murderball - Ed). After about twenty minutes of this training session, Cyril ran past me and said that he'd brought Alan and me to the club, but he didn't know who to leave out for us. I just said that it was his decision.

"Anyway, five minutes later, Cyril just launched into a tackle on Graeme Aldred and laid the lad out. He had to be stretchered away. Cyril turned round to me, and said, "I'll leave him out"!

"We went to Wigan the next day, and took the lead early in the game through Steve Tupling, and were playing quite well.

"There was a long clearance from their keeper, and Steve Carney, who was playing centre half, ducked under the ball, and it bounced into Fred Barber's hands. I thought to myself that Steve used pretty good judgement there. He did it again a few minutes later, and Fred collected the ball.

"Steve did it twice more in the game, and cost us two goals.

"We lost the game 5-1, and afterwards Cyril went ballistic with him in the dressing room.

"Steve turned round and told him that he had a cut on his forehead, and didn't want to head the ball! Needless to say, I didn't play many more games with Steve."

Quakers struggled near the bottom of the league in season 1986-87, and after a run of six home games without a win, Cyril and coach John Craggs were sacked.

"John went to the ground one Monday morning and was called in to see the chairman, Archie Heaton, who told him that he was dismissed. John was on his way out of the ground, when Cyril came along. He stormed in to see the chairman, and

Paul Ward fires goalwards - but where's the crowd!

was told that he was also sacked.

"The chairman came to see me, and asked if I would take training along with Peter Robinson as we were the senior players. We'd only been up training for twenty minutes, when Brian Anderson, the secretary, arrived and asked me to go back to the ground.

"Archie saw me, and said that there was a problem appointing a new manager. He then asked me if I would take it on, and I said yes.

"When I realised what it would entail, it didn't faze me, but in the back of my mind I thought a lot would depend on the reaction of the players.

"I never got back to training to finish the session, and when the players returned to the ground, they were called into a meeting.

"My opening statement to them was "You're not going to believe this, but I'm your new manager."

"After a few minutes stunned silence, they started asking questions. Deep down,

I thought to myself that if I was going to get a poor response, I would have gone back to the chairman and told him that appointing me manager wasn't a very good idea.

"But the players' response was very good. I told them that there were two ways to approach the rest of the season. Either become a laughing stock or knuckle down, win some pride, and if we were going down, then at least we would hold our heads up high.

"They wanted to go down fighting. Four or five players who were on the transfer list came up to me and asked if they could tear their letters up. The players' attitude was first class."

Paul was aged just 23, and there was a huge amount of media attention as he was billed as the youngest ever manager in the Football League, a record that might never be beaten.

"Jack Watson was a tower of strength to me and took a lot of the pressure off. Our first game was at Bournemouth, who at the time were top of the table. We lost, but only by an own goal by Mark Hine.

"Harry Redknapp, who was manager there, came up to me afterwards and said it was the hardest game they'd had all season, and I don't think he was being patronising.

"Middlesbrough was our next game, and I went to the chairman and asked if we could have an overnight, so we stopped in the Blackwell Grange.

"We drew 1-1 at Boro, Alan Roberts scoring for us. We had a bit of a run after that. We won our first away game of the season at Port Vale and won three or four more games.

"Maybe when I took over, people thought that we would win no more matches. But even though we went down, we achieved what we set out to do - to go with our heads held high."

The board of directors decided to advertise the post during the summer.

"When I took over, it was on the understanding that it was until the end of the season. After our last game, I sat in my office with Jack Watson, and he asked me what I was going to do.

"I replied that it would be sensible for me to go back to being a player. But Jack said that he was impressed by the way I'd gone about doing the job, and that I should apply for it.

69

"After the initial interviews, only two people were left, me and Dave Booth, and Dave got it.

"Despite what happened under Dave, I still feel that the board made the right decision at the time. I still think that I would have given it a good go, but at the age of 23, it was maybe too soon for me and I still had a few years ahead of me as a player.

"I thought I might have become player-coach, but Dave wanted to bring his own people in, so Phil Bonnyman arrived. I had no problems with Dave. We had a chat early on, and I said there was no malice and would work with him."

During that summer, there was speculation that Sunderland were going to sign Paul.

"Sunderland had just dropped into the old Third Division for the first time in their history, and there were rumours that I was going to be Denis Smith's first signing.

"I spoke to him and he told me that wanted to sign me when he'd managed to sell Mark Proctor to Sheffield Wednesday.

"Sunderland and Darlington agreed a fee, and when Proctor moved, I just sat back and waited for the call.

"It didn't come, and I read in the Northern Echo "Smith does a U-turn on Ward."

"So I went back to Darlington, and agreed a one year deal with Dave Booth."

Quakers were drawn at Sunderland in the first round of the 1986-87 FA Cup.

"We spent all week practising free kicks and corner routines.

"We won a free kick just outside the area at the Fulwell End, and we were all in the correct positions to try one of the setpieces.

"Kevin Stonehouse charged in, tried to blast it and the ball finished high up in the Fulwell End. Kevin turned round and said "I got carried away!"

When the season finished, Paul went to Leyton Orient.

"I returned the following season, when Orient won 3-1. It was obvious that things weren't going well for Darlington, and that day I felt the same as Denis Law did when he scored for Manchester City against his beloved Manchester United."

Chapter 3

Quaker characters

Dick Corden

DICK Corden was club chairman when Quakers won the GM Vauxhall Conference and Fourth Division titles in 1990 and 1991, possibly the most exciting years in the club's history.

He brought Brian Little to the club as manager in February 1989, and gave him encouragement to build a side to bounce back from relegation to the Conference on that sad day in May 1989.

Dick, owner of a scaffolding company, had joined the board following a meeting at the old Little Chef restaurant on the A66 near Sadberge.

"I met director Peter Boddy there and he said the board needed new blood.

Soon after I arrived, we lost at home to Leyton Orient, and were bottom of the League. We had a board meeting straight after the game, and decided to sack manager Dave Booth.

"Archie Heaton, chairman at the time, wanted Billy Bremner to replace Booth, but he, and other possibilities, might want an arm and a leg.

"Just before that, Brian Little had left Middlesbrough. We wanted somebody hungry to make a name for himself, so I suggested Brian. Archie said: "all right, clever fella, go and get him." This was at 11pm after the Orient game. I didn't know how to find Brian, so the next day rang everybody of that surname in the Middlesbrough phone book. I started at 10am, and at 1pm rang a chap who said that Brian was no relation, but he gave me a number for him in the Midlands.

"Having contacted him, I travelled down immediately. He said that he would take the job until the end of the season. He travelled back with me, and the following morning we met Archie at the Blackwell Grange Hotel.

"Brian wondered what salary he should ask for. I knew that Booth had been on £15,000 per year, so I suggested £20,000".

"Archie didn't want to pay it on principle; so he paid fifty pence per week less! Then we took Brian to meet the players. I said to them: "Here's your new manager" and left Brian to get on with it. Archie stood by the dressing room door,

We've done it! Chairman Dick Corden celebrates Quakers winning the 1990 Conference title

and I told him to come with me, as Brian didn't need him there."

Little almost saved the club from relegation. But the question was - should Quakers go part time, like the rest of the Conference clubs?

Dick said: "Archie resigned, and the directors asked me to take over. I told them I was heavily involved in my business, but they persuaded me. I wanted the club to stay full-time for a couple of years, to give us a chance of returning to the League. Brian felt that if we went part-time, he might not be able to get the players necessary to strengthen the team."

He brought in Kevan Smith, Andy Toman and John Borthwick among others. Winning the Conference took priority, but Quakers also set their sights on a big pay day by reaching the FA Trophy final at Wembley.

"We thought we could make £100,000 out of it, and budgeted for it," said Dick.

"We were favourites for both competitions, but in the Trophy lost at Leek Town, two divisions below us, in the quarter final."

However, Quakers clinched promotion on the last day of the season.

"That was one of the greatest days in my life. I enjoyed the Conference, and we came across some good people," said Dick. "I never thought we'd miss out, even though Barnet gave us a run for our money. We let in the fewest goals in the league, and Brian always did his homework. He said before the season that if he built a defence, he would win promotion."

There were one or two scares, not least when Wycombe, managed by Martin O'Neill - who later made his name at Leicester and Celtic - won 1-0 at Feethams with six games remaining to give chasing Barnet hope.

"They scored in the first minute, and we didn't come near equalising. I thought we'd blown promotion, and was wound up. I went into my old office and sat in the dark.

"The door opened, and in came Brian - I didn't know it, but he used to escape to my old office for reflection as well!"

Quakers kept up their momentum, went up, and the following season stormed through the old Fourth Division.

"At Christmas, I told Brian we could win promotion. He asked if we could afford it, and I told him that we could.

"In that season, he added only Mick Tait to the squad. The spirit in the dressing room was fantastic."

Quakers clinched the title on a nail-biting last day, when defeat could have meant the play-offs.

They beat Rochdale 2-0 in front of a 9,160 crowd, an attendance never since surpassed at Feethams.

The chairman/manager relationship worked, but Little's success attracted bigger clubs.

"Leicester chairman, Eddie George rang me, and asked for permission to speak to Brian. I told him that if I said no, he would approach him anyway.

"I told Brian, who said: "Oh, no, I don't know what to do."

"I replied: "My heart says stay, my head says go." So Brian went, after two fantastic years."

His assistant Frank Gray, also a player, succeeded Little.

Dick was heavily criticised by fans for a programme piece he wrote at the start of the following season, stating he would be delighted to finish one place above a relegation spot, because the Third Division was the limit for the club.

Dick reflected: "Stockport, in the same division, splashed out £250,000 for a player, and that was something we couldn't compete with. I got a sackful of mail, but was only being realistic.

"Maybe if Brian had stayed, we would have finished in the top half."

It wasn't a good season under Gray, and after a 3-0 defeat at Torquay in February 1992, he was sacked, with Ray Hankin appointed as replacement.

"Frank told me that it wasn't a good weekend for him, because his wife had left him while he was in Torquay."

Dick denied the rumour that Gray returned to Feethams after the last game of that season, and collected his severance pay in cash in a black bin bag. "That never happened," says Dick. "He took the club to court, and was paid by cheque."

There were money problems all through that season, and crowds dwindled by around half.

Quakers made a desperate attempt to avoid relegation, by signing striker Nick Cusack from Motherwell for £95,000, a club record fee, which still stands. Cusack, featured elsewhere in the book, couldn't save the club from relegation.

At the end of the season - 1991-92 - Dick asked the bank to back the club throughout the close season, pointing out that Quakers had valuable youngsters such as Sean Gregan.

"But the bank manager told us that for the club to survive, the directors each had to pay £50,000 and hand over the deeds of their houses.

"He told us that if the club went bankrupt, the bank would sell our properties.

"I resigned there and then, because I couldn't afford that."

It was a sad end to Dick's reign, because without his drive and enthusiasm, Quakers might never have recovered from their relegation to the Conference.

Harry Robinson

HARRY was chairman of the club in the mid sixties after taking over from John Neasham, and was a member of the board when Quakers drew at Chelsea in 1958.

"Chelsea were very hospitable. They invited us to lunch before the game in the boardroom - it was silver service, and we were waited on hand and foot," he recalled.

"But when we came in at half time with the team in the lead, the Chelsea directors didn't want to know us.

"Before the match, our secretary, Charlie Brand, announced that he had the replay tickets. Chelsea thought that we were being arrogant, but they had to accept them in the end."

As part of the build up for the Chelsea game, the team spent a few days on the south coast training at Brighton, and manager Dickie Duckworth asked for another seaside trip before the next game at Wolves.

"Normally, we would have thought twice of spending that amount of money, but we thought that since we'd won at Chelsea, we might as well do it again.

"Mind you, when Dickie first asked me for a trip to the seaside, I thought he meant Skegness!

"Dickie knew every train connection that mattered. We went to a game at Gillingham once, and we took the train to King's Cross, where we had hired a coach.

"With the coach, there was a team of outriders, who escorted us across London to Gillingham. The lead rider said when he got us there: "I've done well there, Mr Duckworth."

"Not many teams got a police escort in those days.

"On another away trip to Colchester in the sixties, we took a wrong turning when we got to Colchester town centre and ended up going down some very narrow streets.

"It was one of those situations where we had to back up, inching out of the tight spot. A policeman came up and asked where we'd come from - and goalkeeper Tony Moor replied "Woolworths!""

Harry was chairman when Lol Morgan was appointed manager, and took the team to promotion.

But Lol left, claiming that he should have been offered a better deal.

"We had no right to stop him moving on if he wanted to get on in the world. He made a good name for himself at Darlington."

Harry Robinson gave this interview shortly before his death in 2002.

New faces: David Hodgson, Chairman Steve Weeks and Jim Platt pictured the day the new management duo were appointed

David Hodgson - Manager, June to November 1995, November 1996 to August 2000.

73

UNDER the often bizarre, and never dull reign of David Hodgson, Darlington fans were treated to a roller coaster ride.

The former Middlesbrough and Liverpool striker was an emotional manager, but always likeable. And he had one quality that perhaps no other manager of the club has ever had, or will ever have - he had no ambition beyond Darlington.

He insisted that he would stay with the club no matter how successful he was. While most managers aimed to use Feethams as a stepping stone to greater things, David never set his sights on the dizzy heights of the Premiership - unless with the Quakers.

He had worked as an agent with a difference, when the spell of Darlington engulfed him.

"Instead of fixing up players with clubs, I fixed up clubs with players," he explained. "I didn't represent players as most agents do. Clubs would ask me for a particular type of player, and I would find one."

He had contacts in many parts of the world, and a series of colourful characters were to wear the white of Darlington.

Portuguese forward Pedro Paulo had the sublime, continental skills that few fans ever imagined would grace Feethams. Jose Quetongo, an Angolan, had one stunning game for the club (at Barnet) before being whisked off to the even more unlikely destination of Hamilton Academicals, before playing Scottish Premier Division football with Hearts.

Portuguese strikers Rui Neves and Ricardo Costa, Austrian goal grabber Mario Dorner and his fellow countryman Franz Resch, Canadian defender Jason DeVos, and goalkeeper Loukas Papaconstantinou came and went with varying success.

Dorner had a marvellous season, DeVos was a colossus, while Papaconstantinou left with the record of never conceding a goal - he played only one game.

DeVos replaced the popular Sean Gregan, was an instant hit, and was sold to Dundee United for £400,000.

Perhaps it was David's misfortune that he managed the club under some strong willed chairmen and owners, whose personalities sometimes clashed with his own.

The discreet, softly spoken Reg Brealey, complete with determined, vociferous right hand man Steve Morgon, Mike Peden, an aggressive Scot whose sudden arrival and ambitious plans took many fans aback, and of course the incomparable George Reynolds.

David survived the Brealey and Peden eras, and his early relationship with Reynolds seemed solid.

But two such forceful characters can rarely exist in harmony, and David's departure was inevitable.

His arrival had come about by chance.

"I was asked, by Barrie Geldart (a scout, and friend of the club) to meet central defender Sean Gregan at Scotch Corner," said David.

"They were friends, and Sean was out of contract. Barrie wanted me to advise Sean. He was on peanuts and I explained to him ways of getting a better deal.

"Out of the blue Barrie told me the club was skint and were desperate for a manager who could bring players in, sell them and balance the books. The next game I attended was Middlesbrough's final match at Ayresome Park, and there was a dinner afterwards at Marton Country Club.

"There I met Gordon Hodgson, a Boro fan and Darlington director. Then Steve

Pedro Paulo in action for Quakers in 1995. Sadly Paulo was killed in a road accident in 1999 in his native Portugal

Weeks, the Darlington chairman phoned me.

"He asked if I would be interested in the job. By then I had talked to my wife Beverley about it. The idea appealed. I had been for an interview at Cambridge, but Tommy Taylor got the job.

"Even though my business was about 50 times as productive as the salary Darlington were to offer, I took the job after meeting Steve Weeks, Steve Morgon, and Gordon Hodgson at Blackwell Grange.

"I remember Morgon asking me I if I could sell players. I said if they had two legs I could. He then asked if I could sell bad players. I said I could improve them by 25 per cent.

"As Darlington had just lost nine out of 11 games, drawing the other two, I reckoned it wouldn't be hard."

David wanted ex-Boro teammate Mark Proctor as player/coach, but Proctor pulled out, and Hodgy rang Weeks to say he was not going to take the job. But by then Jim Platt was involved, and he advised Hodgy to go for it.

"Jim was older and wiser than me, and convinced me that I would always regret it, if I didn't go for it. So I took it, and Jim came too."

But David regretted it on the first day. "It was the middle of summer, and I sat in the office all day with nothing happening. I had gone from being on the phone for 12 hours a day, to suddenly sitting in silence.

"I found out later that I had one fax message that day, but the office staff hadn't given it to me. I went crazy with them!"

One of the first things David did was sell defender Adam Reed to Blackburn for around £180,000. The new manager had never seen Adam play, but had to balance the books. There was also a transfer embargo on the club and the money was needed to pay debts.

Sunderland boss Peter Reid had offered £50,000 for Adam, but Hodgy knew that Blackburn wanted a young central defender, and that gave the manager the chance to prove to Morgon that he could sell players.

"Morgon said I had saved the club from going bust. Nobody had done that for 10 years. We could finish bottom and I would still be in a job.

"My next task was to persuade Sean Gregan to take £200 a week - just a few days earlier before I took the job I had advised him to hold out for £500."

Of Morgon, who was running the club, Hodgy said: "He had the same business policy as George Reynolds and was very good. Steve Weeks had told me of Reg Brealey's involvement. I found him to be a gentleman - polite and well spoken."

The manager's first signing was Gary Bannister from Lincoln. Hodgson paid out of his own pocket for Bannister's removal expenses, and the player repaid him with wonderful displays.

Many players who drop into the third division from the top level are a disappointment. Bannister was a gem.

The 1995/6 season started well, with victory at Exeter, Paul Olsson scoring the winner. Pedro Paulo - who has since died in a car accident - had an outstanding debut.

But a home defeat to Rochdale followed, and the team drew five and lost one of their next six games.

"Reg phoned and said I was doing fine. He added that everybody said we were playing good football, and not to worry," said David.

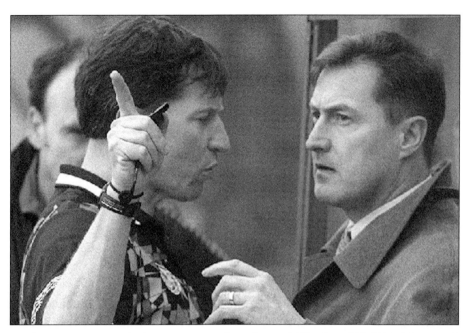

David Hodgson was an emotional manager as many referees discovered. This referee, Eddie Wolstenholme, sent off three Darlington players in one game at Scarborough

75

Brealey rarely attended games, a fact that made fans suspicious of his involvement. But Hodgy was determined to win, despite Brealey's reassuring words.

After a home defeat to Scarborough, the new manager put the entire team on the transfer list.

"I had to work out how I could make the players click. They were fantastic on the training ground, but didn't produce in matches. They lacked that killer instinct.

"I had to play mind games, and broke all the rules. Before the next game, at Barnet, I got them all in a room. I bought 40 cans of beer, wine and champagne.

"I told them if, by having a go at them, I had offended their wives and girlfriends, then I was sorry. But I pointed out that the players were offending their families by not winning, when they knew they were capable of it.

"I knew by giving them a drink, it would loosen their tongues. We drew at Barnet, and then won five games on the trot."

On November 25, Darlington lost 4-1 at Chester, in what was their only away

Farewell to Feethams | a collection of Darlington FC memories

defeat in the entire league campaign. But a week later David walked out.

The team had won 4-2 at Hartlepool in the FA Cup and were drawn at Rochdale in the second round. At half time at Rochdale he resigned.

"I was going to do it before the Chester game. The reason was because Morgon told me he had sold goalkeeper Mike Pollitt. I was furious because I had been led to believe that the money for Reed was all that was required that season.

"Morgon told me if he had revealed the full extent of the debts, then I wouldn't have taken the job. He was wrong - I would have done."

Quakers received £75,000 from Notts County for Pollitt, and David revealed: "I knew County were thinking of selling keeper Darren Ward. If they had, I would have got £200,000 for Pollitt. That's when I decided to leave. I wanted to pressurise the club into not selling so many players.

"I had put my own money into the club, and wanted to win promotion. I would have resigned there and then, but took a break in Cyprus.

"But when I returned I felt just the same, although I knew that if we beat Rochdale there could be big money from a lucrative cup tie. But at half time, I sent a letter of resignation to the chairman with instructions that it must not be opened until the end of the game."

Darlington were drawn against Liverpool in the third round, and David revealed: "Beverley begged me to withdraw my resignation and go to my former club Liverpool as a manager, but I wouldn't."

As it turned out, Quakers, with veteran John Burridge in goal in place of Pollitt, lost 1-0 to Rochdale in the Feethams' replay.

Under Jim Platt - who David wanted to resign with him - Quakers went on to reach the play-off final at Wembley, where they lost to Plymouth.

David was delighted - not bitter - that the players got there, and disappointed that they lost. "Mark Barnard lived in the same village as me, while Gregan and Matty Appleby often phoned me," said Hodgy.

The manager returned 11 months later, after Platt was harshly sacked.

"I had been offered the job a month earlier, but refused because Jim was winning. I said that if the club lost five straight games under him, I would return, but wouldn't play any role in seeing a winning manager kicked out.

"One of the directors rang me before the game at Lincoln and said that Jim was going, whether I came or not."

Platt was then sacked. Within days David sold Gregan to Preston for around £300,000. Then in came Jason DeVos, from Montreal Impact, Hodgy paying for the defender.

"Steve Morgon said he would leave because he felt I could make the club financially secure, while it would have been difficult for the two of us to work together after what we had been through. It was amicable. I have spoken to him several times since and we get on well."

On his return David gave the bank manager a list of players and their values. The bank was satisfied that their relationship with the club would be sound.

Soon afterwards the manager received a call from chairman Bernard Lowery, asking him to come and meet Mike Peden, who was to be the new owner.

"Peden told me he would be a hands on owner. I told him he could have his hands on what he wanted, but not the football team.

"I delved into his background, and by chance discovered that a contact of mine was a neighbour of Peden's. I had my doubts as to whether he had enough money for the task he had taken on."

A lot of players came and went that season, and the following season was patchy, again Quakers rallying to stay clear of trouble, the goals of Darren Roberts and Mario Dorner proving crucial.

By now the East Stand had been demolished and the changing rooms were in orange temporary cabins beside the West Stand or as it was nicknamed 'The Olympic Village.' On the surface everything was rosy. The new stand was planned, and to Peden's credit he did build the new stand - though the debts incurred in the process allegedly became one of the reasons he sold to George Reynolds.

It was built by the start of the following campaign (1998-9), by which time David had made an inspirational signing - Marco Gabbiadini.

"I had loads of players who were fabulous to work with on the training ground, but couldn't transfer it to the pitch," said Hodgy. "Gabbers could be awkward in training, but was fabulous in games. He scored 52 goals in two seasons and must have created 50 of them himself."

The team was soon flying, winning five successive league games, and going top with a 2-1 win at Plymouth, Gabbiadini scoring a wonder goal, and DeVos heading the winner.

But trouble was to rear its head.

David had been doing the job without wages, because he was advised by the Football Association not to accept payment from the club until he had handed his agent's licence back.

But even with that saving, cash flow problems were showing. "On the way to a game at Brentford, DeVos checked with the bank and found he hadn't been paid. We stopped the bus, and checked with the club. We were told that the players would be paid on the Monday," said David.

"We lost 3-0. I sold Jason, and soon afterwards James Coppinger and Paul Robinson went to Newcastle. I wanted to make sure that Darlington earned as much as possible, and the pair went for a total of £600,000.

"Tommy Taylor, now manager at Leyton Orient, wanted Gabbiadini, but there was no way I would let that happen."

But despite the influx of cash, Hodgy knew that all was not well, so was relieved when he heard of George Reynolds' interest.

"I was with youth team coach Stuart Gibson, driving to Middlesbrough. I remember exactly where we were. It was Neasham Road roundabout on the bypass - just where the new stadium would be built.

"George phoned and said if I met him, he would tell me whether he would buy the club. It was 7pm and I got home at 4am. I woke Beverley because I was so excited. We talked for two hours, and she had to bring me down to earth.

"I really felt this was it. Everything I had been waiting for. George had said we would never have to sell a player, but he would admire me, if I didn't have to spend. Every word he said stuck, and I never doubted him. I told him we needed five good players, and that I wouldn't have to buy them."

Darlington won their first three games, and the first three quarters of the season were excellent. But a home defeat by Northampton, who would finally pip Darlington to the third promotion place, and a draw at a poor Carlisle side, cost dearly.

Gabbiadini missed the game against Northampton - who he later joined - through suspension, while David was going to leave him out of the side at Carlisle, explaining: "He had gone off the boil. People said we couldn't play without him, and in the end I backed down. But I think I was right. I substituted him when we were 1-0 down and we drew, Glenn Naylor equalising.

"If the game had gone on another couple of minutes we would have won, and gone up, but a draw was not enough, even though we won our final game with Lincoln. Martin Gray lifted the lads for that game, and we murdered Lincoln.

"But we needed Torquay to beat Northampton, and they didn't. A few weeks earlier I had warned the players that they had lost their way because they believed they were certain to go up. I was proved right.

"But as soon as we heard in the dressing room after the final game, that we had got Hartlepool in the play-offs, the place was buzzing. I knew we would win. The players knew it too, though the atmosphere during the 2-0 first leg at Victoria Park game was tense.

"The second leg at Feethams was a formality once Gary Strodder scored the own goal, but there was no jamboree, for we focussed on winning at Wembley. We quietly went to Norton to train. Food was brought over, and preparations were professional and low key.

"When we got to Wembley we couldn't believe it was waterlogged. Under normal circumstances the game would have been postponed. I could tell there was doubt in the minds of the players.

"Even so we should have been two or three up at half time, Peter Duffield missed when I would have put my house on him scoring. As we walked off at half time Barry Fry, the Peterborough manager, said he couldn't believe it was 0-0.

"In the second half we lost Paul Heckingbottom, while Craig Liddle, Steve Tutill and Neil Aspin were struggling with injuries. If Hecky could have stayed on, Peterborough wouldn't have scored the only goal of the game.

"When the whistle went it was my lowest moment in football. I couldn't come to terms with the fact that the game had gone, and that we couldn't have a replay.

"Thoughts flooded into my head as I lay awake for hours that night. But I never thought of quitting. I went on holiday, and when I came back the relationship between me and George broke down.

"He would not sanction deals for certain players and I realised I could not go on. In the end it was a relief to leave - even though I had always said I would have to be sacked or carried out in a wooden box.

"But I love the club as much as ever. It's still 'we' and I have my mobile phone set so that wherever I am, I know how 'we' are doing.

"It was a pleasure to work with the players, and often a nightmare to have to deal with other goings on at the club. But I look back on great times, and great players.

"In my years away from the playing side of football, I had dreamt what I would do as a manager. The way Gary Bannister played was the way I dreamt it would be. His passing, movement, goals were that dream turned into reality.

"Appleby, Gregan, Liddle, and Gabbiadini were others I will remember with pleasure.

"Then there was Tutill, Aspin and Neil Heaney who were smashing too.

"Of those who were not always so popular with the fans, Paul Olsson did a great job, as did Phil Brumwell. Whether I left him on the bench or dropped him altogether, he bounced back. He had an incredible attitude.

"The one I would love to have kept was Coppinger. It would have been a pleasure to work with him and see him mature into an exciting player. He would have been great for Darlington - which is all that mattered to me."

Hodgson had many backroom battles, but throughout the interview he didn't, even off the record, knock any of the characters who ran the club. Some matters cannot be revealed for legal reasons, but one story sums up the hand to mouth existence of the club at times.

He relates: "An individual within the club asked if I could lend him £50,000. I was dubious, but said all right, as long as his solicitor and mine made sure it was above board.

"His face fell, and he left the room. Very soon afterwards, another individual asked if I could lend him £50,000. I said: "That's strange. I've just had an identical request from XXXX." He scuttled away. They were trying to borrow from one another left right and centre, and it seemed nobody had the cash."

Jack Watson

JACK never played for Darlington, but he was caretaker manager five times as well as chief scout under several managers, proof of the respect which his deep knowledge of the game commanded.

He was at Feethams when Quakers beat Chelsea 4-1 in January 1958.

"The scores were 1-1 after extra time, and Harry Bell, the skipper, decided to change formation in extra time. It worked very well, and we went on to win. After the game, Dickie Duckworth grabbed Harry, and told him that when he was talking

to the press, he should say that it was he, Dickie, who had changed the team."

Jack can also remember an unusual style of coaching by Duckworth. "He used to have a megaphone to shout instructions."

There was another "DD" that Jack knew - trainer Dickie Deacon.

"Dickie was a real character, and people reckoned that he kept his job for so many years because he was the only one who knew how to work the boiler.

"He used to take results seriously, He used to say that if Darlington won, he'd walk down the front street, but if they lost, he would go down the back street."

Jack struck up a good relationship with Lol Morgan, who took Quakers to promotion in 1966. "Lol was a real gentleman, somebody who got the best out of his players.

"Near the end of Lol's first season, he was undecided about whether to continue the same tactics and formation.

"I told him that it was the result that mattered. It was better to win 1-0, than to lose 4-3."

Ray Yeoman, who was manager in 1968, asked Jack to watch their opponents in the Football League Cup, Leicester City, in action.

"I went to watch Leicester City at Filbert Street, and when I went to collect my ticket, the gateman said that he didn't know how I had the cheek to go and watch them!"

Even though Jack was caretaker manager five times, he also turned down the manager's job.

"One day, I got a call from the secretary to meet the chairman at the time, George Tait at Ramside Hall.

"I told the secretary, Charlie Brand, that I couldn't because I was going to watch a game at Grimsby. But I got another call from Mr Tait telling me to be there.

"I went to Ramside Hall, and Mr Tait told me that he was going to sack Len Richley, and offered me the job.

"But I turned it down, and the next morning, I sent a letter of resignation to Charlie Brand. I would never take a job if there was somebody else in the position."

Jack came back to Feethams, as chief scout, under Cyril Knowles, and continued when Knowles left in 1987, Paul Ward succeeding him.

"Paul should have had the job on a permanent basis. He excelled himself, even though he was the youngest manager in the league. He behaved with dignity. I remember that we played at Middlesbrough in the league, and after the game, the press asked Bruce Rioch if Paul could do the manager's job, and Bruce said yes, as long as I (Jack) was helping him."

Jack left the club again in the late eighties, but was brought back by Alan Murray in 1993 for another five year spell.

Ken Lonsdale

KEN was the first public address announcer at Feethams, being appointed in 1959. Before then, public information inside the ground was broadcast by word of mouth, and the team was usually printed in the Northern Echo and Evening Gazette the day before.

But Ken changed all that.

"I started with a sound system at the back of the stand, out of view of the pitch, where Charles Brand counted the gate money. It wasn't at the top of the stand to begin with, and I could only watch the game from the tunnel.

"And because we didn't know the half time scores until the second half had started in our game, one of the ballboys, whose name was George, used to walk around the ground with a board on his shoulder which informed the crowd.

"Some of the music was bad, so after a few months I took my own records to games. The club used to pay me five bob (25p) to do the job, and let me watch the game for nothing.

"As a young teenager, my mother wouldn't let me go to away games, but she decided to go with me to Wolves for the big FA Cup tie, and she thoroughly enjoyed it."

Ken's success as a PA announcer eventually merited a place of work at the top of the stand for the West Ham League Cup tie in October 1960.

"I had a much better view of the game from up there. We beat West Ham 3-2 that night, and I can remember Ray Spencer receiving the ball in the centre circle, running towards the Park End, and then scoring with a shot into the top corner of the net - it brought the house down."

In another exciting game when Darlington scored, Ken forgot about the cramped environment of the PA system booth.

"I can't remember who it was against, but when we scored, I leaped up in the air,

banged my head on the stanchion and was carted off to hospital. I had to wear a neck brace for ages after that!"

Of course, even the lofty heights of the East Stand were no good on foggy days.

"There was one day when we played Chester, and it was so foggy, that we couldn't see either end of the pitch.

"Most of the crowd didn't know what was going on, unless the ball was right in front of them. So George, the ballboy, ran behind the goal when we heard the crowd cheer, found out who scored, then came back to tell me! We won 5-1 that day, and I didn't see any of the goals - nor did many other people."

Andrew Thompson

ANDREW - or "Tommo" as he is known to everyone (including his mother!) - has been mascot and groundsman at Feethams.

One of his most memorable times as mascot was the FA Cup ties against Middlesbrough in 1985.

"We were brilliant. Ayresome Park was covered in slushy snow, and Fred Barber had the game of his life in goal for us, pulling off a couple of great saves.

"For the replay, I helped clear snow off the pitch, then watched our win from the top right corner of the old East Stand."

Tommo wanted to be groundsman. "I used to help groundsman Colin Gray with all sorts of jobs. One frosty day we put straw and hessian sacks all over the pitch so we could play York. Unfortunately, we can't do that now in case the straw has been treated with chemicals. If a player becomes infected, he can sue."

Nothing could have prepared him though for the pitch problems in 1998.

"There was no indication at all of the problems to come, until we built the new East stand in August 1998. Early that season the pitch was brown, because we didn't have a sprinkler or irrigation facilities.

"But the first sign we had that real trouble was looming, was after a midweek game against Carlisle. The water was coming up from the pitch, and covering my feet.

"It snowballed. We had the drains up and, re-turfed the pitch, which was so rotten, the water was stagnant. The pitch was made up of clay, and I still maintain that all the boreholes that were drilled for the stand, altered the water table."

79

Groundsman Andrew Thompson is pictured in his cub's uniform, making tea in 1982, with Alan Walsh playing mum

80

and wouldn't take a stud, the other half was soaked.

"I felt like walking away at times. I was arriving for work at 7am, and not going till 10pm. I couldn't sleep some nights because of the worry - especially when I heard rain beating against the windows. I used to watch with dread when the weather forecast came on television.

"Mike Peden, club owner, threatened to sack me, but it was obvious that the water wouldn't go away. We had sponge rollers, mops, all sorts.

"The players and staff were sympathetic and gave me brilliant backing, but some people at the top of the club weren't working hard enough to help me.

"We had to cover the pitch every night with sheets, held down with stones. I had regular call outs on windy nights to put the sheets back on."

The arrival of George Reynolds eased Tommo's problems.

"I was delighted he bought a pitch balloon. He was the only one who took a real interest in my problems. Earlier when we brought in the groundsman from Middlesbrough, people at the top weren't interested in what he was suggesting."

Reynolds paid for the pitch to be completely dug up in the summer of 2000.

"I was pleased when it was all over. There were times when I wondered what I'd done wrong, but it has helped me because I know that having got through that, I can get through most things.

"I've got no regrets about doing the job. I couldn't play the game, so for me, being a groundsman has been the next best thing."

The club bought thousands of worms to try to aerate the soil. The story achieved national publicity, and still makes him and many other fans cringe with embarrassment.

"I just did as I was told," says Tommo. "The episode was a shambles. I was filmed with a bucketful of worms in my hand, but I knew the idea wasn't going to work.

"Worms had been used at Old Trafford, but Manchester United's problems were different to ours."

It came to a head after the home game with Scarborough. "Mick Wadsworth, the Scarborough manager, complained to the League about the pitch, and we had to stage the Burnley FA Cup game at Middlesbrough's Riverside."

Half the Feethams pitch was relaid in November 1998. "Part of it went from being sodden, to bone hard. In effect, I had two pitches. One half was flat and hard,

The Evening Despatch Appeal

THE club always seemed to have financial problems in the sixties and seventies, but none of them were serious enough to threaten the future of the club.

But the moment Darlington fans dreaded, suddenly reared its ugly head in the spring of 1982.

There had been appeals for cash or financial help before; this one was the most passionate yet. Find £100,000 or the club will cease to exist.

The headline in the Evening Despatch on Monday January 25, 1982, read: "It's the end of league soccer in Darlington - Centenary disaster faces club."

And Despatch editor, Robin Thompson, explained: "A £60,000 overdraft limit imposed by the club's bank, will be broken tomorrow when the players' wages are paid."

He went on to explain that several bills were outstanding, and that ten suppliers had started proceedings to recover money owed.

The plan was to raise £50,000 in six weeks, and another £50,000 by the end of the summer - or the club's £4000 per week wage bill for 33 players would have to be halved. The supporters club gave £400 on the first day, closely followed by £100

Darlington fans and Station Taxis join the fundraising in 1982

Two youngsters who wanted to 'Save The Quakers'

from Wearside League club South Shields.

The Evening Despatch mounted a fund raising campaign to help the club, and they encouraged the townsfolk to take part with a whole range of fund raising ideas. Fans of all ages swam, sold and sung for the Despatch's "Save it" campaign, and steadily the cash mounted up.

But the big fundraising event was the game against First Division leaders Southampton, then managed by Lawrie McMenemy. The Saints included several big names in their side, among them Kevin Keegan, Alan Ball, Mick Channon, and Mick Mills, but it was Darlington's David Speedie who grabbed the headlines with a superb hat trick in the 5-2 win in front of a 9,000 crowd - Quakers biggest at the time since the Bradford City game in 1969.

And within days, there was talk of the little Scotsman going to Sunderland, but he eventually signed for Chelsea for £60,000 - enough to keep the club going.

The Despatch, with the help of the fans, had saved the club.

Ironically, the club lasted longer than the Despatch, which folded in 1985. Nobody saved it.

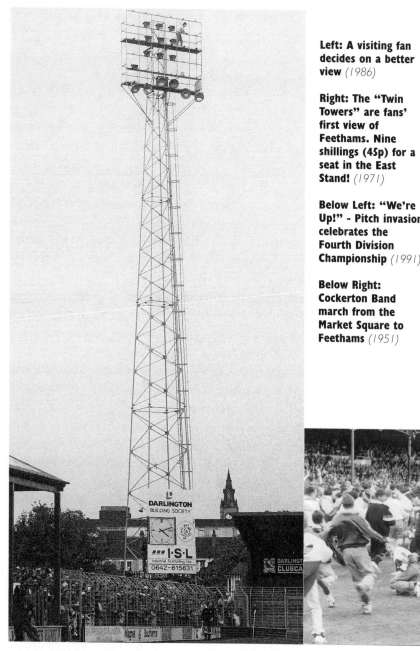

Left: A visiting fan decides on a better view (1986)

Right: The "Twin Towers" are fans' first view of Feethams. Nine shillings (45p) for a seat in the East Stand! (1971)

Below Left: "We're Up!" - Pitch invasion celebrates the Fourth Division Championship (1991)

Below Right: Cockerton Band march from the Market Square to Feethams (1951)

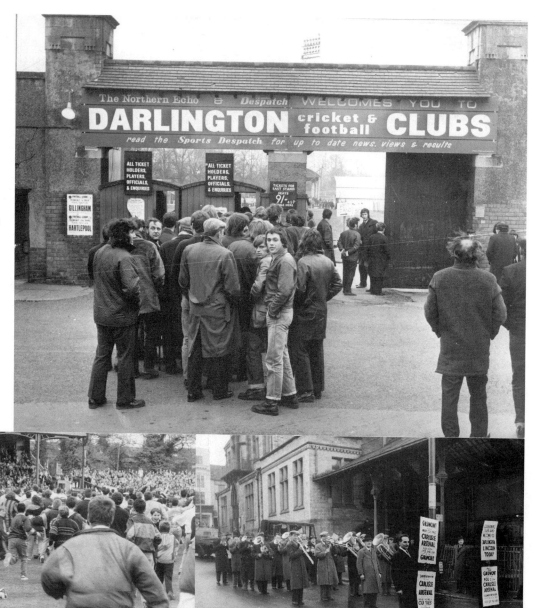

Farewell to Feethams | a collection of Darlington FC memories

Les Abbott

I WENT to Stamford Bridge with my father for the FA Cup tie. We were seated in the back row of the stand, and my father finished with three large bumps on his head, one for each Darlington goal, because right above him was a girder.

Unfortunately, I couldn't go to the replay as my headmaster at Eastbourne School threatened reprisals on whoever was missing on the Wednesday afternoon!

Ken Anderson

ONE of my favourite recollections was when the League Cup was in its infancy and Darlington had games against first division giants West Ham and Bolton Wanderers in 1960.

After a high ball was thumped into the West Ham penalty area, the Darlington warhorse and local dentist Lance Robson rose to the occasion alongside the West Ham goalkeeper and defender resulting in the three of them landing in a heap on the floor, the ball bouncing near them for what seemed an age. What Lance lacked in skill was always made up for by his strength and tenacity and when he got up first to crack in a goal, I have never heard a roar like it at Feethams before or since.

Ted Blair

I COULDN'T face going to the Scunthorpe v Darlington game in 1989. It was our last away game of the season, and we needed to win to keep our slim survival hopes alive. I'd rarely seen them win that year and just couldn't face the drama. I'd rather have missed a famous victory than witness the end of our Football League membership. That for me came in the home game versus Colchester before the Scunthorpe trip when we lost 2-1 and then the final home game to Carlisle, our last in the Football League at that time.

Scunthorpe v Darlington May 4, 1996

We went to Scunthorpe on the last day of the season, needing a win to go up in the third automatic promotion spot. The place was packed with Darlo fans - a lot of unfamiliar faces.

The key thing I remember that day is the anguish on Robbie Blake's face just as he missed scoring by a few inches in the dying seconds when the score was 3-3.

Darlington v Sheffield Wednesday FA Cup second round December 15, 1976

One of my all time memories of Darlo is the time we beat Sheff Wed in the FA Cup 1-0 in December 1976.

Not a lot of the game lingers in the memory except for the 40 - 50 yarder (depends on who you ask) from Ron Ferguson - which seemed to fly into the top of the net.

Ferguson was later quoted as saying he never missed from 50 yards.

It was still possible at that time for everyone to walk from end to end around Feethams. This allowed a bunch of none-too-happy Wednesday fans to sneak into the Tin Shed - where were the police then - and beat up a few Darlo fans.

I took a punch to the nose which left me dazed and bloody but at that age it was more like a badge of honour than anything to worry about. I didn't wash off the blood before going to school the next day, as I was desperate to show it off!

Northampton v Darlington April 27, 1990

One of my best memories is the 3-0 win at Northampton's old County Ground. It was a glorious spring day and there was a large Darlo contingent as we were still on the crest of a wave after coming back from the Conference.

To take a 3-0 lead after 20 minutes was unbelievable but the third goal remains the best I have ever seen in all my years as a Darlo fan. I bought the video from Northampton so I would have a record of it.

As I remember, Mark Prudhoe threw the ball out to Andy Toman outside the penalty box - he moved forward and passed to Les McJannet on the right wing. Les ran down the wing and put across a great ball which Mitch Cook volleyed in from the edge of the box. Sensational.

83

Everything was right that day - great beers beforehand, the lovely weather, the mood of the Darlo fans and the game itself (well, the first 20 minutes). Oh for more like that.

Dave Burdon

I WAS at Stamford Bridge, for the unforgettable cup game of 1958, going by train to Kings Cross. Being 3-0 up at one stage was unbelievable, but the second half was very different, Chelsea pounding the Quakers and drawing level. My father was at St James Park, Newcastle, and said the biggest cheer there was when the score went up on the board at half time.

I was an apprentice at North Road works, and the replay was held on a Wednesday afternoon. I plucked up the courage to ask the foreman, Ossie Parks, for a passout as I had to go to the dentist. He signed the slip without question except to comment: "There's a lot with toothache today, son."

John Carter

WHEN Arsenal played at Darlington in the league cup in 1965, the Gunners team walked all the way to Bank Top Station after the game. I was collecting autographs at the time, and all I got out of Ian Ure, their centre half, was: "Mind ma feet."

In 1967 we hired a minibus to go to Derby for the League cup quarter final. About a dozen of us were threatened with the sack from Cleveland Bridge if we knocked off early.

What a match. 1-0 up at half time, then 5-2 down and a fight back to 5-4. I'm sure if the match had gone another five minutes we would have won. That was the only time I came away from a match so hoarse that I could hardly speak. We certainly gave Brian Clough an early scare in his managerial days - plus we didn't get the sack when we returned to work the next morning.

In October 1976 we were 3-0 up at half time against Bournemouth in a match in which there was not a single corner. We won 4-0, and it was only the second time in history in which a game had no corners.

When I went to Sheffield Wednesday for a cup replay in 1976, the game went to a penalty shootout and I missed my train back to Darlington. I had to get a taxi to York, and it cost me £18.

Eric Caygill

I went to my first match when I was just four years old, was a gateman at the Polam Lane end when I was 15, and I'm in my sixties now.

It was wartime football when I first went to Feethams, and I remember seeing Cyril Sidlow, a Welsh international goalkeeper, and Jimmy Mullen playing for Darlington.

We saw them in town one day on the way to a game. My mum, Eva, said to Jimmy: "Who's in goal today?" "Cyril", he replied. My mum, not realising it was Sidlow standing next to us, said "Oh no, not him."

We used to stand behind the dug out. Some of the players saw her as a mother figure. Later she used to sit at the back corner of the East Stand. A lot of the young players used to sit around her, and they said to her at one game: "You never come to see us play for the reserves."

So she came to the next reserve game on a Tuesday evening - and collapsed and died the following morning. Some of the players were bearers at her funeral.

She was always popular with the players, and I remember one day we were due to play against a strong side, and Tommy Ward, a good old fashioned inside right, promised my mum he would get us a penalty. A corner came over at the Shed End, down he went, and when the referee pointed to the spot he raced over to my mum and said: "Told you."

We used to play on Christmas Day and Boxing Day, and I recall going to Hull for a game on a train of 10 coaches, yet there were only 19 of us on board, so we were all given complimentary tickets. Football came first in our house.

It was a different story when we played at Chelsea and Wolves. The station will never again see an exodus like that.

They were great days. On one occasion after we played at Bradford, Ronnie Harbertson was going to be late for his shift at the colliery where he worked - so we rushed him back in the car.

Editors note: Eric is now the press box steward, and is always on hand to help with whatever jobs need doing at the club on match days or at any other time.

84

Martin Deans

THE fanatical Londoner travels to every match from his home in Uxbridge, yet the nearest he has ever lived to Darlington is Mansfield. And he moved there only to be nearer the Quakers.

He has missed only about eight games in 20 years, and while the passing of time makes the travel more tiresome, his spirits have never flagged.

"I hate 1-0 home defeats," he said. "They are the most frustrating. But I never leave a game wishing I hadn't come, because I know that I have got more out of supporting Darlington than any Manchester United or Arsenal fan has from following their club.

"I feel part of the club, and have got to know players and staff. How can you feel that way if you are one among a million Manchester United fans?"

But how could somebody with no connections, end up travelling tens of thousands of miles a season to watch Darlington?

"I sometimes went to Brentford in my teens and had a soft spot for Chelsea. But every time I looked at the league table, Darlington seemed to be bottom," said Martin.

"I started following their results, then wished I was there when they played at home to Aldershot one Monday night. So I decided to come to a game. I had no idea what it would lead to."

Martin cannot remember his first game, but said: "When I arrived I felt it was a club I could feel part off. Then it became an obsession."

Very occasionally he has missed a game by being on holiday, but even on a sun-kissed foreign beach his thoughts turn to the Quakers, and he admits to being hell to live with from kick off time until he finds out the result.

But despite his fanaticism, Martin is not blinkered. He is kind, modest and friendly, and appreciates that his 'hobby' is extreme.

"I didn't get married because it wouldn't be fair. Colleagues and friends latch onto my devotion, and sometimes ask if they can come to games.

"Take the distance away, and I'm like any other fan - down when the team loses, up after a win. Socially it affects me on Friday nights. I can never stay out late or drink too much because I have to be up the next day.

"There have been a few 6am returns when I've gone straight into work from the

Adam Reed seems to have found an unwanted rival for his Darlington shirt

station after a midweek Feethams game - and that gets harder as the years pass. I once moved jobs to Mansfield to be more central for games. I stayed four years, but missed London, family and friends, so I moved back."

While other fans hope for a home draw in cup ties, Martin prefers a London game. And one of the closest is Wembley. While he thoroughly enjoyed Darlington's first visit, the second was one of his lowest points.

"Once we had beaten Hartlepool in the semi-final, I was sure we would be promoted. But it was another 1-0 defeat. I was gutted when we lost. Manager David Hodgson said to me afterwards that the team would go up the following year. He had such resolve. Phil Brumwell asked me to come back to the team hotel, but I couldn't face it. I went home in the rain."

Of course Martin has seen the other side of life - when Quakers drew 2-2 at Crewe to win promotion in 1985.

"At the end I jumped onto the pitch - something I have never done before. Phil Lloyd and Steve Tupling took me past the stewards and into the changing room where the lads were celebrating with champagne. I have a bottle signed by Cyril Knowles and John Craggs."

Farewell to Feethams | a collection of Darlington FC memories

85

Martin was at Scunthorpe the day Darlington were relegated from the league, and admitted: "I saw people crying. I don't cry easily but was close to tears. I didn't think we would get back into the league.

"I had to go to a wedding reception that evening - and look happy after Darlington had just lost their league status."

But for every down there is an up - and it came at Welling 12 months later.

"I was with the players again and got slaughtered in the Black Prince at Bexley Heath. I threw up on the train home! That was one of the great highlights." (The match, not the train journey).

Martin latched onto the side because they were failures, and in a perverse way, the reason for his support ceases to exist when they are winning.

"In November of the season when we clinched promotion at Crewe, we beat Wrexham at Feethams, and I thought after that game that there was no point in coming. But the appeal quickly returned. It was just a blip."

He has spent a fortune, but has not counted how much. He would like one day to go to South America, but that dream will stay on hold while exotic places like Rochdale and Macclesfield still beckon.

He recalls being at Halifax when 403 fans saw Darlington lose 4-1 in the Freight Rover Trophy (the late Graeme Aldred scoring his only goal for the club). And Martin was at Feethams as Quakers won the second leg 7-0!

Even worse than 1-0 defeats, are postponed games after he has travelled.

"If it's nobody's fault I accept it, but I get annoyed when I feel the game either could have been played, or called off earlier. Torquay in the 2000/1 season was a bad one because it was a night match postponed just before kick off. The same season we travelled to Exeter on an icy day. I kept ringing the ground and they kept saying it was on - but when I saw the pitch there was no chance. That was very annoying."

Martin has become firm friends with many of the players - and used to pick Phil Lloyd up at Ferrybridge on home matchdays. He has sometimes taken players home when they are injured - "Can you imagine a Manchester United fan doing that for David Beckham?" he mused.

Martin was invited to the wedding of former Quakers and Southampton keeper Keith Granger, recalling: "I sat with Frances Benali, and met Matt le Tissier. Keith was so appreciative of my support that he mentioned it in his speech. I was

embarrassed, but it was a lovely thing to do. But it shows fans that the players do appreciate their support.

"Phil Lloyd would always thank me for coming to games, and Adam Reed does the same."

Over the last few years Martin has been a steward at Feethams. His post is the end of the tunnel, so he sees the game. "I told them there was no way I wanted to be on a turnstile - I'm not going to travel this far to miss the match."

He had a perfect view when referee Tom Fitzpatrick was hit by an apple thrown from the East Stand after the official had sent off a couple of Darlington players. "Hardly the right thing to do, but you couldn't help but admire the shot," laughed Martin.

He collects all the programmes which are lined up alphabetically on his shelves. But he doesn't have Sky TV - too busy travelling, to watch it.

He may retire to Darlington, and get to know more of the north east. "I've seen very little of it, but I love the Yorkshire Dales."

The Quakers line-up for the 1990 Conference Season

"I stayed at Askrigg one Christmas so that I could get to the games over the Holiday period."

Like all fans Martin will miss Feethams, but is excited by the new stadium. Ever the optimist, he added: "You never know. Maybe my last ever game will be watching Darlington in the Premier League. That would be a good one to go out on."

Brian Doughty

THE Conference Season was easily the most enjoyable I have had following Darlington. In a way, it was refreshing to visit new grounds in the non league world, but we all knew that promotion was the aim.

At Wycombe, their old ground, the slope was too much for my friend Dennis and during our pre-match inspection of the pitch he slipped over into the dugouts! The Boston pitch was as smooth as any snooker table and at Enfield a stroll around the outside of the ground before the game meant the kids came home with loads of conkers

There were some long trips and we bought a portable black and white television to keep the kids amused in the back of the car - but even that would not work on the horrendous trip in the torrential rain to Cheltenham. The journey was worthwhile when Paul Emson ran from the half-way line to score but Les McJannet probably still doesn't know why he got sent off that day!

That match was the one in which Andy Gray (yes, him of SKY fame) refereed the first half, although he was actually playing for Cheltenham at the time, and spent so much time telling the official referee how to do his job, that he was substituted in the second half.

Runcorn was easily the coldest match, but I still recall being able to watch the game from inside the 'toilets' - the breeze block walls were only shoulder height! We lost 1-2 on a 'ploughed field' and to totally sicken us we had a row with a Chief Inspector who insisted we walk half a mile around an estate back to our car rather than past the Runcorn fans - all 10 of them!

Barrow away. Rain, rain and more rain. They had removed the roof of the stand we were in and by half time even my coat pockets were full of water! The Chairman of our Supporters Club had a collection towards the cost of a new roof and I think the bucket ended up full of water - and the roof still hasn't been replaced!

At Sutton United we arrived early and a welcoming steward told us to go into the bar and he would make sure we all got a cup of tea. That is the only time I have walked straight into a briefing of the match stewards by a police inspector, but after beating a hasty retreat we were well looked after. The biggest roar at that match came as Postman Pat was walking around the ground before the game and as he got to us the crowd was fairly quiet and some wag at the back shouted 'hey Pat, your cat's dead!' - the timing was brilliant. We lost 2-1 - Sutton had rolled the ground so hard we couldn't cope with the high bouncing balls.

We went to Leek Town for the FA Trophy 4th Round thinking it was a formality and we would be going to Wembley. The referee was the notorious Jim Parker and he gave Leek a 'drop ball' direct to their feet and they promptly scored to win 1-0. When Dennis and myself barracked the man as he ran past us on the edge of the pitch and told him he couldn't do that he shouted: 'it's in the book lads, it's in the book' - I haven't found it in the book yet.

Altrincham away produced a classic incident. Someone kicked the ball out of the ground and as play moved to the other end with a new ball the first ball came back over the Stand onto the pitch in front of Kevan Smith. Play was approaching Smithy and he went to kick the stray ball away - I think he had already been booked - and even the home players had to stop the referee sending him off!

At Telford, on Easter Monday, we won 1-0 but memories of David Corner's winning goal are erased by the sickening sound of Jimmy Willis' breaking leg. The sound cracked across the ground and the following silence was deafening.

Welling. Little needs to be said except that the fingernails were well chewed down that day. Rumours of scores from Barnet's game were rife but when Gary Coatsworth scored the winner the ground erupted! The Welling fans congratulated us and it is the only time I can recall my wife jumping the boundary fence and running onto the pitch at the final whistle!

John Dunn

I was squashed amongst the 11,631 crowd when Quakers took on Bradford City at Feethams for a promotion place on May 9, 1969.

I was perhaps a bit paranoid about Bradford fans. I had been punched at Bradford when following the lads in the 1965-66 season, the only time I'd ever been hit at a match.

Fans spill onto the pitch at Feethams during the promotion battle against Bradford City

88

is that Melling got to the ball in the air but it went up rather than horizontally but then fell onto some part of Melling's anatomy (I have over the years become convinced that it hit his stomach which was of sizeable proportions) and ended up in the net.

At this the Darlo fans left the South Terrace and came down both sides, i.e. behind both the East & West stands to re-take the Tin Shed!

The Bradford fans were pretty lively and one or two bottles were waved in the area where I was (though none of them in any way threatened me. They seemed as I recall, to be getting ready to repel the oncoming Darlo fans).

The one thing that was obvious was that the Tin Shed was pretty full already. The upshot was that people ended up on the pitch and a general melee ensued.

The game was stopped and I think that both managers came onto the pitch and the Bradford manager persuaded their fans to vacate the Tin Shed and go to the now pretty empty South Terrace, which they duly did, running across the pitch.

One of the bottles being waved about by a Bradford fan was dropped beside me and I foolishly picked it up. Quickly realising that this might well be misconstrued by the police I took the opportunity to run to the front of the now empty terracing and handed the aforementioned bottle to one of the police officers! I think this was mentioned in the next day's Echo (or Despatch) report where it was said that a bottle was recovered by the police.

I also remember the Darlington v Leicester League Cup second round tie on September 4th 1968.

There were 11,653 inside Feethams. I remember one of the Allan Clarke goals vividly. I was at the front of the Shed against the barrier behind the goal. For one of the goals he received the ball inside the penalty area with his back to goal, with a defender behind him and very tight on him. The next thing was that he seemed to have somehow, almost magically, turned through 180 degrees and was now facing goal with the said defender STILL stuck to his back! I just could not see how he'd done it but there he was eight to ten yards out with a clear chance.

The late Lance Robson missed a good chance in the last minute for Darlo. The ball came from the right and Robson met it while running towards the six yard box at the Shed end. He hit it on the volley with his left foot, but it sailed well over the bar.

Robson came out of retirement - he had set up business as a dentist in

I arrived early and became concerned as I found myself surrounded by more and more Bradford fans. They took over the whole of the Tin Shed apart from a few Darlo fans, who, like me, had arrived early. The main body of Darlo fans ended up on the South Terrace – I stayed where I was and kept my mouth shut!.

The main problem was the numbers trying to get into the Tin Shed after we scored. I don't think that there was any violence, just pushing and shoving until people ended up on the pitch. I was wearing a Darlo scarf and I was still growing (I'm not that tall now!) and the Bradford fans all seemed pretty hard looking to me, but clearly they were not out for violence. But I think they wanted to stay where they were, because their team was attacking towards the Shed.

Darlo took the lead through Terry Melling. As I recall there was either a corner or a cross from the right and Terry went up for it with their keeper. My recollection

Alan Sproates with Pele

they all seemed to go six to 12 inches over the bar.

Brian Keeble – very dependable full back.

Ray Yeoman – hard man.

Ron Greener & Joe Jacques – solid in the middle of the defence Jacques also had a classy edge to the hardness.

George McGeachie – skill personified. Only his ICI career stopped him going higher. It was like having our own Jimmy Johnstone on the wing, could get to the by line with skill and he delivered consistently dangerous crosses.

Les O'Neill – hard working and no mean skill.

Bobby Cummings – goals goals goals with feet and head. I don't think he was tall, but could he jump.

Alan Sproates – really classy left foot, hit crossfield balls with pinpoint accuracy.

Eric Johnstone – another skilful player.

It would be unfair to single any of them out but if I had to I would say that Moor seemed almost superhuman. I could not believe that he could be beaten and was always a bit surprised when anyone did. Why he stayed at Darlington I do not know. He must have had opportunities to play at a higher level.

McGeachie was also a favourite. I was there on the cold night he injured his knee which put an end to his career.

I think that I really got excited about that season after the Swindon Town games in the League cup. I did not go to the away match,

(I rang the Echo office at full time to find out the score before any results were announced on the TV or Radio) but at the home game Jim Lawton (who was a bit of an on/off player and was affectionately referred to as Spud Lawton) played an absolute blinder and Swindon decided that they wanted him.

We got Alan Sproates plus cash. I was just getting used to seeing the classy Sproates and thinking what a good deal we had done when we also signed Bobby Cummings. This was fantastic and I really thought we were going places.

I think missed penalties cost us the championship that year (one miss by Johnston was so bad that he may be the only player to put a penalty over the bar AND the Tin Shed.)

Misses against Bradford City (away) by Yeoman who hit the bar (and I got thumped) and by Cummings in a really exciting night match against Colchester, I think it ended 2-2. I think Cummings scored with one penalty. The other he hit very

Darlington - for the second round league cup tie against Everton on September 3rd 1970.

He played in midfield on that occasion. A lot was made, before the match of a likely confrontation between the hard man Lance Robson and the fiery Alan Ball. I remember Lance running, seemingly at full pelt, at the ball with Alan Ball running in to challenge him. We all thought a big crunch was going to result but Lance actually sold Ball a dummy and left him tackling thin air.

In the 1965-66 promotion team I recall the players in the following way:

Tony Moor – unbeatable, big but very quick to get down to low shots as well as being a major presence in the air.

John Peverell – used to take free kicks with phenomenal power, unfortunately hard and straight. Their goalie knew nothing about it but Bobby had hit it too hard and too straight and had not given their keeper any chance of diving to get out of the way. As I recall the ball hit him on the knee and flew high into the air

One other game I do remember which was not good news for us was an FA cup match in 1963 against Gateshead at home. They were non league and we were expected to beat them easily. Unfortunately they had ageing ex-Newcastle winger Bobby Mitchell on the left wing. He ran the game with an exhibition of classy controlled wing play throughout the match sending in cross after cross.

I can remember the David Frost documentary. I was at university in Manchester at the time and watched it with my new found mates. One abiding memory is the Darlo "wall" which gave Ernie Adams no protection. The film footage shows the wall lining up and the players in it linking arms before the free kick was taken. As their player ran up to shoot, the Darlo player at one end of the wall (I think Colin Sinclair) moved well before the ball was kicked. Unfortunately, rather than attacking the ball he seemed to be ensuring that it went nowhere near him and he actually took off towards the corner flag pulling the wall apart as he did so! Our keeper had no chance!

Gavin Ellis

MY love affair with Darlington started in 1970, when, aged nine, I remember my dad taking me to watch a league cup first round replay between Darlington and Doncaster. Although Darlington won 3-1, I remember the busiest people in the ground being the ball boys because on a blustery night, both sides managed to contrive to kick the ball out of the ground on several occasions. On the way home that Monday evening the bells of St Cuthberts were peeling loudly. I asked dad why they were ringing, and he replied that they always rung when Darlington win. Even at the time, I thought he was only joking.

Cap in hand appeals for re-election followed in the mid to late seventies with the boredom only briefly interrupted by the odd cup run. One memorable occasion was the FA Cup tie against Sheffield Wednesday after we beat Scarborough in the first round. After a goalless first half thanks to the heroics of Alan Ogley, the ground erupted at half time as both sets of supporters began a pitched battle behind the Tin Shed goal. When order was restored, Feethams was treated to one of its best ever goals, when Ronnie Ferguson belted a shot from nigh on the halfway line

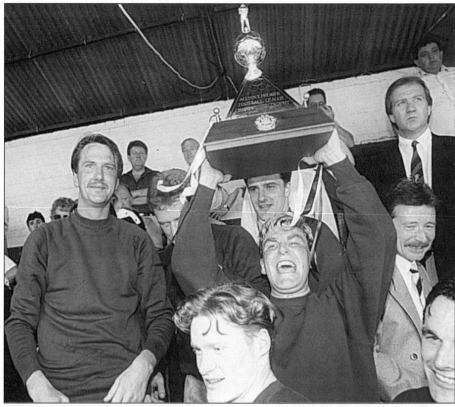

Quakers celebrated two consecutive championships

which sailed straight over the Owls keeper and into the top corner.

As we exited Feethams and approached the bus station, I encountered a Wednesday fan, who was best described as a brick outhouse.

"Bloody robbed tonight, weren't we?" he snarled.

Putting on as gruff a Yorkshire accent as I could, I replied "Aye"

He then proceeded to literally pick up the nearest Darlo fan and tossed him ten feet in the air and about ten yards across the road.

Just after Cyril Knowles was appointed manager in 1983, the players found that he hadn't come to Feethams for an easy time.

A lacklustre first half performance against Chester one day saw us trailing 1-0 in the pouring rain. As the players made their way back up the tunnel, Cyril pointed to them to get back on the pitch, where they were thrown footballs to juggle whilst getting a good soaking. The shock method worked, as we stormed back to win 2-1 and we didn't trail again at the interval for a few weeks.

Cyril's second season saw us win our first promotion for nineteen years and embark on a peculiar FA Cup run which saw the club despatch Second Division Middlesbrough before succumbing to non league Telford, which cost us a money-spinning tie at Everton.

1985-86 unbelievably saw big names such as Bolton, Wolves and Derby beaten before reality returned and we embarked on a downward spiral that was to eventually cost us our Football League place.

By the time Cyril's successor, David Booth, was sacked in 1989, most of Cyril's stars had been sold - the likes of Kevan Smith, Kevin Todd, Peter Johnson, Fred Barber, David Currie and Carl Airey - to balance the books and leave us with football's version of Dad's Army and results which were as comical.

Brian Little stopped the rot to a degree, but our first ever visit to Scunthorpe's Glanford Park was our swansong as we crashed 5-1 and lost our league status. I remember 40 and 50 year old men running to hide in the toilets because they were ashamed of crying, and coming out and saying that there were 60 and 70 year olds in there crying!

Nobody in the summer of 1989 could have imagined the roller coaster ride Darlington were about to embark upon under the stewardship of Brian Little and Frank Gray. Quakers suffered only two home defeats at Feethams as they stormed back into the league at the first attempt. Other memories of the Conference season included thrashing Halifax Town 3-0 and a memorable run in the FA Trophy, but no true fan will ever forget Gary Coatsworth's looping header at Welling.

Our return to the Football League incredibly fetched another championship, and I was to learn later that that a couple of Darlo fans, after our demise in 1989 had put tenners on the club to win two consecutive championships at 4000-1.

The inevitable decline set in again before the club brought in Alan Murray whose first game in charge was against Colchester. Darlo won 7-3, but it could have been 10-10, because both sides were pathetic.

I also remember in that season going to Doncaster the day after Boxing Day to play for the supporters, but we ended up clearing the pitch of snow. Imagine our despair when with Quakers 2-0 up the floodlights failed. Thankfully the fault was rectified and Darlo went on to win 3-1.

We had two play off finals in the following years.

After overcoming Hereford over two legs making our first ever visit to Wembley, where the rumour was that the team were told to throw the match against Plymouth, and they certainly played as if so.

Then there was the sodden Friday night when the FA had the brazen cheek to consider to bring the game forward as they considered a friendly international more important than the Third Division's premier game of the season.

We all know what happened that night.

Doug Embleton

The four months of September to December in the 1960-61 season are possibly the most eventful ever at Feethams.

The Tin Shed was completed; the first floodlights opened; the West Stand burned down; a crowd record of 21,000 was set at home against Bolton Wanderers; the team surged towards the top of the League; then an epic FA Cup Tie against Hull City went to an amazing four midweek replays.

For years, Feethams had been relatively neglected and the cricket field end had simply been a few concrete steps, then a small bank of cinders (to just below the height of the current Tin Shed steps), with occasional wooden barriers along the cinder bank. In the early and latter months of the season fans could turn round and watch the cricket if the football was poor. Rumours of the installation of swivel seats for this purpose were never confirmed. There were no rear barriers.... just a sheer drop.

The South Terrace (then called 'The South Park End'), whilst much larger, was similar. Most people had favourite spots. The paddock in front of the small West Stand was usually full. (It remains the same today, for the insurance policy after the fire insisted on the same design, size and materials).

The corner which now accommodates the Quaker Centre was known as 'Spratt's Corner' because of a large brick wall of a building which carried an advert (white paint on a black background) for "Spratt's Pet Foods". Some of the old sages used to gather by this wall.

Tickets were bought at the Twin Towers and additional small amounts were paid at separate turnstiles for the paddocks. When I became a regular in the mid-50s,

91

junior admission was one shilling and threepence…approximately 6 and a half pence.

In the 1960-61 season the opening home game against Doncaster drew 7,890, and the first away game at Crystal Palace attracted 21,784.

The Tin Shed was nearing completion and the fascination with it emerged because it was a 'cantilever' design - no support posts to block the view. It rapidly became the place where younger Quaker supporters served their apprenticeship. Before the corrugated sheeting was installed, you could see the cantilever roof supports.

After an indifferent start (including a 0-5 thumping at Hartlepool.... but fear not .... they went on to finish second bottom), the corner turned with a 4-1 win at Southport.

The floodlights were opened on a Monday evening of torrential rain as 6,168 saw Darlo beat Millwall 5-2. The novelty of evening floodlit games was tremendous but the event was marred by news the next day. As a result of faulty cabling or a spark, the West Stand had been badly damaged by fire. The next months would be played out, often in front of big crowds, with just the empty, burned out shell of the West Stand.

The team was beginning to balance with the arrival of Ray Spencer, a left-sided wing half. 'Keeper Colin Tinsley had played for Grimsby and was safe if unspectacular. Brian Henderson (nicknamed 'Gento' based upon Real Madrid's Brazilian winger and in recognition of the surging runs down the wing, which Brian would make whenever the chips were down) formed an uncompromising full-back partnership with George Mulholland. The half back line was a list of Feethams legends. Ken Furphy at right half, Ron Greener at centre half and Spencer at left half.

Joe Rayment was a fast, diminutive right winger; Jim Milner a striker-cum-schemer inside right; Dave Carr a no-nonsense centre forward (who was injured just as the famous 'run' began); Bobby Baxter was the son of a Scottish international and a scheming plus goalscoring inside forward with an educated left foot. Left wing was allocated to Brian Redfearn, father of Neil Redfearn and nicknamed 'Cheyenne' because his huge frame and appearance resembled a TV cowboy character of the time. He was injured and his place went to Keith Morton, a versatile striker.

Feethams games in winter kicked off at 2pm and ended in 'half-light'. The extra time cup win over Chelsea in 1958 ended almost in darkness.

So floodlights, to coincide with the new opportunities in the League Cup, were a big thrill. We had a new strip which paid homage to the fashion for V-necks and short sleeves…Darlo's white shirt carried thick black segments around the 'V' and around the end of the short sleeve …There was even a 'trendy' new sock, white apart from one thin black line at the top fold.

Results improved and when Darlo beat Crystal Palace then West Ham at Feethams in the League Cup, the lack of stewarding led to logjams of people at the corners of the ground. Somehow everybody packed in.

Bolton were drawn next and the police set a 21,000 all-ticket capacity. In the meantime, Grimsby were beaten 2-0 at Feethams in the FA Cup in front of 12,357. I remember Lance Robson scoring with a trick of his by chasing a back pass, then seeming to extend his leg to scoop the ball in.

The Darlo surge was feeling unstoppable. Many of the players lived in club houses, particularly in the Yarm Road area. Rumours abounded on the basis of 'Player x' said…and buses and bus stops were the next best thing to a Darlo website! A favourite quote was…"Ken Furphy said that at the moment Darlo are unbeatable". For a few glorious weeks that was how it seemed.

In November, a Feethams game against Chester was played in fog which would have abandoned any game today. As many fans as possible crowded behind the Chester goal. The 'Pink' had to be consulted for the final score (2-1 to Darlington) and my abiding memory is of shadows of players emerging from the foggy backdrop of the burned out shell of the West Stand.

November was the month it began to come off the rails .... but not before 21,023 crowded into Feethams to see Bolton Wanderers and the famous England internationals Nat Lofthouse (centre forward) and Eddie Hopkinson (keeper) beat us 2-1. It would be fair to say that you could not swing a cat.

In the second round of the FA Cup against Hull City, came a defining moment. With time running out and us losing 0-1, Bobby Baxter pumped a speculative shot towards the Tin Shed. The ball went over the bar (I was at the front, behind the net, so had a good view) and with the ref walking back to the centre and looking at his watch, one of our group from the old Darlington Grammar School (who will remain nameless) pushed the ball under the net to get the goalkick taken quickly.

As the referee turned round, he saw the Hull 'keeper bending to pick the ball out of the net .... and blew for a goal.

This quirk of fate set up a series of four replays.

Around then the railway system came into its own and I feel that Darlo should never allow the 'steam train' symbol to disappear from its club crest. It is important that a football retains contact with its 'roots'.

In 1960 Darlington was the railway town. This is reflected in my memories of the replays. 'Football Specials' were efficiently and quickly arranged from Bank Top Station. Indeed, the first replay at Hull was on the Monday following the 1-1 home draw. Diesel trains (usually) left the station at tea-time. Most travelling fans came directly from work or school. The aroma was a mix of factory grease, thermos flask tea and various 'bait box sandwiches'. The 'reading material' was the Evening Despatch.

Travel was easy in 1960. For the first replay, trains took people directly to the Hull ground (are you listening, GNER?!) then home. A 1-1 draw in front of 18,125.

The second and third replays at Leeds and Doncaster (1-1 and 0-0 respectively) also involved 'Special Trains'. On arrival, there were long queues of 'Football Special' buses outside the station which would take everyone straight to the ground for a few more pence. If you consider that the first two games were played on a Saturday and then the following Monday, and that replays three and four were played on a Tuesday (Doncaster) and Thursday (Ayresome Park), it makes a mockery of modern day complexities. Today's transport system and all-ticket arrangements would not cope.

By the time the saga reached Ayresome for the fourth replay, Hull made five changes to counteract exhaustion. Against a largely unchanged Quakers, Hull won 3-0 in front of 19,366 fans.

Darlo had by then played eight cup games by mid-December. The squad (only 23 players made first team appearances in the season) was exhausted and then lost 0-4 at Doncaster and a 1-5 at table-topping new boys Peterborough.

But I remember Hartlepool being mercilessly beaten 4-0 at home on New Year's Eve.

Sadly by the end of that memorable season, Darlo finished seventh, and crowds were down to 4-5,000.

Nevertheless, as the "'Spatch" and the Gazette "Pink" confirmed in those

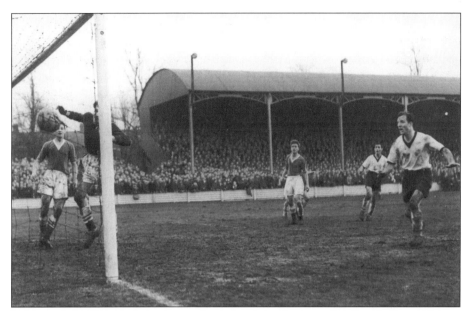

Quakers knock the mighty Chelsea out of the FA Cup in 1958

93

months from September to December, Darlo were near invincible and the memories of the crowds, goals and players will last a lifetime.

Dean Guy

ONE of the funniest moments for me was a game in the mid-eighties, a depressing 1-0 defeat was taking place against Halifax when an incident happened which brought much light relief to the Polam End. An opposition player had gone down injured - right by the by-line at the Polam End, cue an entry onto the field of the oldest physio I think I'd ever seen.

This caught everyone's eye to start with. He then attended to the player, packed his bag and proceeded to jog away. As he did so, he turned to the crowd and coughed. His false teeth flew out of his mouth at an alarming speed. Amazingly, the old boy flung out his hand and caught them in mid-air! He shoved them straight back into his mouth and tried to continue his jog to the dug out as if nothing had happened - fatal! There was a brief moment - seconds only - when most of the crowd couldn't believe what they'd seen, followed by much raucous laughter.

Andrew Heap

I have a lovely memory of the 1982 fundraising campaign (doesn't £50,000 seem such a paltry amount now?) A group of us from Haughton school arranged a sponsored penalty shootout against the Darlo keeper at the time - shows you how impressed we were with him - I can't remember his name. Anyway, we turned up at Feethams on the appointed afternoon, but he didn't. The only player in the ground was Dave Speedie, who quick as a flash volunteered to do the penalty shoot in his place.

At the time I knew he could jump, but I didn't know he used to play in between the sticks for Spennymoor, so it was a pleasant surprise to see him take it seriously and stop half the shots. He was so good we had to fiddle the result to maximise the sponsorship returns! Speedie was already a Darlo hero, but this elevated him to God status. My mate Carol fell in love with him - got him to sign her coat (we had no paper) and never washed it again.

Alf Hutchinson

IN January 1958 I was a National Serviceman stationed at RAF Wunstorf near Hanover in West Germany.

On the afternoon of the Darlington v Chelsea replay, I played football for my section in the Station Inter-Squadron league, along with one of my best friends, Phil Peel, who was a Chelsea supporter.

After our game, we all returned to our accommodation block where we listened to second half commentary of the game on British Forces Network.

Most of the other lads who had no affinity for either team were cheering for the Quakers, as they were the underdogs. At the end of ninety minutes with the score 1-1, it was time to go to the mess for our afternoon meal, but as BFN continued with the commentary I decided to keep listening, along with a few of the other lads.

Phil, however, stated that Chelsea's superior fitness and general all round superiority would see them win, and he left for his meal.

Those of us who remained, especially myself, could scarcely believe what we were hearing as Quakers went on to score three times in extra time. When Phil returned we all managed to look glum and when he asked what the score was, I muttered, 4-1.

He laughed and said: "What did I tell you".

When we said the score was in Darlington's favour, it took quite some time before he would believe us. When he eventually realised the truth, he was most upset, and barely spoke to me for days afterwards.

I've supported Darlington for over fifty years, but that day is one of my special memories - of a game I didn't even see.

Paul Hutchinson

I WAS at the Darlington v Leicester League Cup tie in September 1968, and as a seven year old, I was in awe of the occasion. I remember Ken Felton shooting powerfully past a youthful Peter Shilton only for the Quakers to go down 2-1.

In March 2001, I was in London to see a play. Making my way across Leicester Square, I noticed a Comic Relief autograph promotion featuring Peter Shilton, so I joined the queue.

Those ahead of me talked about memories of his England exploits or his days at Nottingham Forest under Brian Clough. When I got to the front, I said: "I remember Ken Felton blasting one past you at Feethams in the late sixties!"

He answered me with a surprising question; "Was he the dentist?"

Pushing disbelief aside, I replied: "That would most likely be Lance Robson, he passed on sometime ago."

Shilton explained: "I was on the ground after diving for a ball that went behind. He came over and stood on my hand! Some dentist he was! Anyway, my lad's playing against your lot today!"

Of course, Sam Shilton would be playing for Hartlepool against Darlo.

I jokingly started backing off. "OK, forget the autograph, then!"

Nothing like a note of friction to end the exchange.

Neil Johnson

MY Norwegian daughter's first match was against Barrow in a non-league cup. She was four and on my shoulders, dropping crisps, juice and wagon wheel bits down the back of my neck for most of the match.

Darlo scored and everyone jumped about shouting. She asked me, in Nowegian, what had happened, and I told her Darlo had scored. She replied: "I liked that

Daddy, make them do it again" - if only! (Darlo put another three in and of course I claimed the credit.)

Editor's note: The game was for the J M Thompson cup, between Darlington (as Conference champions) and Barrow (as Bob Lord Trophy winners). The game was played at Holker Street, Barrow and Quakers won 4-0. John Borthwick (2), Andy Toman and Steve Mardenborough were the scorers.

Ian Kenyon (of BBC Radio Cleveland)

IN one of the final professional games to take place at the National Stadium before it was ripped down, Darlington were beaten by Peterborough, in that now infamous Third Division Play Off Final.

On a cold wet Friday we'd travelled down to the capital full of optimism after such an impressive season, and with fresh memories of Hartlepool disposed of in the semi-final over two legs.

I had the job of Tunnel reporter for the evening, involving reaction before, during and after the game from the Wembley pitchside. As a result of some Gremlins I hadn't been "on-air" much all evening, but I managed with the help of a BBC engineer, to get the line working again just before the final whistle. This meant I heard the closing stages (albeit on a phone line via Middlesbrough) and was then asked to report on the scenes around.

The Darlington supporters were at the Tunnel End and I was standing near a group of grown men with tears in their eyes as the whistle was blown.

I reported a short piece, and as soon as I started talking, Marco Gabbiadini walked past and live on-air I asked him for an interview. Marco refused, but I could never hold it against him.

Marco had been there before, losing at Wembley that is, and he was hurting. He was in no fit state to speak to anyone. It was then I realised his team-mates weren't following. He had left the pitch, and his colleagues to suffer on his own. He couldn't talk to his fellow players, nor his manager and chairman, let alone the media.

Supporter Neil Johnson

To those who ever thought, that in walking away from Darlington, Marco didn't care for the club, you are wrong. Marco was hurt, upset and as disappointed as everyone else. Everyone else, that is, other than manager David Hodgson, who was distraught.

I handed back to our commentary team of Paul Addison, Ray Simpson and Paul Cross. They were as shell shocked as me, and they continued to assess the damage while keeping a keen eye on the pitch, and watching for David Hodgson to make his way down the Tunnel.

As he emerged into the expanse of the concrete tunnel, he was mobbed by reporters shouting at him for an interview. Reporters from Sky TV, BBC TV and national radio, Century Radio and TFM were all made to wait though, because I calmly called over, caught his eye, and he came to speak to me.

Why me? Radio Cleveland had been speaking to him all season, through highs, and lows. The others only jumped on the "Band-Wagon" with a final in sight. David and I have always got on. It was to become the best interview I have ever done, albeit in a short career. The interview was special because the interviewee was honest, truthful and spoke from the heart.

Reporters often complain that what they hear from managers, players, chairmen and press officers alike, is spin. Not lies as such, but failure to tell the whole story, a compulsion to always want to make situations sound better than they are. David Hodgson didn't do that on that Friday.

I began with the all too easy "David, you must be disappointed?" The next two minutes almost brought me to tears. Imagine if you will the voice of Hodgy with a tear in his eye almost unable to speak through the sobs.

"I can't find the words to be honest. I thought the arena, the stadium, the pitch would be right up our street. I thought the lads did exceptionally well. The work rate was there and the opportunities came to them. We were always a little concerned with their little bit of extra pace up front. All credit to Peterborough, they soaked the pressure up, we were made to battle away and we did, we think we were the better side over the ninety minutes, however they had their chances as well, we didn't take ours, they took theirs. They've made it to the second division while we're left to fight another stinking season in the third. I apologise for everybody who has love or any feeling for Darlington Football Club, in a way we've let them down, we should have been out of this division back in April."

95

96

Lee Nogan in action in the defeat by Peterborough in the infamous 3rd Division play-off final at Wembley

As far as the fans were concerned David always took an interest in how they felt. He paid tribute to their support: "It's absolutely chucking it down out there. It's six or seven hours drive from home. They were magnificent and the most disappointing thing is, we didn't re-pay them with a victory. To be honest with you, I'm ashamed we were beaten tonight, I'm ashamed!"

The interview went on for a while and I handed back to the press box, desperate not to have to speak, with the threat of tears hanging over me. I should admit that until coming to BBC Radio Cleveland, I didn't really care about Darlington. That now just isn't true. The trials and tribulations of that season and since, have made me as much a supporter of the Quakers as you. I can't claim to have followed them for years, but I can say that night I only wanted David Hodgson, his team, George Reynolds, Darlington Football club, and you, to make it up. Who knows where we would be now?

Marco Gabbiadini did speak to me that night. He allowed me to conduct an interview late on, after everybody had left but the teams. He was devastated.

I spoke to David Hodgson a few times during the summer as he prepared for the new season. I had no idea he would leave just before the new season started.

Daniel King

SEASON 1996/1997 wasn't one of the more glorious in Darlington's history. A long battle against relegation; the dismantling of the previous year's great team; the sacking of hugely popular manager Jim Platt; and the introduction of the embarrassing fluffy mascot thing, Mr Q.

But every season has its high points, and this one contained one of the highest points in club's recent history. It bore parallels with the 2000/2001 season, in that a largely awful season was punctuated with a great cup memory - in that case, it was the 2-1 win at Forest. This time, it was a 2-2 draw at Leeds United.

We'd knocked out Rotherham United in the first round of the Coca Cola Cup. I listened to the second leg on the radio. When we were paired with Leeds, I remember being a bit apprehensive about it - although I was looking forward to a trip to Elland Road, I thought we'd get hammered.

The best thing about the opening exchanges was the witty songs coming from the 2,000 or so Darlo fans; some were about George Graham, some were about Lee Sharpe, all are inappropriate for this book.

Rod Wallace put Leeds in front with a route-one goal, and it was a fair reflection at that time. Gary Twynham had probably his best game for Darlo and showed what he could have been capable of. Soon it was all Darlo, and it reminded me of the second half of the 3-3 draw at Scunthorpe where we were just camped in the opposition half.

At half time after Darren Roberts equalised I was trying to take it all in. It looked great on their state-of-the-art electronic scoreboard: Leeds United 1 - Darlington 1.

Sadly, that score changed within minutes of the restart, Wallace scoring his second and earning a place in my all time list of players that I really hate. The scoreboard changed again before long, showing 3-1 to Leeds for a few seconds as Rush had the ball in the net again, but as I slumped back in my seat, everyone started jumping up and down - the goal had been ruled out for offside. Cue some

Jim Platt

uncomplimentary songs about the moustachioed Welsh striker.

The disallowed goal seemed to lift everyone. The army of fans behind Nigel Martyn's goal really got behind the team - I was sitting (or mostly standing) behind some blokes who kept on turning round and yelling 'sing your hearts out for the lads', and most people did. This had the effect of spurring on the players, and slowly but surely we got back on top.

Jim Platt knew that we were still in with a chance of pulling level, and he replaced young Blake with Robbie Painter. This proved to be a masterstroke. Twynham played a great through ball to him, and Super Robbie rounded Martyn and rolled the ball goalwards. The ball took forever to go in - you could see every bump and every divot the ball took - but eventually, it did. To make it even better, it was in the goal which we were all seated behind. This led to mass delirium, and people were just jumping about and hugging strangers. Personally I think I was grabbed by the bloke in front of me. His mate was busy trying to invade the pitch. But I wasn't bothered, I'd have celebrated that goal with Saddam Hussein if he'd been standing near me.

At the end Nigel Martyn applauded the Darlo fans behind his goal for the constant noise they'd made, and he probably got a few claps in return, but you couldn't really tell as the heroic Darlo players had by now come to soak up the adulation. They were dancing about like they'd won the Cup, but then again, a result like this is like winning the Cup for a club like Darlington. Jim Platt came over too - little did we know that he was going to be sacked just over a month later.

That was one of my first away trips. My dad told me: "They won't all be like this". And of course, he was right. But perhaps that's a good thing - if every game was like this, then the memories wouldn't be so good.

David Cork celebrates his goal against Rochdale as Darlington won 2-0 to lift the Division 4 title in front of over 9,000 fans

Colin Leek

MY best memory was when Darlington played Boston United in the Conference. We won 6-1, and David Cork scored four. It was a dreadful night and rained from start to finish, but Darlington were superb.

One of Corky's goals was one of the best ever scored at Feethams. In front of the Tin Shed in the second half, he chased a through ball, controlling it on the bye line just inside the 18 yard box with two defenders on his back.

He beat the defenders as if they weren't there, and with his left foot from a very tight angle curled the ball over the keeper and into the top right corner. The Tin Shed went wild, even though we were all soaked.

David Lippett

THE last game of the 1991/2 season when Darlo were relegated from the old Third to the new Third Division was at home to Exeter. After two successive championship seasons, followed by the departure of Brian Little to Leicester, lack of success was something of a novelty - particularly to those fans who had joined the bandwagon during the previous two seasons.

Our relegation was confirmed long before this final game, so little sorrow remained amongst the Darlo fans who had turned up to witness our swansong in the Third. Not only was the crowd swelled by the usual morbid curiosity, but also by a large travelling support from Exeter - how often is a large Exeter contingent seen at Feethams? Exeter needed a win to be certain of avoiding relegation alongside us. Everyone seemed determined to enjoy the occasion whatever the result, and probably because many newer Darlo fans had only ever celebrated on the last day of the season, there was an oddly misplaced good mood in the Tin Shed. The warm sunny weather no doubt lifted everyone too.

Due to Exeter's greater need for a win, it was almost a foregone conclusion that we would allow them to have it. However, an odd thing happened - our star striker, who had been signed for a record fee (a fee! Imagine that!), Nick Cusack, decided that his last game for the club he had helped relegate was the perfect time to score two. The look on his face as he approached the Tin Shed has stayed with me ever since. He had finally done his record-signing tag justice and showed us what he could do. The trouble was, nobody cared anymore - it was his last game for Darlo. Still, he lapped it all up, and so did we. After a season of defeat after defeat, it was one hell of a tonic to run out 5-2 winners. The final whistle blew to the annual chorus of "Champions!" and the obligatory pitch invasion. The players even came back out to milk the applause! Anyone watching would have thought we really were champions.

The Exeter players and crowd were utterly deflated. Results elsewhere meant that they were relegated too, and once our "celebrations" had abated slightly, we began to make our way over to where they were fenced in by the Sports Centre. The Exeter fans also spilled out of the gate and onto the pitch, and we started to shake hands. "Sorry lads", "Thanks for the win though" and "See you next season unfortunately" were interspersed with tears and swapping of fanzines and scarves.

Then one of theirs cried out, just as our announcer was reporting that Exeter's great rivals at Torquay had lost (presumably to a last gasp goal) - meaning that Exeter were staying up at Torquay's expense! Cue the strange sight of opposing fans all celebrating together under the bemused eye of the police, after one side had just hammered the other! I think we could relate to their joy by imagining Hartlepool as Torquay, and us as Exeter.

I left the ground from the away end in Polam Lane that day, with three Exeter fans who were promising to come and support us when we went to Torquay next season. A truly odd but wonderful day with such a mixture of emotions and friendliness between fans. I remember the occasion every time I see or hear of violence at matches - just to remind myself of how it can and should be.

Dennis Metcalfe

BILLY McEwan was manager, and in a game against Rochdale at Feethams, one of our central defenders was having a terrible day. Late in the game when we were losing 4-0, the referee gave the visitors a corner at the Tin Shed end and then came to stand on the bye line. At this point a wag in the crowd leaned over to the ref and said to him "For God's sake ref send our centre half off". The crowd just erupted into laughter and the ref had a grin as wide as the pitch.

Regretfully he didn't take any notice.

Dave O'Neil

I FIRST started watching the Quakers in 1973/4. It was near the end of the season and, as usual, the team were facing a battle against having to apply for re-election.

I was still at school and felt that I had to go and watch, before League football was lost from Darlington forever.

I went to see the last three home games of that season, and those games have encompassed what it has been like supporting the club over the last 28 seasons.

The first was against Newport County which Darlington dominated, but finally lost 1-0 against 10 men.

The second was a 1-1 draw against Hartlepool. And the final game of that season was a thrilling 4-2 win against Barnsley, which meant no re-election application for that season.

After that Barnsley game I was hooked and I have supported the lads through thin and thinner ever since.

The exasperation of the Newport game (how many more have we suffered before and since), the passion and excitement of a derby game against Hartlepool, and the rare occasions when the team plays beyond expectations and lifts the mind and the spirit as it did for me against Barnsley.

Since then I keep going to matches hoping to be uplifted as I was on the last day of season 1973/74, and sometimes I am, which makes the pilgrimage worthwhile, and keeps me going through the disappointments to the next "Barnsley" game.

Richard Pinkney

I REMEMBER all too clearly the Scunthorpe v Darlo game on May 6 1989. It was a beautiful day in sunny Scunny, but that couldn't detract from the general air of resignation, which turned to despair as the goals flew in (Andy Flounders got a hat-trick as I recall).

League exit - despair after defeat at Scunthorpe

We were hopeless, as we had been for most of the season - that team of 89 was very poor (improving only marginally after Brian Little took over) and we deserved to finish bottom. I felt totally ashamed and had to suffer months of jibes as a result of relegation, although pride was restored at the end of the following season!

The only bright spot on an afternoon of gloom was Paul Willis' superb consolation goal near the end - it's a pity he never fulfilled his early potential. At the final whistle I recall scarves being thrown on the pitch in disgust, while many people were crying. To cap it all, there were a couple of train cancellations on the journey home - it took me six hours to get back to Lancaster where I was a student at the time - my housemates were worried that I had thrown myself off a bridge as I was so late!! We then hit the late bars in an effort to drown my sorrows.

I remember the headlines in the paper the next day: 'Darlo Flounder out of the League!!!'

Whenever I return to Scunthorpe I remember that fateful day and I shudder at the possibility that we could ever go down again.

Guy Rennison

ALAN Murray's first home game in charge when Darlington beat Colchester 7-3 on a Tuesday night sticks in my memory.

We had been trounced 3-0 at Scunthorpe three days earlier in his first game in the hot seat. We'd scored only seven league goals so far that season (in 13 games) but in one game we doubled that. It was one of the most memorable games I've ever seen, a typical Darlo classic. From being diabolical all season, then playing such attacking, open, entertaining football was just...well...er...Darlington.

Alan Robson

I THINK this story restores faith in football support. My father bought four tickets for the play-off final of 2000.

He posted two to my brother in Wokingham, and two to me in Walsall. My brother's arrived the next day. Mine did not. So my friend and I went to Wembley having decided to write off the money and pay again.

Needless to say my brother was having a good time taking the mickey, showing me what a ticket looked like.

We were about to decide on one more pint or go to the ground when I met a Peterborough supporter in the pub (The Old Post Office). He wished me luck and hoped we would lose. I explained that luck was not on my side as my tickets were lost. He then produced two tickets to the Olympic Gallery, right over the half way line.

"You may as well have these" he said. "My daughter works for Sky and got them free, but I want to sit with my mates". He would not accept any payment, or even that last pint we were going to have.

I had a good time showing my brother what a ticket for the best seats in the ground looked like. But for the result that was the best day out at a match I have had. I never even found out his name. If ever he reads this, thanks once again.

99

Richard Simpson

My best memory of following the Quakers was Welling away. From the moment we set off, five of us in a car at 7.30 in the morning, until we arrived back in Darlington, it was the perfect day.

Arriving in Welling about midday we found a local pub, the weather was scorching and the beer flowing. The ground itself was set in Welling's equivalent to the South Park. I was stuck outside until 2.55pm, waiting with tickets, for two mates coming from Birmingham.

Dave Corner enjoys a drink with Richard Simpson, far right, and friends after the Welling match

I have never experienced tension at a football match like that day in Welling. People with radios clamped to their ears listening for the Barnet result, rumours floating round the ground, and then eventually it happened, Gary Coatsworth with an unbelievable looping header that seemed to take an age to float in. You could feel the collective sigh of relief and then a massive surge of elation kicked in – people jumping onto the pitch, everyone hugging each other – it was the best goal celebration I've ever been in.

After the match all the cars streaming out of Welling had their horns blaring, people hanging out of windows singing, it was fantastic.

But the day wasn't over yet. We had three cars so we decided to stop at the last pub before the motorway as Murph and Sticky were going back to Birmingham Poly and Pete, Chris and Monk were heading back into London. We parked in the Black Prince, Bexley Heath and sat outside for a few drinks, just as we were getting ready to set off for home the Darlo team bus pulls into the car park. There were about 25 fans sat outside and everyone stood up clapping and cheering the lads. The players were great, they stood chatting with us, everyone really buzzing. We had our pictures taken with the trophy and the players.

What a cracking day.

Chris Sowerby

Sitting, thinking about the highs and lows of following Darlington for over 30 years makes me appreciate how much of an influence this crazy pastime has been on my family to date. I can clearly remember as a small child my father and grandfather leaving our home in Geneva Road to catch the number 1 or number 9 bus to the town centre. Their returns in the mid to late 60's were a mixture of happiness and despair, and boiled eggs for tea, but what was this all about?

Unfortunately no one can remember when I actually visited my first home game but it was around 1969. Shortly afterwards I clearly remember sitting in the West Stand watching a spirited performance against Everton. Chances were missed by several Darlington players, with Lance Robson the greatest culprit. My Dad and granddad were kind enough to educate me in the fine language of a frustrated football supporter that evening, a skill I have continued to perfect during the stressful 70's, 80's and 90's.

My early memories of supporting the Quakers in the 70's were mainly disappointing. Managers came and went, most were quickly forgettable and chairmen never seemed to be investing in the team or club. But, we did not care because expectations were never too high. Standing in the south east corner then, I can remember some memorable games. On one occasion over 6000 Hartlepool fans in an 8000 crowd inundated us. On taking the lead I was very nervous about over celebrating surrounded by so many away fans.

My first visit to Hartlepool for a league clash in the mid 70's was memorable for many reasons. Initially my dad would not let me go, but decided to come along to keep an eye on me. After being attacked in the ground and finding us 2-0 down a kind official from Hartlepool moved the scant few of us to the safety of the stand. This must have inspired the team as second half goals from Clive Nattress, Willie Coulson and Colin Sinclair resulted in a rare away victory.

During one spell in 70's the team were so bad we lost two games 7-0. This was the closest I ever came to packing the whole thing in.

My next memory of a big cup game pitched Quakers against a quality second division Luton side with the famous Ron and Paul Futcher within its ranks. Luton took the lead in this encounter and nobody gave Darlo any hope of turning this game around. Enter the famous Stan Webb, a right foot drive and a brilliant header

Gary Bennett scores in the FA Cup tie with Manchester City at Feethams

gave Darlo a victory, my first taste of giant killing by my team.

During the early 70's a school friend of mine, Keith Manson, announced that his family were to offer lodgings to Darlo players. The sight of Peter Graham drinking a cup of tea and Mickey Wright and the brilliant Ron Ferguson watching TV left me star struck.

The cup games against Sheffield Wednesday and Everton were special, especially after we beat Sheffield Wednesday despite a 2-0 first leg defeat. Striker Eddie Rowles promised me we would turn it round and he was dead right.

My love for the club led me to chose Quakers as my GCSE PE project. I was allowed a free hand within Feethams to complete this masterpiece which I only got a 'B' for - a bitter disappointment.

One of the saddest but proudest moments of supporting Darlo came in the March 83 when after a series of poor results only 950 or so people turned up for a home game with Mansfield. This was probably the club's lowest hour and thankfully we have never looked like repeating this again.

During my years of following Darlington I have always tried to attend every FA Cup first round game, home and away. Good trips to non league grounds,

Scarborough and Hyde, come to mind, but in 1984 after we beat the mighty Mossley, Altrincham and Maidstone, a draw with Plymouth away came out of the hat. Off we went via British Rail to the other end of the country. After being greeted by the local constabulary the small band of Darlington faithful was frog marched to the stadium. As in these situations the weather decided to change for the worst, so for 90 minutes we all got wet. The rain did not matter to us when Kevin Todd flicked in from a free kick to give Quakers the lead. But, after Plymouth equalised later on, the nerves set in. Just as we were looking forward to a warm British Rail cuppa Plymouth scored the winner to send the faithful home very disappointed.

Throughout my 31 years of following the team the local rivalry with Hartlepool has never diminished. It was the norm for many years for Darlo to win at Pools only for the result to be reversed at Feethams.

In the late 80's a very good Darlo team hammered Pools 5-2 at Victoria Park, with Quakers hero to be Mark Prudhoe suffering in the Pools goal. As well as the result, I can remember Quakers winger Alan Roberts picking the ball up 50 yards from goal beating numerous defenders before shooting past Prudhoe.

The mid 80's promotion team also secured a memorable victory at Pools. After trailing for most of the game a lucky cross-shot from Peter Johnson and a classic tap in from the legendary Carl Airey sent the Darlo contingent home ecstatic.

The same team under the leadership of Cyril Knowles were paired with Middlesbrough in the FA Cup. On arrival at Ayresome Park for some mysterious reason I along with my dad, granddad and brother found ourselves standing in the famous Boro section called the chicken run. As the only Darlo fans for yards around we were made very unwelcome especially when the famous Boro could not break Darlo down for the 90 minutes. Still we had no chance in the replay at Feethams, did we? On a cold wet evening the replay proved to be one of the proudest moments of my time following the Quakers.

Promotions during my time following the club have been very rare but the Cyril Knowles squad in the mid 80's achieved what seemed to be the impossible by going up. On a great evening in May, Quakers secured promotion at Crewe. The 2000 plus Darlo supporters had a brilliant time after Carl Airey scored to secure the vital point required and we celebrated wildly behind a large steel fence.

Division Three was a completely new experience with league games against the

101

mighty Derby County and Wolves and it was great to finish the season in mid table. Unfortunately the second term in the higher division found us with more players injured than fit. All of these problems meant the highlight of the season for me was a surprising 1-1 draw with Boro after their relegation to Division Three, with Alan Roberts scoring with a left foot shot. This game also saw the late Steve Bell playing against his former club. After the dizzy heights of Division 3 the late 80's saw the unthinkable happen, when Quakers were relegated to the Conference. The appointment of Brian Little came too late to save us. The feeling on the last day of the season was awful but we knew there was hope with Little in charge.

Memories from our year in the Conference are mainly good with Cork and Borthwick helping themselves to plenty of goals. A brilliant 2-0 victory at Barnet still lingers in my mind with Borthwick and David Corner scoring .

The final day of the season's win at Welling will remain as one of the most stressful experiences of my time following the team. So much so that for 90 minutes I didn't realise I had kept my sunglasses on until the final whistle blew and we jumped on the pitch and they fell off and were trampled by the hoards of Quakers fans...but hey who cares...we won and we were promoted.

During the disastrous 1993 season, in a weak moment, I agreed to a week's holiday in Cyprus in November...we never go on holiday during the season...to my horror a mid week game was scheduled against Colchester. After a terrible run of results I feared the worst. Back in those days communication was not as advanced as it is today, Sky television had not been heard of. So the morning after the game I still had no

John Borthwick

idea of the result until I switched on the BBC World Service who on a slow news and sport day actually featured the amazing 7-3 victory by Quakers to my delight and amazement. To this day I have never had a weak moment with regard to going out of the country on holiday during the season.

The greatest feeling for any fan must be the walk up Wembley way, which on a sunny May afternoon was brilliant. Meeting friends and fellow supporters was a memorable time for everybody. Nothing was going to spoil the occasion of a lifetime in May 1996.

As the teams warmed up I recall full back Mark Barnard greeting his father. The proud look on Keith Barnard's face was a picture and both Keith and I have discussed this several times as both of them have been friends and business acquaintances of mine for many years.

Later in the FA Cup we were paired against Solihull Borough. After a dismal 1-1 draw at Feethams the return leg turned out to be quite an experience. As my job took me to the Black Country on the day of the replay I decided to travel to the game on my own. On arrival at Solihull Borough FC's ground I was informed that the tie was to be played several miles away. A quick dash across the Midlands got me to the ground just before kick-off. But if my timing was poor the famous Uriah Rennie put me to shame, adding 12 minutes injury time, only blowing after Solihull levelled. After extra time including Lee Turnbull`s sending off the tie was decided by some cool penalties from our boys.

1998 saw the arrival of the finest striker to play for Quakers in my 30 some years of following them, Marco Gabbiadini. After a slow start he developed into a 30 goal a season striker who could win games single-handed with his brilliance.

The FA Cup tie with Man City put Quakers in front of a live Sky audience for the first time. After Gary Bennett scored from a corner it looked like we were about to cause an upset until Paul Dickov levelled late on. The replay at an empty Maine Road saw Quakers eventually lose after Marco was harshly sent off.

David Hodgson's side of 1999-2000 was an outstanding team and the investment in quality players paid dividends. To this day I firmly believe that if we could have played our home games on a decent pitch we would have been promoted easily.

This period was a strange time for the seasoned Darlo fan. Queues to get in, an excellent team and winning games along with plans for a new stadium all looked like the foundations to push Quakers up the leagues...or so we thought.

Marco Gabbiadini congratulates Gary Bennett after scoring against the old enemy Hartlepool

After being knocked out of the FA Cup the wild card available was handed to Quakers. George Reynolds' direct line to God had given us a great tie away to Aston Villa. The trip to Villa was a brilliant occasion and the 5000 plus Darlo fans were not let down by the boys on the pitch. Unfortunately at 2-0 down our spirits were low but when Paul Heckingbottom followed up a Peter Duffield penalty to score for Quakers we all went wild. John Gregory's decision to leave the dug out early and show no respect and praise for Darlo's performance still angers me.

Towards the end of the season our form and some of Hodgy's tactics took a turn for the worse. With the loss of Marco for a couple of games towards the end of the season our form dipped allowing Northampton to squeeze past us which sentenced us to the dreaded play-offs again.

Drawing Pools in the play-off semi-final was as nervy as any game could be. The sight of Sky'S Jeff Stelling and the rest of the panel of experts wearing blue carnations in support of the Pools only increased everyone's desire to win this tie. The atmosphere behind the Darlo goal was brilliant and when Craig Liddle

volleyed home in the first half the scene was set for a famous victory, made even better when Marco slotted in a second half penalty to earn Quakers a 2-0 advantage. Four days later a packed Feethams saw a brilliant Gary Strodder own goal set Quakers on their way to Wembley. Surely this time it would be our day?

In all of the years of Wembley Stadium the hallowed turf had never been so wet. Watching the lads warm-up it was obvious the pitch would not suit our slick passing game. The match itself proved to be the most frustrating I had ever seen with Darlo dominating in every department but unable to score. The second half saw my son managing to fall asleep which I was pleased about as his dad was about to become the most unhappy football fan in the world. Andy Clarke's goal robbed Darlo of promotion and the look on the players faces made it obvious this was the end of this wonderful team. As the Posh players climbed the steps to receive this meaningless trophy I could honestly say I could have cried like a baby.

But sweet times were to return. I journeyed to Nottingham Forest for a Worthington Cup tie, with my brother-in-law, John and my nephew, Lee who are life long Forest fans. The conversation on the journey was about how many Darlo would lose by and when Stern John scored early on it looked very bleak. Nobody in the ground could have anticipated the brilliant fight back Quakers put up in the second half. When Stuart Elliott scored the winner for us from 50 yards, the look on Forest keeper Dave Beasant's face was worth a million pounds.

Dave Sowerby (The Missionary Position)

Only another Darlington supporter could truly understand what it is to follow the Quakers. Despite years of traumas off the field, and disasters on it, the hardened Feethams regular stubbornly delights in refusing to face up to reality, and spend his Saturday afternoons somewhere less likely to ruin his weekend. Who else but this special breed of masochist would contribute to a book devoted to memories from a football ground once described by a club director as a "Victorian Dump".

Despite this ingrained cynicism, some would say pragmatic realism, a chance meeting on a Thornaby bound train led to the formation of Darlington's original fanzine 'Mission Impossible'. Ten years, seventy issues and thousands of pints later, Steve Harland and Steve Raine can be proud that a 'one off' collaboration, brought about to chronicle the Quakers' slide into the Conference, developed into a much

103

loved Darlo institution. Back in those pre-Microsoft days, Steve Raine painstakingly cobbled each issue together on a battered old typewriter that would not have looked out of place on the Antiques Roadshow. However, the advent of the Personal Computer, coupled with the obvious benefits of 'spell check' meant that any Tom, Dick or Harry Charlton could realistically aspire to be the next Nick Hornby. Before long the fanzine had attracted a talented team of writers (some say whingers) with such luminaries as David Ovens, David Smith, Kevin Darlo and Robin Coultherd contributing regular, often bizarre, insights into their own feelings for the club. Steve Harland eventually stepped up to replace Steve Raine as editor, but the direction of the fanzine continued to roll relentlessly on towards its inevitable conclusion - a head-on collision with the club.

Two AGMs in 1996 (only Darlo could have two) at which answers, which were unsatisfactory in our view, were given to some questions, set the tone for all subsequent meetings between the fanzine and the club. The relationship never really recovered though it was not for the want of trying. Various sponsorship schemes were set up by the fanzine, and groups such as DAFTS which benefited the club financially. However, we continued to be at best ignored and sometimes criticised by the club.

It was against this background that Mission Impossible campaigned in the hope that one day we would be told what we felt was the truth. For the most part I believe we succeeded in informing the supporters of the latest developments at crisis-riddled Feethams. Winding up petitions came and went, as did the majority of good footballers, with the frequency of Kevan Smith back passes.

Around this time my own involvement with Mission Impossible began to exact a heavy price. After an edition of the magazine with a particularly strong theme I received an irate phone call from a club official. To say he was upset would be something of an understatement. After much soul searching, a begrudging apology was published in the next issue, from Steve Raine. A written apology from Steve is a wonderfully ambiguous thing. While the text contains all the right words, the poor recipient is left under no illusion that he was still being mercilessly mocked. On this occasion, much to our relief, we managed to stave off the solicitors, but, years later, this climb-down was to have disastrous results for Steve Harland when a club official played the legal card. The whole sorry affair lasted months and drained Steve of any enthusiasm left for the club, or the fanzine, and was, in effect,

the final nail in Mission Impossible's coffin.

So what changed? Well the answer was us, the fans. People who had spent years grumbling to each other suddenly realised they had a voice, and the fanzines, Mission Impossible and the excellent Where's The Money Gone, became obvious outlets.

It would be remiss of me not to mention the good times, and there were many. The Conference and Third Division titles in successive seasons, the two play off victories which secured our place at Wembley with the second one having the bonus of coming against our loveable simian rivals from up the A19. The night at Elland Road when 2000 Darlo fans outsung the Leeds faithful while the team outplayed their supposed Premier League betters. As for Wembley the joy of actually getting there rather outshone the reality of playing in London's very own 'Victorian Dump'. In hindsight the result on both occasions was too important and the defeat against Peterborough will be remembered by most supporters as the end of the Gabbiadini-Hodgson era.

For me the most important memories of Feethams will centre on the people. From my early visits with my grandfather, father, and older brother, a trip to Feethams was something to be savoured. The changing of ends at half-time, the smell of tobacco and Bovril and the forbidden attraction of the Tin Shed made Saturday afternoons eagerly awaited. Even my father's constant threats to stop torturing himself every other weekend, (a threat that he only recently carried out) failed to dampen my enthusiasm. All these factors played a big part in my early football experience, as did the frequent enthusiasm-sapping applications for re-election. If I'm honest the promotion under Cyril Knowles came as a big surprise and for the first time instilled in me the idea that we were not always destined to be also-rans.

It should also be stated that not all contact between the fanzine and the board was hostile either. Gordon Hodgson and Bernard Lowery, both still directors, were always open and friendly and more importantly both were willing to take time to communicate with supporters, even when at times you could sense they were as frustrated as we were. In general the people I met through the fanzine remain friends, and the decision to stop Mission Impossible brought a strange sense of relief. The idea of a subversive, leftfield, alternative look at life inside Feethams had run its course, and the advent of the internet meant information could be relayed in minutes as opposed to once a month in inky black and white.

Thanks for great memories to Marco Gabbiadini, David Speedie, Colin Sinclair, David Currie, Don Burluraux, Gary Bannister, Mark Prudhoe, Brian Little, Craig Liddle, Sean Gregan, and for that looping header Gary Coatsworth. Congratulations to groundsman Tommo, for managing to wear the same bloody hat for what seems an eternity.

Let's hope that our new home will eventually become as much loved as Feethams with hopefully a little more success on the pitch to help fill all those shiny new seats! Feethams was special in many ways as perhaps this one example may help convey...

On August 13th 1942 Feethams played host to the North of England Finals of the British Sheepdog trials. The event attracted 3000 spectators. Forty years later Kevan Smith appeared at Feethams with what looked like a sheepdog on his head. Unfortunately the attendances remained much lower.

Craig Stoddart

I went to Scunthorpe - far from our happiest hunting ground - in 1996 in typically pessimistic mood, even though a win would guarantee promotion.

It wasn't such a surprise to see us fall 2-0 behind but that is not to say I wasn't feeling despondent at watching promotion being lost before my eyes.

I had hoped that we'd cast away the usual disappointing Darlo tag, and for once live the dream of promotion on the last day of the season.

No chance. Not us, we're Darlo and we don't have success. It's not allowed. It says so in the big FA rule book.

But what's this? Miracle of miracles, Darlo decided to rekindle those promotion dreams by pulling level, with time on the clock and the dream reignited.

We required one more goal to complete a comeback of Escape To Victory proportions.

Sit down! Stop getting excited, put the champagne away and remember exactly who you support. There are teams who bask in glory every couple of years - we aren't one of them and we should know better by now.

Scunthorpe's third goal duly arrived. But that could mean the play-offs and Wembley I hear you cry.

So close to promotion - action from the 3-3 draw at Scunthorpe in 1996

Pack it in, Darlo don't get to Wembley either. That's also in that rule book, just underneath the rule on promotion and above the 'not allowed leading scorers' guidelines.

I felt that yet again, we'd been let down. I've supported this lot for years and this happens. We even had a stocked-up mini-bus to return to.

Mark Barnard thought differently though. After being level at 2-2, and thus one goal at that stage would've sealed the dream, we had decided to let Scunthorpe score a third BEFORE we did.

And Barnard had the audacity to score now when it was too late to grab a winner. I was so annoyed, I punched the wall behind me. A couple of Darlo fans for the day didn't understand my frustration but it was no use explaining. To fully comprehend what it meant to see your team fall at the last, required several years of bloody minded commitment to the cause.

I felt that 3-3 meant nothing. It was the same as a 3-2 defeat or even a 7-0 hammering. Barnard needn't have bothered scoring.

Bury duly beat Doncaster to deny us third spot, so it was off to the play-offs.

Farewell to Feethams | a collection of Darlington FC memories

105

Tony Swann

I WAS in the RAF stationed at Colerne in Somerset when Darlington played Chelsea in the FA cup. My dad and father-in-law travelled down from Darlington and I travelled up from Colerne to meet them, went to the match and had a few drinks afterwards - we had something to celebrate as well.

I saw them on to the train at Kings Cross and I went back to camp.

One of my pals in the office was a lad called Jimmy Nicholls and I think he had a trial for Darlington before going for his national service. On the Monday morning after the match he said to me, that someone with the same surname as me had fallen out of the train at Hatfield and was found in a dazed condition wandering along the line - fortunately for him there had been a speed restriction on this part of the track and he survived. The railway authorities stopped the train at Peterborough and woke my father-in-law who had slept through all this and asked him if he had the train tickets, which he had - I think they thought my dad was trying to get off without paying!

I immediately got compassionate leave and travelled home to see that he was OK, which he was. We didn't get to the replay because he wasn't up to it, but living in Hutton Avenue at the time, we heard the roar of the crowds when Darlington went on to beat Chelsea 4-1 in the replay.

Dave Taylor

A GREAT memory for me was when Cyril Knowles was manager. I remember we had been on a poor run in our promotion year. Defeats by Blackpool and Chesterfield, both heavy and at home 4-0 and 3-1. It was a night match against Hereford. We were 1-0 down for what seemed like a lifetime. Then came a Dave McLean curler from outside the box that seemed to take ages to go in. I think it was in the last minute. After that the self belief came back.

Another memory from that season was away to Crewe. The last away game when we got promotion. We were not at the game (Dad wouldn't let me go on my own!) so my friends and I decided to go to the fields near Patons in Darlington and listen to the match on Radio Cleveland while we acted out the game (as you do as a child). I can remember the result - a 2-2 draw. All I can remember was us three three joyous lads running round the field cheering at the final whistle. Great times. To return soon I hope.

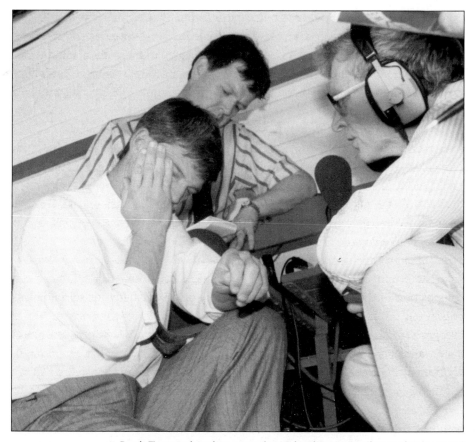

Dennis Thompson interviews an emotional Brian Little - as Ray Simpson pinches a quote!

Dennis Thompson (former BBC Radio Cleveland reporter)

F OR some the Saturday ritual at Feethams involved much more than the events on the pitch. The afternoon would be incomplete without meat pies and Oxo. There are supporters who, deprived of this gourmet cuisine, could in no way survive a couple of hours on the terraces.

Even such hallowed ground as Feethams can suffer from the petty criminal and at one game in the 1960s, intruders broke into the Tea Bar and made off with the ultimate in treasure, a box of Meat Pies. They must have been disturbed getting their loot over the wall and as they legged it in the direction of South Park, they abandoned their ill-gotten gains. "You saved the day for the fans," I said to one of the bobbies on duty just before kick-off. "They were facing the dilemma of a pie-less afternoon, now they're happily stuffing their faces. Don't you fancy a pie?"

"Not really" came the reply. " They're like a few of the Darlo team, well past their sell-by date!"

It was during the War Years, that I got my first glimpse of Feethams.

The train was crowded with good-natured fans, all male, all mufflered and flat-capped. As with most football followers in those days, each one peered through a thick blue cloud of Woodbine smoke. The atmosphere as the fans streamed down the hill from the station to the ground may not have had the electricity of Roker or St. James's but believe me there was a tingle in the air that we lads hadn't experienced before.

In those austere days clubs fielded a motley collection of old sweats, promising youngsters and guest players from the services. Most clubs didn't know the composition of their side until just before kick off. Availability for selection was dependent on service duties, working patterns and of course, transport. Nearly everyone travelled by bus or train. No surprise to see Bill Forrest, the Boro half-back walking down from the station, carrying his boots in a bag. I don't think he received any special attention from the fans. Nor did the soldier heading for the gates. "He's a famous international," said my pal Pete and I believed him even though this khaki-clad star didn't appear to be carrying any kit. " They'll fix him up with some spare boots I imagine. He'll still run rings round the Boro," said Pete, whose Dad knew lots of footballers and was considered by we urchins to be very knowledgeable on such matters.

The queues at the turnstiles were bigger than any I'd seen before. Going to be a huge crowd I thought, we'll never be able to see. But see we did after scrambling through the turnstiles and sprinting round the cricket field to the terrace.

A regular visitor to Ayresome, I was unprepared for the compact little ground with the spectators close to the action. The atmosphere was something special and I was hooked. Of the game I remember little. It was a draw, I think, but memories are of a perfect mid-winter day with the low sun causing problems for the Boro keeper Middleton, who was in constant action. Quakers could field star-studded teams in those days and I remember being particularly impressed by a Scottish left

back (Smith from St Mirren I think) whose tackling and clearances looked awesome to we impressionable schoolboys. In later years I was to enthuse over many other full backs Davison, Mason, Cochrane, Craggs, Jones, Johnson and Gray.

Fifty years later saw me passing through the gates for my last ever visit to Feethams as enthusiastic as ever. Ask me now and I couldn't tell you who played full back that day. However, I'll bet some starry-eyed youngster, in the crowd for the first time, will have no difficulty remembering half a century on.

George Thompson

I STARTED supporting the Quakers in 1975, and the first match I saw was a 1-0 defeat against Northampton. The team was third in the league prior to this match, but unfortunately things took a downward spiral from then on and this set the pattern for the remainder of the season. At that time, the team went seven consecutive games without scoring.

Derek Craig

I didn't see my first Darlington goal for over a month until the 25th October when Derek Craig scored a great header in a 2-2 draw against Doncaster (Doncaster's last minute equaliser that day was scored by Alan Murray, later to become manager).

There are two highlights which stick in my mind. The first was the derby match with Hartlepool in February 1976 when we came back from a two goal half time deficit to win 3-2 with goals from Clive Nattress, Billy Coulson (who had one of the sweetest left feet I've ever seen) and Colin Sinclair.

Sinclair was worth his weight in gold. He played in an ordinary side yet managed to score regularly.

Frank Tweddle

THE Quakers played in hoops when I first went to Feethams with my father in the mid-Fifties. We watched from the West Stand as we played the likes of Accrington Stanley and Gateshead. I still vividly recall seeing a player sent off for the first time - Mansfield player-manager Charlie Mitton for aiming a kick at Dickie Davis.

The formation of the Fourth Division brought a whole host of new clubs to Feethams. I remember being crushed in Spratt's Corner in the record crowd against Bolton.

Then in 1966 came a completely unknown phenomenon to a Darlington fan of that era - promotion.

The heady build up over those last few home games of the season was terrific, and then came the relief when we finally did it in the last match of the season against Torquay.

The following season was dismal, but taught me what being a Darlington fan was all about. I was in the crowd of 18,144 on Boxing Day for the visit of Boro - Ron Greener's 500th game.

The Seventies was an era that tested the patience of even the most committed supporter, but it made me even more intent on sticking with the Quakers. Every point was precious as we battled to keep out of the dreaded bottom four. To this day I feel for the fans of Bradford Park Avenue, Barrow, Southport and Workington, who lost their league status.

The goals of chirpy Scot Colin Sinclair, and the uncompromising defending of Colin Blant stick in my memory, but towards the end of the decade came Ronnie Ferguson's spectacular long range goal against Sheffield Wednesday.

I remember a pal of mine commenting as Ronnie lined up to shoot, "What's the clown doing...he's scored!"

One of the advantages of the layout of Feethams was that you could switch ends at half time to watch the Quakers attack in both halves (or if you were a masochist the defence). Feethams was never quite the same once fans couldn't switch.

In the financial crisis of the Eighties. I remember a friend phoning me at work when the news broke. I took the call in the office of the boss. "Not bad news," he enquired as I put the phone down. "Yes, terrible news," I replied as I walked out, leaving him thinking there must have been a death in the family.

I was in the West Stand when we beat Boro in the FA Cup, and recall being bear-hugged by a complete stranger, who proceeded to jig me up and down when Phil Lloyd scored.

The despair of relegation to the Conference, followed by successive promotions then relegation again were unbelievable times, but reaching Wembley for the first time topped the lot. That is probably the pinnacle in all those years supporting the club.

I've enjoyed the excellent view from the East Stand for the last four years - with none of those awkward supports in your line of vision.

I'll miss Feethams after coming for almost 50 years, but perhaps after 119 years it's time for an upgrade as nostalgia tends to tinge one's view of a place.

Dave Watson

MY first Darlington match was against Carlisle on 20 December 1947. My father took me as we lived in Barnard Castle then and I, aged nine, was one of a crowd of 7138. I remember standing on a kind of embankment behind the corner flag between the east stand and now the Tin Shed end. I could hardly see a thing but I was at the right end to see Darlington's last three goals: two as a result of corner kicks right in front of me.

Beforehand, obviously I was very excited that I was going to see my first match and watch Darlington but the two players I was eagerly wanting to see were Darlington goalkeeper Norman Tapken because he had been on the books of Manchester United and Newcastle, and Ivor Broadis, Carlisle's player-manager (I believe he was only in his mid-twenties at the time). Later he played for Sunderland and England.

Most of the excitement took place in the last five minutes. Spectators had been leaving in droves but I was hooked. This was Harry Clarke's first game of the season and he scored the first goal with the other goals coming from Ken Bower (2) and Bobby Sinclair.

Home games were preceded with Cockerton Silver Band playing and marching through the town and playing both before the match and at the interval.

It was not unusual to see some well-known names playing in the Third Division especially in the early 1950's: those coming towards the end of their careers and dropping a division or two for example. George Hardwick played for Oldham in their 5-0 win at Feethams; Raich Carter for Hull City; Freddie Steele, centre forward ex-Stoke playing for Port Vale.

Cliff Mason was a sound and dependable left back. I lived and worked in

108

Sheffield for five years and I met him on a few occasions at the Abbeydale Sports Club where he played tennis and I cricket. He told me on one occasion that he always dreaded an injury when playing for the Quakers because the trainer, Dickie Deacon, (the person who was virtually everything else in those days) had fingers like nails and after he had dealt with an injured player, the player felt worse than what he had when he was first injured.

I was in the crowd for the league cup tie against Bolton in November 1960. Nowadays to think of 21,000 in the ground beggars belief. I was in the paddock of the East Stand, and we were fairly crushed but were able to move without too much difficulty. Darlington played well that evening and with a slightly better goalkeeper might have won as I felt he might have saved one of the goals.

I seem to think that Ron Harbertson was a slow developer. If I remember rightly he had had several clubs before coming to Feethams where he came into his own. Hard-working, skilful, direct with a hard shot he was an idol with the crowd. It was reported at the time that he was transferred for £5,000 to Lincoln which many, including me, thought was very much below his true value. This was somewhat proved with the excellent contribution he made at Sincil Bank, where he helped to save them from relegation.

Simon Weatherill

MY first visit to Feethams was on the last day of the 1970-71 season against Brentford, when we won 2-1.

I remember that the whole day out cost me just 50p pocket money. A half-cheap day return ticket from Northallerton to Darlington was 19p, admission to the ground was 22p and a programme was 5p. This left me with 4p change, either for a Mars bar on the way home, or for something in the programme shop at the Tin Shed end of the East Stand.

My personal list of triumph and disaster:

6 Jan 1973 Darlington 0 Southport 7

One of the worst ever seasons when we finished bottom of Division Four. We had been beaten 7-0 at Bradford in the previous game, so Ernie Adams was left out and Phil Owers was given his debut in goal. I'm afraid I can't comment on how well he performed because I couldn't see anything at his end of the ground. A thick fog

You can't stop me! Striker David Currie dances away from a defender

descended on Feethams and from behind the goal you could just make out the halfway line. In those days you could always stand behind the goal that Darlington were attacking - we didn't see much of the ball that day.

It would disappear into the gloom at the other end of the pitch and then the Southport players would come jogging back, congratulating each other. There were seven goals scored, and I didn't see any of them!

15 May 1982 Darlington 0 Sheffield United 2

United came to town, needing to win to clinch the championship. They brought around 10,000 supporters. They took over the whole ground and brought a fantastic party atmosphere to the game. Many of them were in fancy dress - I remember standing next to three gorillas at one point. The Darlington team lined the tunnel at the start of the game to applaud United onto the pitch. While they waited they performed various warming up exercises and I can remember Batman and Robin coming out of the stand to join them!

3 March 1985 Darlington 7 Halifax 0

Already 4-1 down from the first leg, this seemed a pointless exercise. It was a wet Sunday afternoon and I can't recall why I bothered. Only 765 of us turned out but those that stayed away missed a treat. A young triallist by the name of John McMahon scored a hat trick as we swept the Shaymen aside.

6 May 1985 Crewe 2 Darlington 2

My first promotion party. A Bank Holiday Monday evening kick off which enabled us to watch Manchester United versus Nottingham Forest on the way down to Crewe. For atmosphere and excitement, Gresty Road was the place to be. Two goals from Carl Airey clinched promotion for us, but the highlight of the night was a thumping Kevan Smith header for one of Crewe's goals - Fred Barber in goal didn't stand a chance.

8 December 1987 Darlington 4 Exeter 1

A game that should never have taken place because the pitch was frozen solid. Exeter had travelled up for the original fixture ten days before, only to find the game postponed because of a frozen pitch. The game went ahead, and it seemed it might develop into complete farce, with players slipping and sliding everywhere - except David Currie. He put in an incredible performance of balance and skill to turn the Exeter defence inside out. He scored two and set up another for Alan Roberts.

26 November 1990 Darlington 0 Manchester United 6 (FA Youth Cup)

A chance to witness the youth team of the biggest club in the country. The match turned into a one man show, with a certain Ryan Giggs playing up front for United. He scored five of their goals. Two days later he signed a five year contract, and two months after that he was in United's first team.

2 November 1993 Darlington 7 Colchester 3

This was our 18th game of the season, and we still hadn't won. Alan Murray had just been appointed manager and this was his first home game. A small crowd assembled more in hope than expectancy, but we were to witness a completely different Darlington. Lee Ellison scored in the first minute. Everything we tried seemed to come off, but we still managed to keep conceding goals and keep it interesting. Pick of the goals was a Gary Chapman diving header five minutes from time. Alan Murray said afterwards "I didn't feel comfortable until we were four goals in front."

18 September 1996 Leeds 2 Darlington 2 (Coca Cola Cup)

The first opportunity I'd ever had to see Darlington play against a top flight side. (I'd missed midweek games at Coventry, Everton and West Ham in the seventies because of school). The celebrations when supersub Robbie Painter rounded Nigel Martyn to score the second equaliser near the end of the game will live with me for the rest of my life.

Alan Wilkinson

IN the early 1930's our area suffered economic hardship. An older friend once said: "If you want to know the meaning of the North East Depression, look at the crowd coming out of Feethams on a winter afternoon."

My memories go back to the 30's, when my father took me from Barnard Castle by train, to watch matches from the Paddock of the East Stand.

If the 'gate' was small we sat on the wooden terracing; if there was a big crowd everybody stood up to see.

There was no terracing on either side of the stand, just grassy (or muddy) slopes. The only secure footing was on the ridge at the top.

I recall war time when the team members varied according to which soldiers were stationed in the neighbourhood.

I saw Leslie Compton of Arsenal and England play at Barnard Castle, so surely some notables played for Darlington, but I can remember only one 'guest' player.

He was called Warburton, normally of Chester City, who impressed me when he beat a full-back by carrying the ball past him on top of his boot, then pulling it back and going round the other side of the defender, still without the ball having touched the ground.

Other memories around and after wartime include players from a higher level closing their careers at Darlington. One was Don Ashman, formerly a Middlesbrough defender. I remember a comment on him in a Darlington match as reported by the Gazette Pink'un. It said that all seemed lost until 'Ashman appeared from nowhere' and cleared a shot off the line.

Later came Dickie Davis from Sunderland and Johnny Spuhler from Middlesbrough. The former was a strongly built player who specialised in the 'flick-on.'

When Spuhler went on a run, he not only had his head over the ball, but, it seemed, the rest of his body. He was difficult to dispossess.

The biggest crowd of which I was a member at Feethams was the cup replay against Chelsea in 1958. I was told that Patons and Baldwins works were closed for the afternoon. My party went to the Polam end, but were separated by the crowd surging at every goalmouth incident.

We re-grouped at half time, and well before the end the crowd was singing: "Who's afraid of the big, bad Wolves?" whom we had to meet in the next round.

More recent memories have included tricky footwork by Alan Roberts, a lobbed goal by Andy Toman, forceful foraging by David Cork and Carl Airey, excellent goalkeeping from Fred Barber, a wonderful goal by David Currie against Wolves, strong clearances by Kevan Smith, a hat-trick by Gary Worthington, goals from Marco Gabbiadini - not just in number, but in quality - and defending by Craig Liddle.

David Currie is the best Darlington player I have seen. He was creative, a team player and an individualist. His goal against Wolves seemed to fly almost parallel to the goalline until nearing the goal, and then swerved past the keeper.

His goal against Scarborough, away, in the first minute, was a one-on-one; he ran half the length of the field, looked as if he was going to shoot, the goalkeeper went down, and only then did Currie shoot.

When we won the Fourth Division Championship, the trophy was handed to Kev Smith.

His play and captaincy had been vital, but marred by dodgy back-passes. As he, beaming, received the trophy, a wag in the crowd shouted, "Don't pass it back, Kev!"

Bad language and inane chanting from the Tin Shed has become worse over the years, while the standard of refereeing has deteriorated. But despite this, after all these years I still look forward to the next Darlo match.

Ray Wilkinson

MY brother and I, along with two more brothers, played together for the reserves in the late fifties. I believe it is the only time two sets of brothers have played for Darlington in the same team. My brother's name is John, while the other brothers were Charlie and Frankie Wayman.

The groundsman, Bernard Flack, was nearly arrested one day. He ran from the West Stand at the end of a game to take the nets down, and was chased by a policeman to the goal at the cricket club end. Bernard explained that he was the groundsman, and the policeman was so surprised and embarrassed as he was watched by the crowd on their way out of the ground.

John Winn

MY first match at Feethams was as a ten year old in January 1954, when, in icy conditions, we played a 1-1 draw with Halifax. So hard was the ground that Darlington's outside right, Jimmy Keers, sustained concussion after a fall and didn't return to the side for nearly two months.

My memories of the Chelsea match are that my Dad and elder brother went to Stamford Bridge leaving me to hear the news on the radio that the Quakers had gone three up, and then the disappointment as Chelsea fought back to force a draw.

For the Wednesday afternoon replay, 'Bug' Allen our Biology master, no football enthusiast, let us listen to the commentary on the Light Programme and joined in the cheers as the Quakers scored three times in extra time to win 4-1.

By this time we knew that the winners of the replay would visit Wolves, at the time the toughest draw imaginable, and my father, never one to make rash promises, had said that he would take me to Molineux if we beat Chelsea, so we joined the great exodus by train to the West Midlands. It seems incredible that some 11,000 made that journey when typically before the cup run league crowds at Feethams were six or seven thousand. After the 6-1 drubbing it seemed a long way back.

Other cup memories include the five matches in 60-61 against Hull City, of which I saw three, and all because the referee allowed an 'equaliser' by Bobby

Baxter in the last minute of the first game to stand, when to most onlookers, including myself standing behind the goal at the South Park End, his shot went over the bar.

The highlights of that first season of floodlight football at Feethams were the league cup matches against West Ham and Bolton. My girlfriend had Bolton connections (her father had gone to the same school as Tommy Lawton) and accompanied me to that match and cheered for the Wanderers!

In 1972 I left Darlington to work in Sussex and visits to Feethams became rarer. The dismal fortunes the team experienced in the seventies tested the loyalty of the keenest supporter and I can recall some depressing experiences at places like Gillingham, Portsmouth, Brentford and indeed most other southern grounds on which we played.

The happiest memory of recent times has to be to that lovely day in May 1990 at Welling when we clinched our return to the Football League. I think for the first time in my life I went onto the pitch at the end of that game and a tear was not far away when I realised that the chants of 'champions, champions' were for the Quakers for the first time since 1925.

Last year my wife and I left the south coast and now live just a 45 minute drive from Darlington and so after almost thirty years I am back as a regular at Feethams, until we move to the new ground. I will miss the old place, its quaint charm and so many memories, but I'll be as keen as the next supporter when we are in the new stadium.

112

Chapter 5

Famous matches

The day we won the cup - the Division Three North Cup in 1934.

SIR is a hero! Pupils must have been delighted when their teacher Dan Cassidy scored a wonder goal to win the cup.

Cassidy was given permission to skip school and play in the May 1 final at Old Trafford.

The 4-3 victory over Stockport gave Quakers their only cup success - except for local north east Trophies such as the Durham Senior Cup.

Defender Cassidy scored with the last kick, after racing past his own forwards and the Stockport defence, which moved up looking for offside. He then sent a rasping drive past keeper Finningan. There wasn't time for Stockport to restart, and the 100 or so Darlington fans went wild, as four minutes earlier their team had been losing.

Stockport went ahead late in the first half, then Quakers' defender Bill Scott

Darlington in 1934-34, the team that won the Third Division North Cup

punched away a goalbound shot (not a red card offence in those days) and Stockport made it 2-0 from the penalty.

But Tom Alderson (60 minutes) pulled one back with a tremendous cross shot. He tried the same again seven minutes later, and although the ball was blocked, John Middleton swooped to equalise.

Again Stockport went in front. However Quakers rallied, Bill Eden's corner four minutes from time being headed home by Jerry Best, setting the scene for Cassidy to have something special to tell his next class.

A crowd of 4640 paid £249 for what was regarded one of the best ever games at Old Trafford.

This was the competition's inaugural season, so Darlington's was the first name inscribed on the trophy. The team was: Beby, Whelan, Scott, Cassidy, Strang, Hodgson, Eden, Middleton, Best, Alderson, Edgar.

One rarity that day was the use of ball boys - they wore long white coats with red collars, and kept the game flowing by always giving the ball to the correct wing half - the player in that position always took throw ins in those days.

There was a crowd of 100,000 in Manchester that day - but they were not interested in the Quakers. They were there to see the Manchester City side return from Wembley with the FA Cup they had won two days earlier by beating Portsmouth 2-1.

J McKenna, president of the Football League, presented the cup to Quakers' skipper Dick Strang, saying how he admired their spirit when losing, and their magnificent finish.

The Quakers had travelled to Manchester on the 12.58pm train, and returned on the midnight train.

Councillor T Rogers said, at a special presentation: "We've always been noted at Darlington for playing a clean game, whether in adversity or victory."

Darlington had seemed to be heading out of the competition at the first hurdle, when they could only draw 1-1 at home to Gateshead.

Having won the replay 3-2 after extra time, they were handed a bye, then played

113

York City at Feethams, winning 4-3 in front of 2,000, paying just £88. Quakers were 3-0 up after 23 minutes, before the jitters set in.

In the semi-final Wrexham were beaten 3-1 at Feethams, all four goals coming in the last 15 minutes.

A crowd of 3823 fans paid £185, but the two clubs received just £37 each after expenses, and pool money which went to all the clubs in the division.

The competition had been organised to raise funds for clubs, and in that respect didn't work. At the start of the cup run the Supporters Club handed over £100 to the club to pay the wages of three new signings until the end of the season, despite having only £209 in the coffers.

And Darlington were far from happy at having to play at Old Trafford. They wanted to toss a coin to play at Feethams or Stockport.

Darlington finished 16th, the cup triumph rescuing a poor season, that carried one particularly awful statistic.

They played Chester three times and lost 8-0 away, 4-0 at home (in the game before the Old Trafford Final), and 6-1 in the FA Cup.

114 FA Cup Run 1958

DARLINGTON'S victory over Chelsea was the most famous cup success the club has enjoyed.

The seven goals that Quakers scored in the 3-3 draw followed by 4-1 triumph, helped reach a tally of 17 FA Cup goals that season - a club record for the competition proper, and beaten only when they started in the qualifying rounds in 1910/11. That season they played 11 cup games - starting with a win over Hartlepool - amassing 24 goals.

Darlington started the 1957/8 FA Cup run with a 2-0 win at Rochdale, Ron Harbertson scoring twice. He was carried off shoulder high by Darlington fans who had no idea of the joy to come.

Rochdale played for 73 minutes with 10 men after Wainwright - trying to score with a diving header - crashed into a concrete post.

Quakers' stalwart Ron Greener played with concussion from the first couple of minutes, in a match in which 8395 fans paid £842.

Darlington were drawn at home to Midland League side Boston, a professional side, who a year earlier had won 6-1 at Derby. Darlington won 5-3.

David Carr, a colliery bricklayer, scored a hat-trick, colliery fitter Harbertson scoring the other two. The crowd of 10,014 (receipts £1,157) saw Darlington progress to a third round trip to Third Division Norwich.

Before the game Dick Duckworth snapped up three players, including, for a substantial fee, Burnley striker James Milner.

On the way to Norwich the team had a scare when a faulty coupling went, splitting the train into two, but none of the squad was injured. Harbertson and Tom Moran scored in front of 24,340 fans. Duckworth said: "We shall give Chelsea a real fright."

Darlington had gone to the pantomime before the Norwich game, so stuck to the same routine before the visit to Stamford Bridge, staying at Brighton.

The Stamford Bridge pitch was in an awful, slushy state following a sudden thaw.

But, in front of 40,759 fans (£5589), Darlington swept long passes down the wings to avoid the worst of the mud.

Keith Morton and Milner combined to set up Harbertson for the first goal after

Moran scores his first against Chelsea

A second for Moran!

four minutes. Chelsea keeper Matthews made two brilliant saves from Carr, but on 28 minutes a defensive mix up enabled Carr to walk the ball into the net. A young Darlington fan ran onto the pitch and pinned his rosette onto the net - play continuing while a policeman led him from the goalmouth.

Harbertson hit the bar, then on 50 minutes Morton scored from Carr's corner to send the 2,000 travelling fans into dreamland.

But suddenly - as in the Jack and the Beanstalk pantomime the players had seen twice - the giant awoke. Lewis (52 mins), Tindall (67) and McNichol (70) levelled the scores.

Quakers dug in. Goalkeeper Turner was excellent, looking safer than Chelsea's £22,000 keeper Matthews, Brian Henderson was a barrier in defence, and Ken Furphy and Don Rutherford looked better wing halves than their Chelsea counterparts. Harbertson's speed was a constant problem for Chelsea, as Darlington forced a replay.

Reflecting on the fact that Quakers led 3-0, Darneton, in the Northern Echo, wrote: "The temerity of it all."

Chelsea were given just 200 tickets for the Feethams replay. The game, on Wednesday, January 29, was brought forward to 2pm as the Corporation Transport Department wanted traffic cleared before schools and works broke up - though how many people were at work or in school that day is debatable.

The Feethams gates opened at 12.30 and there was a scramble for a good view. Messages of support flooded in, one Darlington fan, H Tomkinson of Buckinghamshire, writing: "You can beat them. Jimmy Greaves, Brabrook and co are nobody when it comes to a sticky wicket. Go to it lads, and let's have some of the old glory back."

A cablegram arrived from Canada, sent by Percy Masterman, a native of Darlington. It read: "Best of luck. Darlingtonians here are pulling for you."

Town centre pubs, The Falchion and The County were given an extension. The police raised no objection, saying: "There will be a lot of hoarse throats."

A crowd of 15,150 (£1999) packed Feethams and saw Moran put Darlington ahead on 35 minutes, and although McNichol equalised three minutes later, Moran, Carr and Harbertson scored in a six minute spell in extra time in front of a delighted cricket field end.

The players were mobbed at the whistle, Joe Turner just having time to do a somersault before being engulfed!

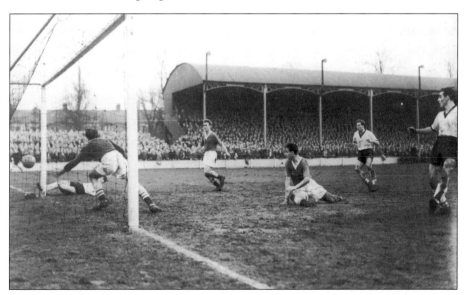

Harbertson completes the rout!

Farewell to Feethams | a collection of Darlington FC memories

"Darlington pension Chelsea off," boomed the Echo. Quakers fielded a team costing just £3,000 and containing six part timers.

Duckworth said: "Towards the end of normal time we were beginning to flag, so I put Carr into the middle, and switched Harbertson to the wing because his injured shoulder was giving him trouble. The move worked."

Chelsea were generous in defeat, chairman Joe Mears admitting: "Darlington played magnificent, open football and were easily the better side."

Darlington visited mighty Wolves in the fifth round - Quakers first time in the last 16 since the 1910/11 season - and returned to Brighton to prepare.

They trained at the greyhound stadium, and at the other end of the arena were West Ham, preparing for their tie with Fulham.

Hammers asked if the sides could practice together, but Duckworth said: "No, we won't test our strength against each other. If we meet later in the competition, all well and good."

The players had salt water baths, and there was yet another trip to see Jack and the Beanstalk. It didn't help that several Darlington stars, especially Harbertson, were rumoured to be the subject of bids from other clubs.

Wolves were unbeaten at home all season, but 5,000 fans made their way from Darlington to the West Midlands by train, and many others by car, including Bill, Colin and Ted Harris in a car lavishly decorated in Darlington's colours.

Nearly half of the Darlington side had flu during the week and were struggling. Turner climbed from his sick bed to play. In front of 55,778 fans (£7,992/6s) Darlington held out for over half an hour, but were three down at half time.

Wolves scored two more before Harry Bell pulled one back to the biggest cheer of the game, but Wolves won 6-1.

Darneton reported: "Neither players nor supporters will have the slightest quibble. They were beaten by a side that played football of a quality they had never met before."

The players shared a bonus of £220, but the memories were more precious still.

Harbertson moved to Lincoln, and the transfer money was put towards the £16,000 floodlights installed to bathe Feethams in light.

But there has yet to be a more illuminating game than that against Chelsea!

Despite their marvellous cup exploits, Quakers finished the season fifth from bottom of the league.

League Cup run 1960

CROWDS flocked to Feethams for a run which ended in heartbreak with a last minute winner for Division One giants Bolton Wanderers, led by Nat Lofthouse.

The 21,023 who gasped in dismay in torrential rain, took the aggregate over three Feethams games to 48,020 - as many as Quakers attracted in an entire season several years later.

The run started with a 2-0 win over Fourth Division Crystal Palace on October 12. The Northern Echo reported: "Darlington showed the converted stay-at-homes that things aint what they used to be. This was a new Darlington, bent on the sort of success which will make the turnstiles click merrier than ever before."

A crowd of 9940 saw Palace's 20-year-old third choice keeper John Swannell play a blinder, until he pushed left winger Keith Morton's 65th minute cross into the path of Joe Rayment, who scored. Four minutes later Ray Spencer clinched it.

West Ham were the next visitors, and the game attracted 17057. Hammers were 12th in Division One, but had lost all seven away games, scoring seven and conceding 21.

Ray Spencer blasted Darlington in front after 20 seconds. The left half sent debutant Lance Robson down the flank, and he crossed for Bobby Baxter to set up Spencer.

West Ham's new 4-2-4 formation struggled, but Dave Dunmore equalised on 23 minutes. Brian Henderson and George Mulholland were outstanding in defence for Quakers.

Keith Morton got round Hammers' skipper John Bond on 53 minutes, and crossed for Robson to set up Joe Rayment, who put Darlington 2-1 ahead.

Bobby Moore, picked earlier in the day for England u-23s, almost equalised with a drive which Colin Tinsley saved. Then Robson latched onto a back pass from John Lyall to make it 3-1. John Dick pulled one back for West Ham on 68 minutes, but Darlington finished on top.

Newcastle manager Charlie Mitton left Feethams pondering the wisdom of having given Robson a free transfer.

The third round brought the mighty Wanderers to Feethams.

116

Talk of switching the tie to Burnden Park was quashed by chairman John Neasham: "It must be played at Darlington. There is no reason why we should not beat them."

Nat Lofthouse had hit a hat-trick in his side's 6-2 win over Grimsby, second in Division Three, to earn the Feethams trip. But Darlington were having their best post war season.

The game was all-ticket with a 21,000 limit, and for the first time stewards were used. After the West Ham game, some fans complained of sore ribs as some sections of the ground were too crowded, while others were not full.

The crowd for Bolton would have been even bigger, but work on the West Stand was not completed. Over half the tickets were snapped up within 24 hours.

Darlington were fifth in Division Four, having just notched their first ever win at Workington, 3-1. Bolton, despite their stars, were third bottom of the first division, with two wins and a draw in eight away games.

The attendance shattered the 35-year-old Feethams record, and the the crowd was thrilled when Rayment, Darlington's smallest player, smashed home Milner's 16th minute cross. Then Lofthouse and Doug Holden, two of five internationals in Bolton's side, saw efforts blocked on the line by skipper Henderson.

An outstanding save from Eddie Hopkinson denied Robson a second. But on 69 minutes a free kick on the flank 35 yards from goal was taken by right back Roy Hartle, the ball slithering in for an equaliser after slipping through Tinsley's grasp.

Bolton sensed victory, and got it on 89 minutes, Holden racing onto Fred Hill's pass to round Tinsley.

By the Saturday fog had replaced the rain, and a bemused Chester City side lost 5-1 at Feethams, though hardly any of the 5521 crowd saw the goals. The surreal world of Darlington FC had returned to normal.

League Cup run 1967

THIS was the Quakers best run in a major competition - the only time they have reached a quarter final.

It started with a 1-0 Feethams win over fellow Fourth Division side York City, but may have ended before it started had striker Bryan Conlon not passed a fitness test on a leg injury just before kick off. For Conlon scored the only goal on 70 minutes, thumping in Don Ratcliffe's cross.

The reward was a first ever trip to Southend, who were second in Division Four, having won all three home games, conceding only one goal.

Darlington were 14th. Southend scored in the first minute - but then came a rare moment in Quakers' history, a referee gave them a huge helping hand.

The official Bob Pritchard got in the way of a Southend clearance, the ball rebounding straight to skipper Ratcliffe, who crossed for Conlon to score a 56th minute equaliser. Ten minutes later Ratcliffe sent Dennis Fidler clear to net the winner.

Next came Portsmouth at Feethams, but four days before the October 11 tie, Darlington lost 2-0 at home to Barnsley.

The fans were angered by the inept display, and bayed for the blood of directors and players. One enraged supporter turned to Echo reporter Bill Mimms and offered him 100-1 on Quakers beating Pompey, adding: "If they win I'll print the money for you myself." Mimms did not take the bet.

Portsmouth were fourth in Division Two and unbeaten away. Quakers were 17th in Division Four and without a home league win.

Only 6192 fans turned up, but were treated to a 4-1 in what was described in the press as "a stupendous footballing feat."

On 47 minutes Fidler set up Les O'Neill to score with an exquisite lob. John Hope, 18, a late replacement for Tony Moor then made a marvellous save to preserve the lead.

Then Harry Kirk crossed for Conlon to score. Ratcliffe's 70th minute penalty made it 3-0, and although Pompey pulled one back, Conlon headed a fourth.

Trevor Atkinson brought in as deputy centre half for Joe Jacques, had an outstanding match.

Millwall were next at Feethams and the Echo was in lyrical mood: "The prize at stake is a passport to the quarter finals of the one-time Cinderella competition, which has rapidly found almost 92 Prince Charmings only too eager to provide a cosy fitting soccer slipper to woo its economic charms."

Manager Jimmy Greenhalgh used more familiar footballing language: "The lads are in the right frame of mind."

They duly beat Second Division Millwall 2-0. With Brian Albeson in particular tackling feverishly on a slippery surface, Darlington went ahead on 20 minutes, when Ratcliffe's cross was deflected to Les O'Neill who hammered the ball in.

Millwall rallied but Tony Moor in goal and Alan Sproates were outstanding in keeping them out.

Two minutes from time, Conlon picked up Ian Davidson's pass and raced 50 yards to fire in a second.

Again the game was seen by a poor crowd of 7732. That, when Darlington drew Derby away, provoked an outspoken response from club secretary Charles Brand, who said: "It's the worst draw we could have got, but frankly our supporters don't deserve another home tie."

Meanwhile Arsenal manager Bertie Mee, whose side were drawn at Burnley, mused: "I'd rather go there than have to play at Darlington."

Darlington's players were on a bonus of £282 a man to win, made up of money carried forward from previous rounds to add to a guaranteed £250 for losing semi-finalists.

Second division Derby were unbeaten at home, winning five of their six games, Darlington were two divisions below in 18th place, but had won three away matches in the league.

The Quakers put up a magnificent show in the Midlands mud. They led at half time, were stung by three Derby goals in two and a half minutes, pulled back to 3-2, went 5-2 down, then roared back to finally lose 5-4 as eight of the nine goals came after half time.

Derby keeper Reg Matthews must have feared the worst as he had been in the Chelsea side hammered by Darlington nine years earlier. He was beaten by Les O'Neill in the last minute of the first half, after the Darlington man jinked past two defenders. But O'Neill deflected Alan Durban's shot past Moor for the equaliser. Within two minutes Derby were 3-1 up, though Bobby Cummings pulled one back.

Derby scored twice more, one an own goal from O'Neill, whose back pass crept into the net.

Still Darlington refused to lie down. On 82 minutes Ratcliffe jinked through to score, then three minutes from time Joe Jacques headed in.

Greenhalgh said: "Three of their goals were virtually own goals, another was very lucky and the other possibly came from a foul. We were just as good a side as Derby."

Even colourful Derby manager Brian Clough said: "It was better than the Palladium. We are through - but just."

Darlington 6 Cambridge 0 Division Four, September 28, 1974

THE hype which preceded the game was more extraordinary than the result. The fun and games started almost a fortnight earlier when cartoonist, publicist and cabaret entertainer Paul Trevillion latched onto the Quakers who were near the bottom of the Fourth Division.

The London born egotist had previously challenged Britain's top golfer Tony Jacklin to a £25,000 bet over a putting contest, and breezed into Darlington predicting the club would shoot up the Fourth Division, and hammer Cambridge 5-0.

He set a top hat on top of some hat boxes on the goalline at Feethams, then challenged Quakers' penalty taker Gordon Cattrell (who features elsewhere in the book) to knock the hat off with one shot from 12 yards.

Cattrell obliged, Trevillion declaring: "That was the finest hat-trick I have seen! The hat represented the Fourth Division and we will take it by storm."

He then challenged any player in the country to come to Feethams, place a £1,000 cheque on the penalty spot, Trevillion doing the same, and if the player emulated Cattrell's feat, then the money went to the penalty taker, if not Trevillion pocketed it.

"Gordon is king, now he has done it. Your Malcolm McDonalds and Pop Robsons might know they can hit it nine times out of 10, but they know there's a chance they might miss, and like Gordon, they get only one chance."

There were no takers, but an upbeat Trevillion continued with his extravaganza, declaring that if Quakers lost to Cambridge the fans could pelt him with tomatoes. He explained that he had fallen for Darlington when driving past Feethams on his way to a cabaret performance. When he returned to the town to boost the side's fortunes he brought with him a wooden crown he claimed had been touched by Henry VIII.

On the pitch things were not going well. Three days before the Cambridge game Quakers were thrashed 4-1 at Exeter.

Singer Kathy Kirby arrived to join Trevillion, who had got companies to sponsor his antics. Cigarettes and crisps were to be handed to the crowd, while the players were to receive cigars and champagne.

Kirby was to present an 'outrageously' expensive mink coat to the wife of the manager of the winning team. Then she would give each Darlington player a kiss and put on a free concert for them.

But Trevillion's plans to let the fans pelt him with tomatoes was quashed by the directors. They feared fans would throw things more dangerous than tomatoes, and the board would be sued for damages.

That morning rumours of romance between Trevillion and Kirby, led to him hurrying home to London to protect his wife and three children from press intrusion.

But he hadn't lost his confidence, declaring: "In two years' time I will be the biggest thing in showbusiness. I will be on at the Palladium and will invite everyone at the Darlington club to come and see me."

Kirby did attend the match in front of a crowd of 2304, no bigger than average. But this was no average Darlington performance.

Don Burluraux put them ahead with a solo effort, then Stan Webb headed home a Cattrell free-kick. Eric Young scored a third. Then Colin Sinclair crashed in the fourth and fifth, and just when Trevillion's prediction seemed set to come true, Billy Yeats spoiled it by sweeping Sinclair's pass into the net to make it six.

Delighted manager Billy Horner said: "Paul is welcome to visit Darlington any time. We've gained publicity, but the players had been threatening a win like this all season."

David Lewis reported in Monday's Echo: "It might have been the ego boosting antics of Trevillion, the presence of glamourous Kirby, or more likely the verbal roasting Horner gave his players before the game. But whatever the reason, something injected a new fire into Darlington."

And Supporters club chairman Barry Weatherill added: "During these comparatively dull days at Feethams, it's nice to think we have friends in people like Paul and Kathy."

After the game, normal service was resumed. Darlington lost their next match, at Southport 1-0, and went down by the same score in the return game at Cambridge the following March.

Rather than take the division by storm, they finished fourth from bottom, and faced another re-election plea.

Trevillion was last heard of working as an artist with a Sunday newspaper. And there are no reports of a mass exodus from Feethams to the London Palladium.

Darlington's 1978 line-up whose League Cup run was finally ended at Everton

League Cup run 1978

A FIRST half header from Derek Craig started Darlington's run. The opening cup game was played before the first league fixture, and Fourth Division Darlington visited Third Division Mansfield on August 12. The centre half's powerful header proved the only goal.

When Darlington came from behind to draw the second leg 2-2 courtesy of goals from John Stone and Barry Lyons, they headed for Second Division Fulham and another 2-2 draw, with Craig and Dennis Wann scoring.

Torrential rain awaited Fulham in the replay on September 5, and the upset came through a Lyons penalty on 63 minutes, after winger Lloyd Maitland had been upended by Kevin Lock in front of the Tin Shed.

Darlington boss Peter Madden told the press: "We were magic. Fulham had no answer to our enthusiasm and determination."

In the month before the date with Everton at Goodison, Quakers won only one of six games - 2-0 at Halifax.

One unusual event did take place on September 23. An It's A Knockout competition was staged between the football and cricket clubs.

Everton looked an awesome proposition. They beat Wimbledon, who were at the top of Division Four, 8-0 in the second round, while Finn Harps were walloped 10-0 in the UEFA Cup.

Darlington took 2,000 fans that Tuesday night, October 3, some visiting the bookmakers, as Quakers were 20-1 to win. Everton were second in Division One, and had a 100 per cent home record, having won all four league games, conceding only one goal. They were unbeaten away too, but Liverpool were ahead of them.

And Reds' boss Billy Shankly visited Quakers dressing room before the game - a tale told by Clive Nattress elsewhere.

The League Cup held memories for Madden, a member of the Rotherham side of 1961 that lost the first final 3-0 at Aston Villa, after winning the first leg 2-0. Everton boss Gordon Lee was in the Villa side. Madden was gunning for revenge: "I don't like getting medals for losing," he said.

Derek Craig was ready for battle with Everton's prolific scorer Bob Latchford, saying: "I'll be fighting for every ball. Someone should tell him I've scored a few goals as well."

Quakers keeper Martin Burleigh was in no mood to be intimidated, after playing at Goodison with Carlisle three years earlier: "The dressing rooms are so big, we'll be able to warm up with a five a side game," he laughed.

Everton winger Dave Thomas was missing, and without him they lacked a creative force.

The travelling fans were crammed in the lower tier of the main stand, by the tunnel. On the edge of them was Andrew Wilkinson, co-author of this book.

"Next to me was a fat, loud Scouser, who stuffed pies the entire game. 'We'll hammer yer,' he said. "But as Darlington snuffed out the dual threat of Latchford and Micky Walsh, my unwanted companion became agitated. 'When the first goes in we'll hammer yer' he said."

But the first wouldn't go in, Jimmy Cochrane making a sliding tackle to take the ball off Latchford in front of goal.

Then on 16 minutes, Jimmy Seal, as he reveals elsewhere, missed a marvellous chance to put Darlington ahead.

Everton were rattled, and when Andy King burst through, Burleigh raced out to make a terrific 37th minute block.

The noise as the teams left the field at half time all came from the Quaker fans, the rest of the 23,682 crowd was stunned.

Everton finally scored the only goal on 54 minutes - with a slice of luck. Colin Todd's cross was deflected to Martin Dobson, who looped a shot over Burleigh.

The pieman piped up: "Told yer," he grinned.

But Darlington then camped in the Everton half. Wann fired a free kick inches wide with keeper George Wood beaten. Then Wood handled outside the area. Lyons' free kick shaved the post, as did another effort from the skipper as Everton hung on.

The final whistle was greeted with a mixture of bristling pride, and heart rending pain for Quakers' players and fans, and the ovation as the team left the field was deafening.

The players were gutted. John Stone said: "We knew if we could contain them for the first 15 minutes of the second half, the match was there for us to take.

"The goal was one of those things. Todd's cross struck a player, then bounced off the shoulder of somebody else straight into Dobson's path. We deserved a draw. In the last 20 minutes we had them on the run. Our supporters were magnificent."

Madden said: "Every one of my players was a gladiator. We came within a coat of paint of getting an equaliser."

Madden was soon to part company with the club. But there was a blessing to go with memories of Goodison.

From the gate receipts of £30,000, Darlington picked up a club record £12,000.

That money helped buy Alan Walsh. It was a final act of genius from Madden, a manager who had lifted the club out of the doldrums.

FA Cup run | 1984/5

TO win promotion and dump Middlesbrough out of the FA Cup in the same season would be deemed too good to be true - yet that's what happened.

Darlington had won three successive league games to go top of the league, as they went into the first round clash with Chester City at Feethams on November 17.

A notable figure in the Chester side was Lee Dixon, later to become an Arsenal star.

Darlington's 1984/85 squad who beat Middlesbrough in the FA Cup

Carl Airey and Gary MacDonald put Quakers two up in 15 minutes. Chester pulled one back, but Airey struck again, before a late Chester rally.

But the 3-2 win was played with Quakers under a cloud, as Colin Ross in his first season at the club, was told the previous day, that a knee injury had ended his career. And a similar fate appeared to be awaiting Mike Angus, who was given the thumbs down by a specialist. The Chester game turned out to be the last for veteran full back John Craggs.

Quakers were drawn at home to non-league Frickley, a Yorkshire town a mile or two from where Darlington manager Cyril Knowles was born. The visitors arrived having won 12 of their previous 15 games, and they played well, going down to Phil Lloyd's 23rd minute header.

Lloyd popped up at the other end to clear after Frickley hit the bar and Knowles confessed: "They deserved a replay."

The day before the game Cyril had picked Graeme Aldred in place of Craggs, asking the former Boro man to hang up his boots and concentrate on his assistant manager's role.

When Quakers were drawn to visit Boro, everybody was thrilled. Among ex-Boro staff now working at Feethams were: Knowles, Craggs, Lloyd, MacDonald,

Peter Johnson, Steve Tupling and Mark Forster.

Boro boss Willie Maddren said: "Middlesbrough should win, but Darlington are the only league side unbeaten away from home. Defeat for us would be humiliating."

Cyril was laid back: "At least we won't need an overnight stop," he quipped.

Dick Corden, a Boro fan later to become Darlington chairman, had just pledged the Teessiders cash backing, after a crowd of just 4,040, the lowest post war crowd at Ayresome, saw Second Division Boro draw 1-1 with Shrewsbury, thanks to a last gasp own goal.

It was announced that Darlington had lost £17,000 the previous year against a £22,000 profit the year before that (how football finances have changed).

Quakers were given 3,000 tickets, and British Rail promised buses from the station to the ground.

Shortly before the game, Mike Angus went to see a Harley Street specialist to confirm the end of his career.

"After a half hour examination, I asked his opinion," said Angus. "And I could hardly believe it when he said: 'Give it another go.'

The jubilant Quakers heroes after drawing 0-0 in the FA Cup tie at Middlesbrough

Garry MacDonald scores Quakers first in the FA Cup replay against Middlesbrough at Feethams

"I rushed to King's Cross Station and phoned Cyril because I knew we had a reserve game the next day. I played in it, scored and felt no reaction." As another former Boro man, Angus relished the Ayresome trip.

The Quakers squad went to a country retreat to prepare. The bookies offered 4-7 Boro, 4-1 Darlington, 11-4 the draw.

Darlington were big news now, and drink company McEwans offered them a lucrative sponsorship deal (which included updating the Quakers Sports Centre) to run to 1987, and the players wore the new logo on their strip for the first time at Ayresome.

The occasion was massive. Boro keeper Kelham O'Hanlon was godfather to Angus' daughter. MacDonald's mum was a Boro fan who couldn't bear to go to the game, but his father went, switching allegiances for the day.

"There's no pressure," said Cyril. "It's all on them. I've even got letters from Middlesbrough people saying they hope we turn them over."

On a foul January 5, a day of mud, snow and sleet, 19,084 fans piled into Ayresome. Quakers' fans had the seats behind the east end. Darlington keeper Fred Barber made an outstanding save from Irving Nattress to earn a 0-0 draw. Angus missed a good chance, while Gary Macdonald saw an effort cleared off the line - a incident that earned Airey a rollicking from Cyril, for claiming a goal, instead of going in the for the kill.

Dave McLean was man of the match, the press reporting: "He played balls out of the midfield bog as if he were at Wembley.

"We were the better side," said Cyril, while Maddren retorted: "The pressure is on Darlington now."

The replay was three days later, and around 50 fans turned up to help groundsman Colin Gray clear snow off Feethams. Club chaplain Raymond Cuthbertson joined in, even though a prior engagement meant he would miss the match. Quakers players returned to their secret retreat, for the calm before the storm. And what a night it was.

The sad statistics were that 15 fans were arrested, three taken to hospital, hundreds of Boro fans spilled onto the pitch when their team was losing, and concrete slabs and iron spikes were hurled at police in fights inside the ground and on the cricket pitch.

Brave referee Norman Wilson, after taking the players off, said if necessary he would wait until midnight to finish the game.

After a tense first half, Macdonald sent the majority of the 14,237 crowd wild, when on 53 minutes, he forced the ball over the line in a scramble. Back came Boro, Barber saving well from David Currie, later to play for Darlington.

At the other end Airey set up MacDonald, whose powerful drive was saved by O'Hanlon. Then on 76 minutes, Mitch Cook's corner fell to Kev Smith who prepared to shoot. But Mike Angus got in his way (possibly deliberately, knowing Smudger's shooting).

Angus squeezed the ball through to Phil Lloyd, who turned it into the net. That was the signal for the Boro fans to flood onto the pitch. But police action, later praised as 'magnificent' by Quakers' chairman Archie Heaton, ensured the players could return.

Quakers' nerves jangled. Tony McAndrew pulled a goal back, then Quaker hearts were in their mouths as Heine Otto went down in a tangle with Angus. The

Phil Lloyd about to score Quakers second against Middlesbrough

referee pointed dramatically for a goal kick, when most of the crowd seemed to think he had pointed to the penalty spot.

The two managers had opposing views, Knowles saying: "The referee kept great control." He sportingly added: "I'm not going to gloat. I have a lot of time for my former club and their manager. There has to be a loser and I feel sorry for Boro and Willie."

Maddren was feeling the pressure, and in an out of character outburst, he said: "The referee did not allow us to compete. We should have had a penalty, but the ref ran away."

Darlington's agony was yet to come as they were beaten by non-league Telford in a fourth round replay, when a trip to Everton beckoned.

Feethams was packed with 11,240 fans on January 29. Telford, whose manager Stan Storton was a former Darlington player, had already beaten Lincoln, Preston

and Bradford, and Knowles warned: "We must not have the same approach as we did against Frickley."

Gola League Telford forced a 1-1 draw, being denied a win by Mark Forster's close range equaliser on 75 minutes.

In the replay Quakers were blown away 3-0 by two tremendous long range goals and a penalty. Telford were beaten 3-0 at Goodison by an Everton side that went on to lose the final to Manchester United.

Incidently, Angus' career did end shortly afterwards, but he played his part in a famous Darlington win. However it brings sadness to reflect on the fact that both Knowles and Maddren have since died from illnesses which claimed them much too soon.

Coca-Cola Cup run 1996

FANS were delighted to have another massive game to savour so soon after Darlington lost at Wembley.

Within four months of that disappointment they made their way back up the A1 after seeing a 2-2 draw at mighty Leeds United. The celebrations from over 2000 Darlington fans when Robbie Painter equalised in front of them was a moment to treasure.

The season started disappointingly, with defeat at Hull City - Quakers first on opening day for six years.

Fuming manager Jim Platt called the players in for Sunday training. "He said at the time: "If I had started on them after the game, we would still have been in Hull."

Three days later Quakers entertained Second Division Rotherham in the Coca-Cola Cup, and Robbie Blake scored the only goal after 90 seconds, latching onto a pass from home debutant Darren Roberts.

What was particularly sweet was that the goal was scored past Steve Cherry, Rotherham's new keeper, who had played for Plymouth against Quakers at Wembley.

In the second leg Darlington also won 1-0, Roberts scoring after 56 minutes.

Darlington skipper Andy Crosby was star man, despite playing with stitches in his ankle. Rotherham was his home town club.

He was even happier when Quakers drew his first club Leeds. On the eve of the

123

Darren Roberts celebrates his equaliser in Darlington's magnificent 2-2 draw at Leeds United

124

trip to Elland Road, Crosby said: "The Leeds fans won't even recognise me, but I've had the landlady from my old digs on the phone for tickets. It will be my first visit since the club let me go. I'm a Leeds fan and all my family will be there.

"I don't think Leeds' striker Ian Rush will have a sleepless night over facing me and Sean Gregan. My fear is that we will get turned over, especially as it is George Graham's first game in charge and the Leeds players will want to impress."

Leeds, the previous season's losing finalists, started brightly, Rush firing over from six yards in their first attack which cut Darlington to ribbons. After 15 minutes Leeds went ahead when Nigel Martyn's clearance was flicked on by Lee Sharpe, for Rod Wallace to fire home from 20 yards.

But the floodgates didn't open. Two minutes later Blake crossed for Gary Twynham to head just wide, then Roberts sent a chip narrowly off target.

And when on 40 minutes Leeds failed to clear a corner, Anthony Carss crossed for Roberts to prod past Martyn. Roberts beamed: "I couldn't believe the space I was given. I thought I was offside."

On 49 minutes Wallace restored Leeds lead from a tight angle. Then Rush had an effort disallowed for offside.

But when Brian Atkinson saw Martyn off his line, the Darlington midfielder was

close to equalising with a 30 yard chip which dipped over the bar.

But the England keeper hadn't learned his lesson, and when substitute Painter latched onto Twynham's pass he scored easily as the keeper rushed out. Darlington held firm, Paul Newell saving a weak header from Rush.

Phil Brumwell, who marked Lee Sharpe effectively despite suffering a heavy cold, said: "Our fans were even noisier than at Wembley. You would have thought we had won the cup. To score twice isn't luck and says so much for our character."

The teams were: LEEDS: Martyn, Kelly, Harte, Ford, Jobson, Wetherall, Grey (Blunt 82), Wallace, Rush Couzens, Sharpe. DARLINGTON: Newell, Brumwell, Barnard, Crosby, Gregan, Twynham (Kelly 81), Oliver, Atkinson, Carss, Roberts, Blake (Painter 68).

Darlington were out of luck in the second leg, losing 2-0. Gregan was forced off with a head injury after 15 minutes, and while he was receiving treatment Wallace scored.

After 24 minutes Gregan returned with a heavily bandaged head, but was helpless to stop Ian Harte scoring six minutes later. In the second half Carlton Palmer knocked Roberts' effort off the line as Darlington rallied. But they had already had their glory, as Gregan said: "We raised eyebrows. It is no disgrace to lose to a Premier League side over two legs. Jim Platt told us at half time that we might as well go down fighting.

"Some of our lads showed they could play at a higher level, but Leeds were strong and Palmer made the difference. When I saw the first goal on television I know that I would have prevented it. I would have been marking the player who got the knock down that set it up."

Within weeks Gregan and Blake had moved on, to Preston and Bradford respectively. Missed by Darlington fans, their contribution to a great night at Leeds would live long in the memory.

Wembley play-off v Plymouth May 1996

DARLINGTON'S first play-off final was everything a trip to Wembley should be - except for the result.

It was a sunny May day, the crowd (43,431) was huge by Third Division play-off standards, and the Twin Towers shone resplendent.

Around 10,000 Darlington fans made the trip. Automatic promotion had hardly been talked about all season until it became a possiblility in the last couple of games.

Before that for half a season or more, Wembley had been the target, and as the dream moved closer everything pointed to the perfect day.

Disappointment at missing out on a top three spot was fleeting, for Hereford in a two leg play-off semi final was all that stood between Darlington and Wembley.

Quakers had beaten Hereford twice during the season. They were to beat them twice more - all four victories by a single goal. Darlington had ensured a play-off spot thanks to Matt Carmichael's goal at Edgar Street on April 23.

Darlington made the trip back there on May 12. The following team: Newell, Carmichael, Barnard, Appleby, Carss, Crosby, Gregan, Blake, Painter, Gaughan, Bannister, was stunned when Dean Smith headed Hereford in front after two minutes.

But Sean Gregan equalised with a looping header on 27 minutes, the central defender's first goal of the season, and 11 minutes later Blake sidefooted in Mark Barnard's cross as Darlington won 2-1.

Gregan told the Evening Gazette: "I was trying to head the ball back into the danger area. It crept in. It was great to score, but I was most pleased at keeping Steve White out, as he has 33 goals this season. He resorted to winding me up and kicking me, but I was determined not to react."

Manager Jim Platt beamed: "The players never fail to amaze me with their attitude and resilience."

Before the second leg, however, the manager was cautious: "We lost to Rochdale at Feethams in the FA Cup earlier this season, when the prize was a trip to Liverpool. Football has a nasty habit of kicking you in the teeth."

Anthony Carss missed the second leg through injury, Phil Brumwell coming in. Hereford piled forward in front of a Feethams crowd of 6584, and created such havoc in the Darlington box, that manager Platt quickly changed tactics.

It had the desired effect. After 17 minutes, Robbie Painter turned in Gary Bannister's angled shot to send the home fans wild. And when Blake was tripped on 47 minutes, Matty Appleby fired home the penalty in front of a packed Tin Shed.

Tony James pulled one back after 65 minutes, but Quakers coasted home, especially after Richard Wilkins was sent off after 83 minutes for a scything tackle

Andy Crosby leads out the Darlington team at Wembley for the 1996 play-off final

125

on Barnard. The force of the challenge shattered the left back's shin pad, and for an awful few seconds, his teammates thought the pad was his bone.

The noise from the crowd built to a crescendo as the seconds ticked away, the whistle being greeted with delight by players and fans.

The Darlington staff were jubilant. General manager Steve Morgon said: "All north east fans are welcome to join us at Wembley for what will be a fantastic day out."

Chairman Bernard Lowery added: "It's a fantastic achievement by Jim Platt and the players. They have brought us the greatest day in the history of the club, and have done it by playing quality football that has been admired everywhere we have gone."

Skipper Andy Crosby said: "When I was appointed skipper, never in my wildest dreams did I think I would be leading the side out at Wembley."

Appleby revealed: "I have never been to Wembley. I made the decision not to go until I was playing."

Hereford manager Graham Turner was dignified in defeat: "Darlington were

Robbie Painter in action at Wembley

126

the better team," he said. He didn't deserve Hereford's relegation to the Conference which came the following season.

Plymouth beat Colchester 3-1 in the second leg of the other semi-final, after Colchester won the first leg 1-0.

Jim Platt told his players to enjoy the build up. It was sound advice in view of the way it ended. The crowd for the final was bigger than for the previous few England internationals. They saw Plymouth triumph courtesy of Ronnie Mauge's near post header early in the second half.

Darlington had come within a whisker of taking a first half lead when Appleby started and finished a flowing move, hitting a shot an inch or two wide.

The team was distraught at the final whistle. As the Plymouth hordes danced, Crosby sat on the lush turf head between his knees, while Gregan lay face down a few yards away.

The players bravely faced the press.

Robbie Painter said: "I'm gutted and so frustrated at not getting a shot on goal.

Getting to Wembley capped a great season, but the fact that we lost overshadowed everything."

Mark Barnard said: "As we drove to the stadium I didn't feel nervous until I saw my mum and dad outside the ground. Our passing was not as good as usual.

"The turning point was Matty's shot which was so close. In the second half the ref (Bill Burns) let us down. There were a lot of late challenges and more decisions should have gone our way."

Midfielder Steve Gaughan said: "The first half passed me by. I thought we had been playing five minutes when I looked up at the clock and it said 34 minutes. People warned me it would go in a blur and they were so right.

"We didn't play as well as we could, but world class players come here and fail to live up to the hype. I'm down, but we will look back in later life and say we played here. Nobody can take that away."

Phil Brumwell, in many fans' eyes, the Man of the Match, said: "It was one of my better games, but it counts for nothing. I'm only 20 and I have played here. Some players never get here, but when the final whistle went I just wanted to crawl into a hole.

"The fans were tremendous. None of them left when the game ended, and they gave us an ovation we will never forget.

Appleby reflected: "If I had scored we would have finished up with two or three."

For Bannister, the only team member to play at Wembley before, it bought painful memories flooding back: "That was 10 years ago, when QPR lost in the League Cup. I had wiped it from my mind, but when Wembley loomed again the memories returned. It hurt then and now. I enjoyed the build up, but the result changes your feelings. We are still in the Third Division."

Blake, like Painter, rued the fact that he didn't manage a shot: "The final ball let us down. It was one of those days when it didn't quite happen. I now know that Wembley is a bad place to lose. I would love to come back one day and win, but I would rather get automatic promotion."

Manager Platt said: "We didn't do ourselves justice. We like to get the ball down and play, but Plymouth didn't let us. We've had a great season. We came from nowhere, but in the end it just wasn't to be."

The Darlington team was: Newell, Brumwell, Barnard, Gregan, Appleby,

Crosby, Bannister, Gaughan (Carmichael 88mins), Painter, Blake, Carss.

They created club history, and to the Darlington fans they stand as heroes alongside the greatest players ever to grace the magical Wembley turf.

Worthington Cup 2000

STUART ELLIOTT'S wonder goal from fully 50 yards completed a sensational victory for Darlington at Nottingham Forest's City Ground on Wednesday, September 6th, 2000.

The two groups of visiting fans (one behind the goal into which Elliott struck and the other high in the stand) leapt to their feet in a mixture of disbelief and uncontrollable glee when the midfielder's 85th minute shot flew into the net to give the visitors a 2-1 win.

Forest keeper Dave Beasant - not for the first time in his career - had sent a clearance from wide on the byeline straight into the path of an opponent who accepted the chance.

But although it was a clanger from the experienced keeper, nothing should detract from the skill of Elliott, who hit the ball first time, from inside the centre circle, with power and precision.

In rounded off a remarkable comeback, from a Darlington side which included several reserve team players.

First Division Forest had taken a ninth minute lead through Stern John, who had outpaced the defence before slipping the ball past Quakers' Dutch keeper Frank van der Geest.

Forest were so dominant that a rout looked a certainty.

Indeed, a radio reporter sitting in the press box next to the authors of this book, told his listeners after around 15 minutes' play: "If you are looking for an upset, look elsewhere. There's no chance of one here. Forest are already one up and looking good for several more."

And he seemed absolutely right at that stage.

But the Forest onslaught, part orchestrated by former Feethams favourite Robbie Blake, who was on loan at the City Ground from Bradford, gradually petered out, and although Darlington rarely got into the Forest half, they reached the interval just one down.

Adam Reed (left) and Stuart Elliott in action at Bradford. The 7-2 scoreline was a fair reflection of the game

Elliott came on for Steve Walklate for the second half, and gradually Darlington began to assert themselves.

After 65 minutes, Richard Hodgson, released by Forest the previous season, crossed from the left for substitute Paul Campbell to equalise with a near post header which looped over Beasant.

Then came the keeper's clanger, after which frantic Forest pressure was met by a determined Darlington rearguard, and superb handling from van der Geest.

The Darlington side was: van der Geest, Liddle, Hodgson, Pepper, Reed, Himsworth, Gray, Walklate (Elliott), Hjorth, Williamson (Campbell), Angel, Zeghdane.

The game was a two-leg affair, the first having been a 2-2 Feethams draw, Elliott (pen) and Glenn Naylor scoring for Darlington.

And there was no question of Forest easing up for the second leg, so Darlington's victory was a major surprise.

After the Feethams draw, a Forest source told the media: "Forest will take the return game very seriously. The club is losing around £100,000 a week, and they see this as a chance of a money spinner as a lot of Premiership clubs will play weakened sides in the competition."

What they didn't expect was to be beaten by an understrength Darlington. Elliott said after his incredible goal: "The ball came perfectly to me. I reacted instinctively and fortunately it went where I wanted it to. To come from a goal down was fantastic. It was a collective effort."

Delighted manager Gary Bennett said: "The players keep surprising me with their workrate and ability. They were brilliant."

It was Darlington's first major cup scalp for some years, though in the previous couple of seasons they had come mightily close to beating Manchester City, Sheffield United and Aston Villa.

But the glory was not to last.

A near full strength team played admirably in losing 1-0 at home to Premier Division side Bradford City in the Feethams leg of the second round.

Again Bennett, with an eye on important league fixtures, rang the changes for the second leg at Valley Parade, leaving out six of the players who drew 1-1 at Macclesfield in a league game three days earlier.

"Our squad are all capable. Those who get the opportunity tonight won't let us down. The fans lifted us at Forest and will lift us again," said the manager.

But there was little the fans could do. They watched their side go three down after nine minutes, and skipper Martin Gray was quickly brought off the bench. He helped stem the tide but Bradford stretched their lead before half time and Darlington were well beaten before goals from Stuart Elliott (60mins) and Mark Angel (63), with his only goal for the club, restored some pride.

The only other thing the 1000 or so travelling fans in a poor crowd of 4751 had to cheer, was a magnificent penalty save from Andy Collett, which denied Benito Carbone a hat-trick.

The 7-2 scoreline was a fair reflection of the game, and Bennett, while defending his decision to leave out key players, stormed: "I thought the side would be good enough to have a chance, but we gave away goals through schoolboy errors. Some of the players let the club down, and I feel sorry for the fans."

Some of the players were soon released, scorers Elliott and Angel included, though their contribution to two extraordinary rounds of the cup, which produced the full range of emotions, will long be remembered.

128